55 5

C000297555

Robert Swain

The production of this volume has been sponsored by Stagecoach
North West.

Stagecoach in Cumbria

Yan Press.

ISBN 0-9540713-0-1

A catalogue record of this book is available from the British Library.

Published by:
Yan Press, 10 The Nook, Bolton-le-Sands, Carnforth. LA5 8DR.
© Robert Swain, 2001.

Walkers should note that rights of way can be changed, temporarily diverted and, subject to an appropriate order, closed. Permissive paths are not rights of way and the routes can be closed or diverted without warning.

CARNMOR PRINT

Printed by Carnmor Print
95/97, London Road, PRESTON, Lancs. PR1 4BA
Tel: 01772 555615

Contents

Walk Maps and Timetables

INTRODUCTION

By doing these walks, the explorer will experience a rich variety of countryside and villages and find many delights on the way. Some of the walks are well known, but several are not. It was only when doing them that the author discovered the several delights between Staveley and Windermere, having previously only used the road up the Kentmere Valley to reach the Garburn Road. As a result, a number of walks as originally planned had to be changed or dropped.

All the walks in this book start and finish at a bus stop on the Stagecoach in Cumbria 555 bus route, which runs between Lancaster and Keswick and is one of the longest stage-carriage services in the country. Some of the walks are circular ones, using the same stop for both the start and finish of the walk. Other walks are linear, using different stops at each end. Generally, the main bus stops in each place are used and not necessarily the nearest. As the walker becomes familiar with the bus route it will become clear which alternative stops can be used to suit individual circumstances.

Car parks are only occasionally mentioned. However, it is appreciated that walkers may have to use a car to reach the bus route. In general, there will be somewhere to park that is not too far away. Much enjoyment can be got from travelling by bus over this route as things are seen from a different perspective, especially from the top deck. Places can be visited without the need to walk back to a car, giving much more freedom to explore the area.

Times given for the walks are very rough. Some walkers may want to spend more time looking at the scenery, flora, wildlife, buildings, etc. than has been allowed whilst others may want to spend less. Also, a party of, say, six crossing some of the paths could take quite a lot longer than one person on his or her own owing to the number of stiles to be crossed. It takes a lot longer for six people to cross one stile than it does for one person on his or her own. The main thing is to allow plenty of time to enjoy your walk.

The principal aim of this book is to help walkers enjoy their ramblings and the countryside and to introduce them to the towns, villages and hamlets on the way without needing to use a car. Most of the paths followed are either rights of way or permissive paths. In the main, roads are only used where necessary, but sometimes a road is used in preference to a path where there is some specific village to visit or something of interest to see.

The walks have been so planned that there is considerable flexibility. In some cases two linear walks can be put together to make for one long round trip walk. In other cases, part of one circular walk can be linked with part of another to make a linear walk, or some other combination of circular walk. At most points where a stretch of the route is used in common with other walks, or where walks cross over each other, there is a numbered reference. These numberings are consecutive and the same reference number is used in the later walk so as to assist any walker wishing to link parts of two walks. In fact, by linking sections of various walks in the book, you are able to do a through walk all the way from Lancaster to Keswick (part of one walk having to be done in reverse) with very little road walking.

All the walks are ones that the author would be happy to do again, and several of them have been done more than once. Whilst the book has been written as though the walks are being done in the holiday season they can provide delightful days out at other times of the year.

Mention must be made that some buses are numbered 556. These travel via Borwick and Priest Hutton, not Tewitfield. Otherwise, there is no variation in the routes followed between the 555 service and the 556 service. The 555 service is virtually the same throughout the year with roughly a bus each hour from the stops on the route. There are various other buses running in the Lancaster area and throughout the Lake District, the peak services being in the height of summer, but they are not used for the purposes of this book.

The sketch maps are not to any scale but are for guidance as to the direction each walk follows and its relationship with other walks.

In doing all these walks, remember you are often going over private property even if it is a right of way. Do not leave any litter. Shut gates after you. Do not cause disturbance to farm stock or damage growing crops, it is the farmer's livelihood. Do not disturb wildlife. Keep dogs on leads at all times; if you meet me my dog will be on a lead. As well as cause trouble if off a lead, dogs themselves can get into unexpected difficulties when on unfamiliar ground and roaming free.

In several places in the book you will be told to pass an attraction. Do not take this too literally, but allow time for visiting it or come again another day.

WALK 1, LANCASTER, GLASSON DOCK, LANCASTER CANAL, LANCASTER.

Easy.
14 miles.
Allow six hours.

Lancaster is a city, being granted this status in 1937 together with its final Charter, which dates back to the Bronze Age, but its story was only of real significance from the times of the Romans who arrived around 70 A.D. They built the first castle in Lancaster with a civilian settlement below on what is now Church Street, and this spread out from there. The Roman port was probably around the site of the bus station in Damside Street. The remains of some of the Roman buildings are still to be seen on some open ground below the Priory Church, but other buildings were lost on the construction of Mitre House car park.

The present castle, which has a keep dating back to Norman times, houses the Shire Hall, round the wall of which are the shields of the High Sheriffs of the county right through the ages, these looking across to the Court. Also, it houses a former Assize Court where many murderers and others were tried. Here, the Pendle Witches were tried and George Fox, founder of the Quaker movement was imprisoned. The castle is still in use as a prison, prisoners arriving and leaving by John o' Gaunt Gate, the imposing main gate looking over Castle Park and Castle Hill. The Norman keep is part of the prison and prisoners have tried to escape from there, not appreciating its height. There are regular guided tours covering the courts and old dungeons.

Beside the Castle is St. Mary's, the Priory and Parish Church of Lancaster, a church founded by Roger of Poitu in 1094 on the site of an earlier Saxon church. The tower dates from the 1750's and replaces a much less ornate original one which would not have stood the weight of the bells.

At the time of the Domesday survey in 1087, Lancaster together with Church Lancaster were two vils within the Manor of Halton.

Lancaster has long been a market town, the markets having occupied various sites over the years, and there are still regular street markets as well as the covered market. The street markets are now on Church Street and Cheapside, but were formerly in Market Square, which is in front of what was the Town Hall, but now houses the City Museum.

Although there has been much development over the years, there are still many traces of Lancaster's past to be found in old buildings and passageways.

Press Gang at Easter Maritime Festival, Lancaster.

St. George's Quay was once bustling with maritime trade, particularly from the West Indies and Canada. Mahogany and other hardwoods for use in the furniture trade by Gillows were landed here. There are some fine examples of Gillow furniture in the Judges' Lodgings, which is now a museum, facing down Church Street and tucked in the shadow of the Castle. Although not in a very large way, Lancaster was involved in the slave trade.

Along St. George's Quay are many of the warehouses associated with the former Maritime Trade, these largely having been converted to other uses. The earlier warehouses were of three storeys and had wooden hoists whilst the later ones had four or five storeys and metal hoists.

In the midst of all these buildings stands the Maritime Museum which occupies the former Custom House and one of the warehouses. This was the third Custom House in Lancaster and was erected in 1764. The Lancaster Port Commissioners, who were established by Act of Parliament in 1749, must have had the building in mind as they left three plots available when the other buildings along the Quay were being laid out.

The building was designed by Richard Gillow, the cabinetmaker and architect, and was to be built in keeping with the best in the town. The specifications show that the Long Room chimneypiece was to have flags the "same pattern of that in the front Parlour at King's Arms". The Long Room is on the first floor of the building and was where the clerks conducted their business and where there was the Collector's Office.

On the ground floor of the Custom House was the weigh house, where goods were weighed and checked before being sent into a bonded warehouse. Here, there was a room providing shelter for boatmen and searchers. There was no direct access between the two floors, this only coming about with the conversion to a museum, which is well worth a visit. Now, over the Easter holiday, there is a Maritime Festival each year with many fine entertainers using Maritime themes, this being centred on the Museum but also using other venues in the city.

Roughly on the site of the Millennium Bridge was the old bridge which crossed the River Lune. It had four arches and had stood there for many years. In 1745 parts of the battlements were removed so as to reveal any of Prince Charles' forces trying to cross over it, and they were never rebuilt. The bridge fell into poor repair. As a result, the present Skerton Bridge was authorised by Act of Parliament in 1782, it being opened in 1788. The bridge has five arches and is said to be the first multi-arched bridge with a level roadway to be built in the country.

The old bridge was reached by Bridge Lane, which was a narrow lane coming down from China Lane, now China Street, and did not follow the line of the present road. A reminder of the old way to the bridge is 'The Three Mariners' a public house set back from the present road, but on the line of the old road. It is reputed to be one of England's oldest haunted pubs.

In 1830 a young man from Keswick was sent to be apprenticed to Lancaster painter and decorator Richard Hutton. This was James Williamson. On completing his apprenticeship he went to London where he saw oilcloth being manufactured and, upon his return to Lancaster, set up his own business. In 1844 Williamson established a small factory on St. George's Quay and ten years later bought land below Carlisle Bridge where he started the construction of St. George's Works. In 1870 he acquired the site of a former shipbuilding company and expanded his works.

Williamson's became a major Lancaster employer, by 1879 having a workforce totalling 2,000. By 1875 Williamson's son, also called James, had taken control of the company and it was he who expanded it until it employed almost a quarter of the Lancaster workforce. James Williamson the second was elected as Liberal MP for Lancaster for several years until his elevation to the peerage in 1895, with the title 'Baron Ashton' after Ashton Hall, a property of his.

Lord Ashton gave various gifts to Lancaster, including the present town hall and the organ in Ashton Hall (part of the town hall building), the statue of Queen Victoria in Dalton Square in front, and the clock in the Priory

Church. He died in 1930 when his estate was said to have been worth £9.5 million. The Ashton Memorial in Williamson Park, which was a gift to the town by his father James Williamson, was erected in memory of Lord Ashton's first wife. It was designed in 1904 by John Belcher, an architect, but slightly revised by his partner J.J. Joass before the commencement of construction work in 1907.

Williamson's factory was connected to the railway at Lancaster Castle station via the line to Glasson Dock. From the line, there were sidings onto St. George's Quay, these terminating by Carlisle Bridge. Now, a considerable part of the factory has been demolished, making way for Lune Industrial Park and the railway tracks have long since been lifted.

Formerly, Lancaster had two railway stations, Lancaster Castle (now Lancaster) on the Lancaster and Carlisle line, which is now part of the West Coast Main Line, and Lancaster Green Ayre, which was on the site of the green area between Skerton Bridge and Sainsburys. That line, part of the North-western Railway line from Yorkshire to Morecambe, was completed in 1850 and later became part of the Midland Railway. The store and its car park occupy part of the site of the station and its yard and turntable. In turn, the station was built on the site of the main Lancaster shipbuilder's yard, Brockbank's Yard. The only reminder of the area once having been a railway station and yard is the crane, which formerly stood in Hornby station yard. (Walk 2 passes over this area.)

From Green Ayre, the railway crossed Greyhound Bridge on its way to Morecambe. The line from Lancaster Castle station to here and on to Morecambe Promenade station was electrified in 1908. The last of the electric trains ran on New Year's Day, 1966. Now, the bridge had been converted for road traffic.

The Brockbank family built several sea-going craft of all sizes. They had built fifty-four vessels between 1779 and 1801, five of which were over 300 tons. Their firm was founded by George Brockbank in the 1730's and later his son and son's nephew came into the business. The old bridge across the Lune caused problems to the yard as fully rigged ships could not pass beneath it. In 1800 John Brockbank purchased the bridge and two years later the first of the arches was removed to allow ships to pass downstream. The second arch fell down in 1807, another was demolished in 1814 and the last arch fell in 1845. After this, John Brockbank gave up all rights to the ruins and site to Lancaster Port Commissioners, his paying them £30 to take over the remains of the old bridge.

To celebrate the Millennium, the River Lune Millennium Park has been brought into being, its comprising the new Millennium Bridge, and cycleways and footways to Caton together with the restoration of the viewpoint at Gray's Seat and various works of art along the way. The bridge was opened on 16 February 2001, a large crowd of pedestrians and cyclists being present to watch and be amongst the first to cross.

Whilst being one of the longest walks in this book, this is also one of the easiest to do.

From Lancaster bus station, cross Cable Street, the main road, via the pedestrian crossing and turn to the left. At the road junction ahead, turn right and follow the road to St. George's Quay. Walk along by the River Lune, passing the Millennium Bridge, former warehouses and the Maritime Museum over to the left and well worth a visit, and then pass under Carlisle Bridge, which takes the West Coast main line across the river.

Continue straight along the road, pass Forbo, the direct descendent of Jas. Williamson and Son, and whose future is in doubt at the time of writing. Pass the entrance to an industrial estate and then pass a warehouse. On reaching Keyline on the right, come to the end of the motor road. Pass to the left of Keyline onto a bridleway for Aldcliffe. The bridleway is at first tarred, but shortly becomes a broad, stony track to follow.

Continue along the bridleway to where it turns left at Aldcliffe Crossing, the site of an old railway crossing for the line from Lancaster to Glasson. (Alternatively, about half a mile from the end of the tarred track, there is a way up to the old railway line on the left and this can be followed to Aldcliffe Crossing.) Cross the remains of the crossing and then turn immediately right onto the old track bed of the railway, which is now part of the Lancashire Coastal Way. It is a very good path to follow.

The path passes along by the tidal River Lune on its way to its estuary. A bridge takes it over a large stream, Burrow Beck, which will be seen again later. Shortly beyond that crossing a house is passed on the left. By here are the remains of the old Ashton Hall station, a private station for the use of Lord Ashton. Now, not much remains to be seen of this feature except for the raised ground that was the site of the platform.

Pass beneath a brick bridge and about half a mile further on is a picnic area on the site of the former Conder Green station and yard. From here, go to the right over the former railway bridge spanning the mouth of the River Conder as it empties its waters into the Lune Estuary.

Follow the path along to its terminus at the Victoria Inn, which is at the end of Victoria Terrace. It is well worth having a look around Glasson Dock before continuing with the walk.

Owing to silting problems with the Lune channel up to Lancaster, the Lancaster Port Commissioners resolved in 1779 to build a wet dock at Glasson, which is about half a mile from the older Old Glasson. The area around was all marsh and fields, there being no road from Conder Green, at that time the only road approach being via Thurnham.

On 20 May 1787 the first ship, the 'Mary' tied up at the newly completed dock, her having been built at the Brockbank yard in 1783 and originally named 'Rebecca'. The dock is 2.706 acres in area and is roughly rectangular. In the late 1980's there were several changes around the dock, the New Quay being built and the entrance enlarged and converted from having conventional double gates to a single gate raised and lowered from the bed of the dock.

Sadly, the old dry dock in the southwest corner can no longer be seen as it was filled in during 1969. It was opened in 1840 and extended in 1852.

At the sea lock there is an electrically operated swing bridge. The former bridge, which was very similar in appearance, used to be operated by capstans. It is at the sea lock that responsibility changes from the Lancaster Port Commissioners who control the dock, to British Waterway Board who control the Lancaster Canal. This lock has two sets of gates at the top, one pair being for very high tides when the water in the dock is higher than the Lancaster Canal in the basin above. Normally, the canal being the higher, the lower pair of gates is in use.

Although authorised by an Act of Parliament of 1793, the construction of the Glasson Arm of the canal was delayed and it was not opened until 16 May, 1826, when the 'Sprightly' a sloop laden with a cargo of stone from Duddon passed through bound for Preston.

The canal basin now houses an extensive marina. In the heyday of commercial traffic over the canal there was a commodious warehouse in the corner by the marina. There were railway lines running down from the station, half a mile away, across what is now a car park, and to the wharf. Surprisingly, it is recorded in 1889 that Glasson drinking water was taken from the canal basin.

Glasson church stands by the canal bank shortly above the basin. It is younger than the canal, only being consecrated in 1840 and extended in 1932.

At high tides the road from Conder Green to Glasson is flooded and traffic should then go round via Thurnham. However, some drivers decide to risk it and can become stuck in the tide. This happened to a bus on 27 January 1936 when the 12.10 p.m. bus from Lancaster had come part way along the road before its engine failed. The passengers had to remain aboard as the water was already too deep for them to alight. At high water, the tide came up to the seats on the bus. It was not until nearly 3.00 p.m. that they were able to alight and the bus be towed back into Lancaster.

For the walk, cross the road from by the Victoria Inn and turn left onto the towpath running beside the canal basin. Go along the path, passing Glasson Church and come to bridge 8, which is skew, unusual for the Lancaster Canal.

Pass Thurnham Mill Hotel and Restaurant by which is the bottom lock of the flight of six locks dropping the Lancaster Canal down from the main line to the sea lock. The entry point and some of the mechanism from when this former corn mill was water powered can still be seen. The former channel taking the water from the canal to the mill is to the left of the towpath as it passes on and past lock five. By the top of lock four there are the remains of the take-off point for the water. The Lancaster Canal Company purchased the mill in 1824 for £1,100 in order that they could get the water rights and divert the millstream into the Glasson Arm below the adjacent lock.

At bridge 4, below lock three is where water from the River Conder is brought into the canal. Lock two is passed and then lock one at the junction with the main line of the Lancaster Canal is reached. Here, there is Junction Bridge, a turnover bridge so designed that horses could be backed over without having to be disconnected from their boats.

At the junction, turn left past the lock-keeper's cottage, which is the residence of the man in charge of the Glasson flight of locks. Continue on along the canal bank, passing Galgate Marina on the way. Galgate village can be visited by crossing the bridge here and then turning left along the main road. For the walk, continue on along the canal bank, passing the gardens of some of the Galgate houses on the far side of the canal.

About a quarter of a mile from the bridge leading to Galgate there is one of John Rennie's "Little Aqueducts" taking the canal over the River Conder. This is the third of four similar aqueducts on the Lancaster Canal, all designed by John Rennie.

After another mile the start of Deep Cutting is reached. This is where the Lancaster Canal passes through a cutting of roughly 1.5 miles. About 150 yards from the beginning, pass under Brant Beck Bridge, which is a standard bridge in design except that it is much higher. The standard bridges are so called because they are all built to a basic design by John Rennie, who was the engineer to the Lancaster Canal between Preston and Tewitfield. More of the story of the canal is told with walk 2.

The canal crosses over Burrow Beck, which is taken under it by a syphon. The lower pool of the syphon and the Beck flowing on its way is easily to be seen by looking over the masonry wall from the towpath.

Pass under Carr Lane or Broken Back Bridge, unusual in that it is a Rennie Standard bridge in design, but instead of the roadway being humped as it crosses the bridge, it dips down to its centre, the roadways either side of the canal being higher.

At the deepest part of the cutting, pass under the widened bridge taking the road for Cockerham and Glasson over the Canal. Continue on to the end of the cutting and pass into the open again before reaching another, much shorter, cutting. The towpath swings right on reaching Aldcliffe Road and then passes under a bridge with no keystone in its arch. Pass Aldcliffe Road Footbridge, which was made from a ship's gangway. Pass under the West Coast main line and then pass the former boathouse for the Swift Boats on the far side of the canal, which has been renovated from its previously ruinous state.

Owing to the threat to passenger traffic on the Lancaster Canal from the railways, a Swift Boat service was introduced on April 1st, 1833, at first just between Lancaster and Preston, but extended to Kendal from July 22nd. This service continued to operate until September 22nd, 1846, when it ceased on the opening of the railway line to Kendal. A replica of a Swift Boat is to be seen in the Maritime Museum.

The next bridge is another turnover bridge and is crossed to join the towpath, which is now on the right of the canal as it passes through a half-mile stretch of Lancaster before changing back again. Only the first part of the stretch is part of this walk. A footbridge by the "Waterwitch" pub, named after one of the Swift Boats, is passed and

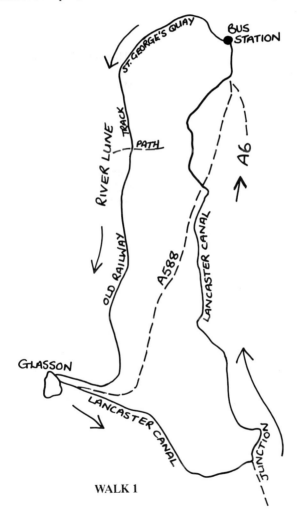

WALK 1

then the slope up to the road at Penny Street Bridge is reached. The pub has been converted from the former canal stables. Opposite are the wharves and basins and it was there that the Lancaster Canal Company had its long since demolished offices. From the bridge, come out onto the road and turn left, cross the pedestrian crossing to the central island and then turn left over another pedestrian crossing. From there, go straight down the road (Penny Street becoming Cheapside) for about half a mile, passing through part of Lancaster's pedestrianised shopping area, to its end and turn left for the bus station.

WALK 2, LANCASTER TO SLYNE AND BOLTON-LE-SANDS.

Easy.
3 miles to Slyne, 4.5 miles to Bolton-le-Sands.
Allow 2 hours to Slyne and a further half to three-quarters of an hour to Bolton-le-Sands.

From the bus station, cross the main road at the pedestrian crossing, turn right, and then left along the short street by the traffic lights just ahead. Join the walkway at the end of the street and turn right. Follow the walkway to the road taking traffic to Morecambe and to the north and then turn right to go beneath it via an underpass. On leaving the underpass, turn left onto the riverside walk and then right to pass along it. This area is the site of the former Green Ayre station on the railway line from Morecambe to Leeds. Ahead is the crane from Hornby station yard and Skerton Bridge taking traffic into Lancaster. From here to Caton this bank of the Lune is part of the Millennium Park with interpretative notice boards and some works of art to be seen along the way.

Pass beneath Skerton Bridge and then follow a walkway close to the banks of the Lune (1). Continue straight along here, the site of the former railway line from Lancaster to Yorkshire. Pass by Skerton Weir,

Across Skerton Weir at Lancaster

which is at the head of the tidal section of the River Lune and continue up to the Lune Aqueduct ahead.

The Lune Aqueduct is the finest structure on the Lancaster Canal and this is an appropriate place for a little of the canal's story.

A number of surveys of a proposed canal linking the industrial towns of Lancashire with Kendal, via Preston and Lancaster had been considered, but nothing had come of them. Patience was running out so that on 4 June 1791 a petition was presented to the Mayor of Lancaster requesting him to convene a public meeting to consider the building of a canal. The meeting was held on 8 June, resulting in further survey work being undertaken. October 1791 saw John Rennie being asked to make a survey. This he did and the proposed canal was to run from West Houghton on the Lancashire coalfield through to Kendal. A subsequent public meeting in Lancaster Town Hall on 7 February 1792 saw its being resolved that the necessary Act of Parliament be obtained. The Act was passed on 25 June 1792 and John Rennie was appointed engineer.

Work on the construction of the Lancaster Canal began in 1793, the first contract covering the stretch from Ellel Grange, not far from Galgate, through to Tewitfield, and was for £52,000 excluding bridges. Only part of the canal from West Houghton to Preston was built. There, a tramroad took goods of the Ribble to the North End, as the section of canal from Preston to Kendal was known, resulting in there being no link by water with the main canal system. There were problems with the contractors, which held up work on the canal's construction, and the Lune Aqueduct had to be built. It was not until the autumn of 1797 that the work was completed and on 22 November the Lancaster Canal was formally opened from Preston to Tewitfield. Six boats took part in the ceremony, but the actual voyage was only for the short distance from Lancaster to the aqueduct and back again.

The Lune Aqueduct is a magnificent structure. It has five semi-circular arches, each of 70 feet, stands 60 feet high and has a total length of 600 feet. The piers for the arches have foundations from 20 feet below the level of Skerton Weir. To provide extra strength, there are inverted arches between the arches, something which is not visible as they are hidden by the spandrels. The aqueduct is topped with a massive cornice carrying the water channel. John Rennie designed the structure and the contractors were Alexander Stevens and Son of Edinburgh. Work on the aqueduct began in January 1794, the last arch was completed in July 1797 and the whole structure finished in the autumn. It was originally estimated that the Lune Aqueduct would cost £18,618-16s-0d, but the final figure was £48,320-18s-10d, the piers alone having cost £14,792-9s-8d. On the southwest side, above the central arch is a Latin inscription translating to:

"Old needs are served; far distant sites are combined; Rivers by art to bring new wealth are joined. A.D. 1797 J. Rennie, engineer. A. Stevens and Son, contractors."

On the northeastern side there is the inscription "To Public Prosperity".

Alexander Stevens never saw the completion of the aqueduct as he died on 29 January 1796 and his son completed the work. Stevens is buried in the Lancaster Priory churchyard and there is a memorial plaque to him in the south wall of the church.

Immediately in front of the aqueduct (2), a path leads to the right and a flight of steps takes it up to the Lancaster Canal towpath. Turn left and walk across the aqueduct (3), under bridge 108, the Halton Road Bridge, to the next bridge, 109 (4). Leave the towpath via the steps, cross the bridge and then turn sharp right onto the track which runs alongside the canal.

At the end of the first field on the left there is a signpost indicating a public footpath. Cross the stile and go straight ahead by the stream to another stile in the corner. It can be an awkward crossing after rain as the stream is also crossed and the ground around here can be very muddy. Once over the stile, go along the field, keeping close by the stream, to where the next stile to cross is in the fence ahead.

Next, go diagonally left up the field towards where there is a piece of old gateway standing on its own. Now, its only purpose is to indicate the right of way. Continue on up towards the hedge and, just before the end of the field, there is a stile leading to the adjacent field to be seen in the hedge. After crossing it, the next stile to be crossed is a few yards further on to the right. This next field is crossed keeping to the hedge on the right, passing a field gate on the way, to another stile in the corner by the hedge in front. Go straight up this field and across the next stile.

Continue straight up this next field, keeping close to the hedge on the right. From here, the Hest Bank Lane area of Slyne, parts of Morecambe Bay and the Lakeland Fells can be seen. After crossing the next stile, bear well left across the field. In the fence on the far side there is a gateway with a stile to cross just to the right of it.

The path goes straight across the next field to another stile in the fence opposite and Slyne is seen in front. From this stile, turn left along by the hedge to another stile, which is nearby, and after crossing it turn right by the fence to the following stile to cross. From this stile, bear diagonally down the slope towards the kissing gate in the hedge in front. From that gate, cross over the field and come out at a stile leading onto the A6. The Cross Keys bus stops are both close by to the right.

For continuing on to Slyne, carry on walking past the bus stops and past the Cross Keys Hotel. Towards the northern end of Slyne there are further bus stops.

Slyne is part of Slyne with Hest. Formerly it was part of the Bolton-le-Sands parish, but, with Hest Bank, is now a parish in its own right. It is an old manorial village, as is shown by its having a manor house and manor farm. Close by them were a malt kiln and a smithy. Across the road from the Cross Keys Hotel are the old village stocks where wrongdoers were imprisoned and which are still in good condition.

For a quiet walk on to Bolton-le-Sands which uses the beginning of walk 4 in reverse, continue along the main road to the far end of Slyne village and then turn right up the Halton road for a few hundred yards. A kissing gate on the left leads to a path which drops down some steps and then goes right, over a stile and across the playing field to a kissing gate. Go straight across the narrow section of the next field to a gate in the hedge and then follow the path by the left-hand hedge to a stile. From there the path, although not clear, then goes straight across the field near the hedge on the right to the large field gate leading onto Ancliffe Lane, named after the farm close by. Turn left along Ancliffe Lane for Bolton-le-Sands village. Cross the main street and go down St. Michael's Lane to the bus stops on the A6 for the 555 buses, to the left for buses south and across at the crossing and then a few yards right for buses north.

Most of walk 4 can be linked with this one from Slyne to make a circular walk from Lancaster.

1. Walk 3 joins here.
2. Walk 3 leaves here.
3. Walk 3 joins the towpath here.
4. Walk 3 passes under this bridge.

WALK 3, LANCASTER, CATON, HALTON, LANCASTER.

Easy
8 miles
Allow 3.75 hours.

From the centre of Lancaster, start as walk 2, if coming from the north alight from the bus at Red Cross and then cross over Skerton Bridge and follow the road round to the left. On shortly reaching a road junction where the traffic goes into town, turn left along a short track to join the riverside path. Turn right along the former railway track, which now has a proper surface and streetlights, and keep going straight along it. Take the left-hand path at a junction, the one to the right being out onto a road. Follow the track along, past Skerton Weir, and come to the Lune Aqueduct (2). Pass under the aqueduct and continue along the track past the back of the Post House Hotel.

After leaving the Post House there are a number of places where the former railway track can be left to follow the old right of way above the River Lune. Turn onto this path before reaching a point where the ground to the left of the railway starts to rise at an old cutting. Follow the riverside path over a wooden stile and across a field with the bridge taking the M6 over the Lune being at its end.

Follow the pathway under the M6 bridge and then cross the adjoining field by the Lune. Over to the right the street lamps on the old railway walkway are to be seen. At the end of the field the path passes through a kissing gate and then continues along the river-bank. Shortly, the former railway track is joined again and it soon comes to a car park. Cross the car park and over Denny Beck Lane and continue straight on past the former Halton railway station. (The village of Halton is across the River Lune and is reached by a bridge at the foot of Denny Beck Lane, making for a shorter walk.)

Whilst there is a path by the river, it can be tricky to follow if the Lune is high, so it is recommended that the old railway line is followed, passing above Halton Rocks in the Lune, until Forge Bank Weir is reached over to the left. On the way, some inverted trees are passed, these being one of the works of art in the Millennium Park and arousing a lot of controversy locally. A roadway for North West Water passes through a gap in the fence on the left close to the Weir. Turn down the roadway and at the bottom turn right to follow the fence, on the other side of which are some of the water company's buildings.

The path goes down to the river-bank again and then along it, over another North-west Water structure and then over a wooden stile into the next field. This is the right of way. Continue over the field above the river, the path not being distinct, and pass a number of trees where erosion has exposed their roots. Cross a small stream and then over a rather muddy stretch where there are several trees with exposed roots and come to an old railway bridge in front.

On reaching the bridge, cross a stile and then turn up the steps to the right to come out onto the old railway track again, where turn left to cross the bridge. Follow the track bed along, under a road bridge, and then turn left to go up to the car park. (By going under the railway bridge there is a diversion to Gray's Seat. Follow the bank of the river, up some steps and through a gate to the right, leading onto the busy road, which is crossed. Turn right for about 100 yards to the entrance to the path leading up to the viewpoint, where there is a seat and an excellent view up the Lune Valley to Ingleborough. Return by the same route to the railway bridge.)

For Caton, instead of turning up to the car park, keep following the track bed along, crossing another bridge spanning the Lune and looking down to Penny Bridge. Continue along the track to where it passes through a gateway onto a roadway. There, turn right, passing Station House, for Caton village. The Domesday Tree is along the road to the right at the entrance to The Croft. Return to the car park by the Lune by the outward route. The diversion to Caton takes about half an hour.

Caton is now largely a dormitory for Lancaster. However, it once had much industry as there were eight mills working in the area. Low Mill will have been seen from the bridge when crossing the Lune, its being the lowest of the Caton mills and the one nearest the river. It has now been converted into residential accommodation and the mill chimney has been demolished. Originally it was powered by a 25.75 feet overshot wheel and a 21 feet undershot wheel and was erected in 1784. Steam power was added in 1819 owing to fluctuating waterpower. At one time half the workforce was made up of apprentices who were orphans and other unwanted children from Liverpool.

Passenger trains ceased to serve Caton on 1 January 1966 and the station buildings were subsequently demolished. However, the goods shed remains, the building having been converted into the Roman Catholic Church for the village in 1963.

Caton is famous for its Fish Ṣtones and Domesday Tree. The stones are stepped and joined by metal ties. It is believed that monks from Cockersands Abbey, which is at the Lune Estuary beyond Glasson Dock, came here in medieval times to sell their surplus fish. Shading the steps is an ancient and twisted oak tree, the Domesday Tree.

In the 19th century Caton was part of the Lancaster parish, but is now a parish in its own right. The parish church is St. Paul's at Brookhouse, one of the four communities making up the village. Whilst there is a relic of the original 12th century building in the form of a Norman Arch, much of the church dates from 1865, when it was consecrated. Most of the original building, apart from the tower, had been demolished owing to its having fallen into disrepair.

Seen from the former railway bridge is Penny Bridge, the road bridge over the river at Crook of Lune and by a popular picnic area in summer. Originally there was no bridge over the river between Caton and Halton and the river had to be forded. In 1806 a toll bridge was opened here, which

Summer at Crook O'Lune, Caton

cost £3,164, including £172 for the tollhouse. This bridge stood until December 1881 when the middle arch collapsed followed by the rest of the structure. It was replaced by the present bridge, which was opened in August 1883.

Back at the car park, go towards the road and turn right to follow a permissive path by the wall, separating it from the road. At the end of the path turn right along the road towards Halton for about forty yards and then cross over to pass through a kissing gate and onto a footpath through the woodland.

Cross a footbridge over a beck and pass over the open field in front, generally keeping close to the river-bank. By Forge Bank Weir the path splits, and the arm turning down to the left is taken. Go down a flight of steps onto a paved area above the Lune and turn right. Along here there used to be mills, but these have been closed and demolished over the years. Pass by Halton Rocks in the river below. Go round a large gate and straight along the roadway in front, passing by some industrial buildings.

The roadway turns to the right and then joins another roadway. Here, turn left and follow this roadway to its end at Station Road, which leads from Halton village and over the river to the former railway station. Turn right along Station Road which comes out onto Low Road, where turn to the left.

Halton was known to the Romans, a Roman altar having been found in the churchyard in 1794. They may well have occupied Castle Hill, which looks down on the churchyard.

Castle Hill is the lowest motte and bailey structure of the Lune Valley, where there are six, it being a small one, a much better example being further up the Lune valley at Hornby. It was the Normans who constructed these 'castles' possibly on Saxon sites. The larger area is the bailey, which was surrounded by a ditch and to which people would retreat in times of trouble. The excavations from the moat would be used to form the motte, the higher defensive point within the bailey and usually towards one end. The motte at Halton is easily recognised as there is the village flagpole on top. The Saxon Earl Tostig, the Earl of Northumbria, may have had his castle here as Halton was his seat. Tostig was the brother of Harold Godwinson (the king of England killed at the Battle of Hastings) and held much of the land in North Lancashire and South Westmorland, which were not then counties in their own right but part of Yorkshire. He was deprived of his Earldom in 1065, leading to his death at the Battle of Stamford Bridge.

Following the Norman Conquest, the whole area of Lonsdale south from the River Keer, apart from the Lordships of Hornby and Whittington, were part of a Royal Forest. This does not necessarily mean that the area was wooded, but harsh forest laws would apply.

Most of Halton now lies to the east of Castle Hill, including modern developments and the shops. Below the hill stands St. Wilfrid's church, the present building being consecrated on 8 October 1877. It replaces a 1792 building, this in turn replacing a building dating from 1539 and which was in a bad state of repair resulting in demolition apart from the tower, which remains. St. Wilfrid was a northern saint who died in 709 and there is a local belief that he founded the original church in Halton.

The remaining parts of Halton Hall stand across from St. Wilfrid's church. Edmund Sharpe purchased the building in 1886 and eight years later the Lordship of the Manor. He was the last Lord of the Manor to live in the hall, which had stood there for 200 years with some parts being still older. He had a Victorian wing added. Following the death of Sharpe, the estate was sold in 1931 and the oldest parts of the hall demolished. Now, only Sharpe's wing and part of a bay window in a bungalow remain, these being seen from across the Lune.

The former railway line and station are across the Lune from the village they served. The present bridge was constructed from parts of the former bridge over the Lune at Green Ayre in Lancaster this being from when it was replaced by the present Greyhound Bridge in 1911. Following its re-erection at Halton, the bridge was opened by Mr. E. W. Sharpe of Halton Hall on 13 February, 1913. Prior to the coming of the railway the Lune was forded at Denny Beck, close to where it is now spanned by the bridge.

Halton station is different from any others on the line. In 1907 a train set the original station alight and it burned down. It was replaced by the brick building, which still stands.

Pass straight through Halton. Above the mini-roundabout at the end of High Road is the site of the former Motte and bailey. St. Wilfrid's Church is passed. Shortly after leaving the last houses of Halton the bridge taking the M6 over the River Lune is again reached. Pass under the bridge and turn left to cross a stile onto Ministry of Defence property. A signpost shows that it is a public footpath.

Go straight along the good roadway just above the river and passing through Halton Camp. On reaching a perimeter fence round buildings on the right, the path continues straight ahead along the river-bank. It is a grassy path to follow. The Lune Aqueduct is to be seen ahead. Before passing under the aqueduct, the outflow from the Lancaster Canal comes down from the right.

Turn up to another path once under the aqueduct. On joining the other path, turn right onto the canal towpath at the end of the aqueduct (3), where turn left. Pass under the Halton road and pass under the following bridge (4). On reaching the next bridge, Beaumont Turnpike, leave the canal towpath for the bus stops, first passing under it if travelling to the north. There are stops to both the left and the right for travelling in either direction. The stops to the north, reached by crossing over the canal bridge, are the nearer, but there is not much in it.

2. Walk 2 leaves here.
3. Walk 2 is joined again here.
4. Walk 2 is left again here.

WALK 4, BOLTON-LE-SANDS, SLYNE, LANCASTER.

Easy
5.5 miles
Allow 2 to 2.5 hours.

Bolton-le-Sands has existed since at least Saxon times, the name coming from Old English words for dwelling and village or hamlet. In the Domesday Book the village is listed as 'Bodeltone'. The addition of 'le-Sands' came about with increasing travel in the nineteenth century so as to identify it from the several other places in the country also named 'Bolton'.

Holy Trinity, the parish church dates back to at least 1094, but it is probable that there was an earlier Saxon church. The building has been extensively altered over the years, the last major works being done in 1880. A number of smaller changes have taken place since that time.

Following the Reformation, the first Roman Catholic Chapel in the village was a converted barn at the corner of The Nook and Ancliffe Lane, this serving from 1868 to 1884. On 6 May 1884 St. Mary of the Angels in the centre of the village was opened for worship by the Bishop of Liverpool.

The first non-conformist church building, which dates from 1910, in the village still exists, its being a corrugated iron building below the Lancaster Canal and opposite to the Packet Boat public house. The 'Tin Tabernacle', as it was known, was never seen as being the permanent church. The present building, Christ Church (United Reformed) was opened in 1935, two major additions having been made since that time.

Bolton-le-Sands was much altered with the building of the Lancaster Canal in 1793. Its line cut the Town End section of the village off from the rest, resulting in the present road by its side, Shady Lane, being built and the road from Lancaster being diverted. The line of the old road can still be seen in the glebe field. The main road through the village went to the right of the Packet Boat, along what is now Packet Lane, and in front of the houses seen down below on the right from Packet Hill. The by-pass road, now part of the A6, was not constructed until 1926, all traffic previously having to pass through the centre of the village. The bridge, which is often known as 'Packet Bridge', is officially 'Bolton Turnpike Bridge' from the days when the road was part of the turnpike to Heron Syke.

Prior to the 20ᵗʰ Century the main occupations of the people of the village were connected with agriculture. Barley was one of the main crops grown and there were malt kilns in the village, by the 1800's the only ones being at St. Michael's Grove and Town End. However, there was also a trade in cockling, particularly in the second half of the nineteenth century, the cockles being transported by packhorse until the coming of the Lancaster Canal.

Another reminder of the agricultural past is the former pinfold, on the west side of the A6 around 100 yards south of the Royal Hotel. This structure was originally circular and where stray animals were impounded until collected by their owners. Road widening has seen part of the pinfold demolished, but the remainder is well preserved.

From the St. Michael's Lane bus stops in Bolton-le-Sands, these being either side of the lane, which crosses the A6 road, go up the eastern part of the lane to the centre of the village. Cross the main village street by St. Mary's church and cross straight over the road the left leading to Nether Kellet and go up The Nook in front. Follow it round the corner, where it becomes Ancliffe Lane.

Go along Ancliffe Lane for about a mile and a quarter to where Ancliffe Hall Farm is up a lane on the left. Opposite the lane is a large metal field gate to pass through and go straight across the field towards the trees ahead to the left. A kissing gate leads into a young plantation by the much older trees. At the end of the plantation there is another kissing gate and then cross the narrow neck of the field to another kissing gate leading into the football field.

Assuming no match is taking place, cross straight over the pitch to a wooden stile and then cross the next field and up some steps to a kissing gate leading out onto the Halton road, where turn right for Slyne.

On dropping down to the A6, turn left to the Cross Keys, passing the main Slyne bus stops for the 555 route on the way. At the Cross Keys (5), turn down the road to the right, passing the old Slyne stocks on the left at the top of the road. Follow the road along and over a crossroads. About half way along the field on the right, and just

Stocks at Slyne

before reaching a roadway to a farm, there is a gate leading into it. Cross straight over the field to the kissing gate in front.

Once through that gate, bear right towards another kissing gate in front, this leading into the trees. Drop down the path and over a footbridge spanning the end of a pond. Once over there, go through a kissing gate and then right across the field following the line of the hedge on the right. On reaching another kissing gate, go through it and along by the ditch by the hedge on the right.

Cross a stile by a field gate and continue along by the hedge until the path turns left to go through a wooden stile and out onto a track where turn left. Follow the track to the bridge over the Lancaster Canal (6), cross it and turn onto the canal bank, where turn right. Go under the next bridge, before which is the sight of old stables for the changing of horses, the buildings having now vanished.

Pass under the next bridge and then as the following bridge is reached Foley Farm is seen over to the left. Leave the canal bank just before reaching the bridge and go straight down the lane from the farm and on reaching the road at the end turn right to pass under the railway.

Once under the railway, turn left at the sign for Watery Lane. Go straight up the path amongst the trees. At the top there is a stile leading out onto Watery Lane. From here, either go straight down Watery Lane or turn left and go down St. Chad's Drive to the Torrisholme to Lancaster road at the bottom, where turn left.

Pass under the railway bridge and then turn right to cross over Ryelands Park, going to the right-hand corner of it. Come out onto the Morecambe to Lancaster road, where there is a pedestrian crossing just after passing under the railway bridge. After crossing the road, turn back under Carlisle Bridge again and go up the steps by it to cross the Lune on a footway by the railway.

After crossing the bridge, turn left along St. George's Quay, for the bus station, passing the Maritime Museum, well worth a visit, on the way. Alternatively, from the steps by Carlisle Bridge, follow the riverside track up the Lune to the Millennium Bridge, cross it and turn left and pass under a former railway bridge and along the road to the bus station.

5. Walk 2 ends here unless going through to Bolton-le-Sands.
6. Walk 5 continues along the track to Bare.

WALK 5, BOLTON-LE-SANDS, BARE, BOLTON-LE-SANDS.

Easy
6.5 miles
Allow two and a half to three hours.

From the St. Michael's Lane bus stops, which are near the Little Chef (northbound stop is to the north of the lane, opposite the car park for the Far Pavilion Restaurant, southbound stop is opposite the Little Chef), go up the road towards where the church with the spire is seen.

Before reaching it, there is a bridge over the Lancaster Canal and the towpath is joined to the right of the bridge. There, turn right and walk along the canal bank.

In about half a mile pass Hatlex Swing Bridge, one of only two such swing bridges now left on the main line of the canal. Pass under the next bridge, Hatlex Bridge (from which Slyne can be reached by crossing it and following the road up to the village), and follow the canal along. Once under the next bridge, there are the boats moored at Hest Bank. Over to the right is Station Road, looking straight down towards the signal box at Hest Bank. A diversion can be made here to the village centre by coming off the canal bank and dropping down the road. For the walk, pass under the following bridge, number 117 and continue onwards past moored boats to the next bridge, 116 (6).

Mute Swan on Lancaster Canal

Hest Bank is part of the parish of Slyne with Hest, but was formerly part of Bolton-le-Sands parish. In former times the Oversands route across Morecambe Bay to Kents Bank started here and there was a special light in one room of the Hest Bank Hotel to guide coaches. Whilst there are no longer coaches crossing the sands of Morecambe Bay, there are regular guided crossings on foot during the summer months, generally to raise money for charities. Crossing the Bay should never be attempted without a guide. There used to be a stone pier here and coastal vessels regularly called and transshipped goods onto the Lancaster Canal, only a quarter of a mile away, for carrying through to Kendal.

The West Coast main railway line passes through Hest Bank, the station long having been closed, and this is the only stretch of the line where it does actually run by the coast on its route from London to Glasgow. In the days of steam trains there were troughs to the north of the crossing, the water for them being drawn from the canal.

At bridge 116, turn off the canal bank onto a good farm track, following it down to the left, away from the canal. As the track reaches the main West Coast railway line, it turns left, following the railway until going under the line at a bridge. Pass into a field and cross to its far side and then go through a kissing gate leading onto another railway line. Cross the line with care as it is used, but not very frequently, even though it may be completely rusty at the time of your crossing a train could be approaching. Go through another kissing gate and turn left down the lane running between the railway and Morecambe Golf Course.

The path crosses a wooden footbridge and then swings right, fairly close to the golf course. Cross another footbridge and then follow the path onwards past some houses on the left. The path turns left and passes round the golf course and then the back of Happy Mount Park before coming out onto a road. Follow the road for about 100 yards to a junction with Elm Grove going to the right. (By going straight ahead the centre of Bare and Princes Crescent with its shops are reached.) Turn down Elm Grove and cross onto the promenade at the crossing to the right, opposite the entrance to Happy Mount Park.

Bare is now a suburb of Morecambe, but used to be a village in its own right, and was surrounded by fields. However, it still retains some of the character of a village as it has a row of varied shops, Princes Crescent, stretching from near the railway station to the promenade. There was a tithebarn opposite the Elms hotel. Outside Bare Post Office is a rather rare type of letter box dating from Queen Victoria's days, its having no royal cipher and no mention of Post Office ownership. Also, the aperture is higher than normal.

The road round the coast is very different from how it is shown on the 1891 map. Marine Drive, as it now is, was Bare Road, leading to Bare and along towards Bare Battery, a short way on from the modern entrance to Happy Mount Park, close to the beach and by which was a magazine. Bare Camp was established in 1886 as a military training ground where soldiers spent two weeks during the summer months. There was no road beyond the battery, only a path round by the shore to Hest Bank. The present Coastal Road linking Morecambe with Bolton-le-Sands was built in the 1920's. Happy Mount Park was opened in 1927.

Turn right along the promenade and see Hest Bank ahead. Where the road starts to bear right away from the sea front and up towards Hest Bank, there is another roadway to its left. Turn along here, using the part for pedestrians, this being part of the Lancashire Coastal Way. Follow the path on, in front of the leisure complex, across some shingle in front of the houses and onto the beach. Ignore a path to the right as it is for Hest Bank, but continue ahead along the beach.

On reaching Hest Bank, turn right towards the railway and signal box, seen earlier from the canal bank, and then left along the roadway before reaching them. Follow the roadway along, with a cafe over to the right. On reaching some houses, a sign indicates that it is a private road. The Coastal Way is just to the left of the road. Continue straight along the pathway which runs along the top of the beach. As a farm is reached, turn to the right towards the roadway. Cross it and pass along by the wall separating the farmland from the shore. Pass through a stile in the wall and go up the field bearing to the left. A stile is reached at the hedge in front. Cross it and bear left through the caravans. On reaching the wall between the shore and the buildings of Red Bank Farm there is a stone stile to cross. Continue straight along from here over a grassy stretch and then along the top of the sea defences to St. Michael's Lane, which is the second turning on the right after leaving the farm. Go straight up the road, over the railway and to the A6 by the Little Chef and the bus stops.

An alternative ending to this walk is to continue straight along the beach after passing the first farm, instead of going through the stile and field. By doing this, a large "erratic" rock, known as "Jumbo Rock", left by a retreating glacier in the Ice Age is passed. Above is Red Bank, a promontory which has changed its appearance over the years owing to erosion. At the end of this stretch of beach, turn onto the embankment of the sea defences by Red Bank Farm and continue along the top to St. Michael's Lane, the second road going off to the right.

6.   Walk 4 turns onto the canal bank here to continue towards Lancaster.

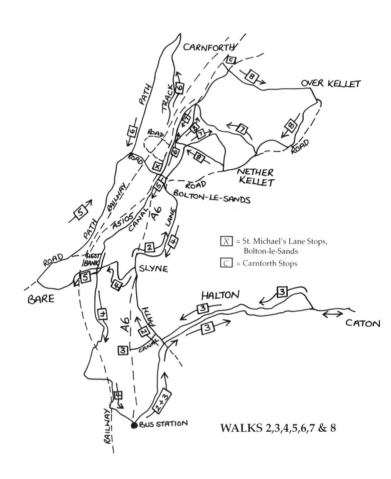

X = St. Michael's Lane Stops,
Bolton-le-Sands

C = Carnforth Stops

WALKS 2,3,4,5,6,7 & 8

WALK 6, BOLTON-LE-SANDS, CRAG BANK, COASTAL WAY, BOLTON-LE-SANDS.

Easy
5.5 to 6 miles
Allow three hours.

From the St. Michael's Lane bus stops, go up the lane towards the centre of the village, where a church spire can be seen. On coming to the bridge over the Lancaster Canal, do not cross it, but join the towpath and turn left. Continue along the canal bank, passing under Bolton Turnpike Bridge, close to the Packet Boat Hotel, Chorley's Bridge, Bolton Cinder Ovens Bridge (7)(8) and continue from there to the next bridge, Barkers Bridge. Here, come off the canal bank and into a lay-by off the A6. Cross the road and turn left until reaching the way to Detron Gate over to the right.

Turn down the lane towards Detron Gate, go over the railway bridge and then, as the road bends left, go over a stile by a field gate on the right. Follow the farm track along to its end. Cross the stile by a field gate and follow the track along by the hedge and wall on the right. The field broadens out and from there pass along by the dyke to the left and not the fence.

At the end of the field there is a metal field gate with a stile by it. Cross into the next field and continue over it by the dyke on the left. At the end there is a wooden footbridge over another dyke at right angles to the one followed. Cross the bridge into the next field and pass straight over it to a wooden stile in the fence. This stile leads onto a lane where turn right for another stile by a field gate leading onto the road at Crag Bank. Turn left along the road, passing a farm, and come to a turning to the right by the North West Water premises. Go up the track for a few yards to a stile by a gate, waymarked, into the field on the left. Go along the field by the wall on the right, looking straight along towards Warton Crag.

At the end of the field there is a stile to cross into the next field and then continue straight ahead. At the end of this next field, by a metal field gate, there is a wooden stile to cross and then bear left past some hawthorns. After passing them, cross a stile and then a footbridge into a marshy area. Here, go along by the hedge on the right for a short distance and then up the field to where a waymarker post is seen at the top.

River Keer and Warton Crag near Galley Hall

Pass the waymarker and then over some rough ground with a marshy type of grass towards another waymarker. On reaching it, bear left to the fence in front, going just above a pond on the left. By the fence there is a plank footbridge leading to the stile which is crossed. Bear right up the field and then towards the right of a brick building of the farm, Galley Hall, in front.

On reaching the building, there is a stile on the far side of which stone steps lead down into the farmyard. Pass through the farmyard, along a farm lane and out onto a road in front. Here, a signpost indicates that it is the Lancashire Coastal Way in either direction. **From here the coastal route is tidal and can be blocked at high tide.** Turn left along the road with the River Keer on the right. Come to where the road bears left. (If not wanting to do the field walk from by the North West Water buildings, continue straight along the road to here.) To the right at that corner there is a field gate with a stile to its right and by it a Coastal Way sign. Cross the stile and then follow the trackway at the left of the ground just by the slope up to the fence. This is at the head of the shoreline.

On reaching a metal field gate in a fence, cross the stile by it. Continue along the shoreline and come to a waymarker indicating that the route is a little to the right, at the end of the grass and at the head of the shore. As the path is followed along, there are a lot of little channels to cross. Pass more waymarkers and then round by the edge of the red sandstone bank of Crag Bank.

Once having passed round the Bank, continue over the grassy ground in front, going at the head of the shore until two gullies have been passed. After that, turn right towards the seaward edge of the grass. There are two paths which can be followed over the next stretch, their merging into one as the grassy foreshore narrows. As the first farm on the left is passed, bear inland and join the roadway before reaching the second farm.

At Wild Duck Hall, the second farm, pass it and onto the shore again, going towards the fence in front. The path then goes along an embankment and round by the fence on the left until it reaches steps up to the sea defences at Bolton-le-Sands. Pass along there until the bottom of St. Michael's Lane is reached on the left. Go straight up the lane for the bus stops, northbound to the left and southbound across the A6 and slightly to the right.

7. This stretch of canal bank is done in reverse in walk 7.
8. Walk 8 uses the road crossing this bridge on its way to Carnforth.

WALK 7, BOLTON-LE-SANDS, NETHER KELLET, BOLTON-LE-SANDS.

Easy
5.5 miles
Allow 2.25 to 2.5 hours.

From the bus stops at St. Michael's Lane, go up the road on the eastern side of the A6 to the centre of the village, crossing the Lancaster Canal on the way. On reaching the top of the lane, cross over and turn right to pass round St. Mary of the Angels church. At the road junction, continue following the left-hand road past the church. On reaching the village school a few hundred yards ahead turn left along Mount Pleasant Lane.

The lane comes to a crossroads where turn right and pass the row of cottages known as Tarn Cottages. Go straight along the track from there, passing a stile on the right on the way. A metal ladder stile at the right of a field gate is reached and crossed. The ground in front can be very soft and muddy, particularly in winter. At the end of this stretch of track there is another metal ladder stile to the left of a gate.

From that stile, cross the remains of an old quarry road and go up the hillside, keeping close to the hedge on the right and come to another ladder stile. Cross it and drop down amongst trees into what was an old sandstone quarry, but which has now been planted. Follow the path along through the plantation, passing over a short stretch of open ground after dropping down from the stile. The path does wind a little amongst the trees until a waymarker post is reached.

Continue straight along the path to a wooden stile in a fence. Cross it and go straight over the field to a pair of wooden stiles, which are also crossed. Bear to the right up the field then entered. At the top of the slope, go towards the far right-hand corner of the field where a stile by a field gate leads onto a lane by the M6. Turn right up the lane to its end and then left over the bridge over the M6 to Nether Kellet.

Nether Kellet is now virtually surrounded by limestone quarries. At the top of the village there is a former lime kiln and the pub, the Lime Burners Arms, reveals that limestone has been one of the two main industries of the village for many years. A number of the paths and roadways have been diverted from their original routes because of limestone workings. The other main industry is agriculture.

Ecclesiastically, Nether Kellet is part of Bolton-le-Sands parish, the vicar of Bolton-le-Sands being the incumbent for both churches. Besides the Anglican church, the village has an independent Congregational church.

Lime Burners' Arms, Nether Kellet

Pass through Nether Kellet village until near the top where there is a road to the left going to Carnforth (9). Turn down that road and follow it to where there is a stile in the hedge on the left. Cross it and down some steps into a field and then diagonally right to a wooden stile leading onto a footbridge, which will have been seen from the road. Go over the bridge and cross the stile into the field at its end. Go straight up the field by the fence on the left to a wooden gate at the top. From the gate, bear right up the next field towards the fence on the right. Continue straight along by the fence. (Note, this fence is at the opposite side of the field you were in earlier and if it is not desired to go to Nether Kellet, cut straight left across the field from the ladder stile instead of dropping down into the former quarry.)

At the end of the fence, a metal ladder stile is crossed and then the grassy field path going to the right is followed. Cross an old quarry roadway and another metal ladder stile into the next field. From there, go towards the top right corner of the field where there is another ladder stile to cross onto a farm track.

Cross the track and another stile and, in the next field, bear left towards a gateway by which there is a squeeze stile onto a farm lane. Here there is a choice of tracks. You can cross the lane and another wooden stile and go down the field to another stile and there turn right along a track towards the canal bridge.

Alternatively, turn right down the farm lane and follow it to the canal bridge, which is crossed. Turn either left or right to join the canal towpath, but once on it turn right for Bolton-le-Sands. The bridge where the towpath is joined is Thwaite Bridge. Pass under four more bridges (7), Barker's Bridge, Bolton Cinder Ovens Bridge (8), Chorley's Bridge and Bolton Turnpike Bridge. On reaching the next bridge, Bolton Church Bridge, go under it and come off the towpath onto St. Michael's Lane. Turn right for the centre of the village or left down to the main A6 for the 555 bus stops.

7. This stretch of canal bank is the reverse of how it was walked in walk 6
8. Walk 8 uses the road crossing this bridge on its way to Carnforth.
9. Here walk 8 is met coming down from Over Kellet.

WALK 8, CARNFORTH, OVER KELLET, NETHER KELLET, BOLTON-LE-SANDS, CARNFORTH.

Easy.
6.5 miles
Allow 3 hours.

Carnforth is famous for the station having been used in the film 'Brief Encounter' and, at the time of writing, work is being undertaken to return it largely to its appearance at that time.

Originally, Carnforth, the name meaning 'heron ford', was part of Warton parish and remained so until 1894. The arrival of the Lancaster Canal had very little effect on the small village of Carnforth, but the coming of the railways did and it was from then that the village developed into the present small town. Most of the village lay along the old coach road, which is now known as North Road.

The Lancaster and Carlisle line between Lancaster and Oxenholme opened 22 September 1846, the special inaugural train to Lancaster stopping at Carnforth for water. The next line to be opened was the Ulverston and Lancaster line in 1857, later to become part of the Furness Railway. The last line to be constructed was the Midland line from Yorkshire, its opening in 1867. It linked with the line from Lancaster Green Ayre at Wennington. Carnforth was then an important railway junction serving three different Companies before the grouping of 1923. There were originally three Motive Power Depots, two now remaining, the 'new' shed dating from 1944 and to be seen from the Warton road and the Midland on the left just before reaching the railway bridge on the way into Carnforth from the north.

The original station at Carnforth, known as 'Carnforth-Yealand' was over half a mile from the village to the north. With the coming of the second line it was necessary to build a new station at the point where the two lines met, resulting in the present station being built and the close by Station Hotel.

1864 saw the Carnforth Haematite Company being formed. The company built its furnaces and ancillary plant on a triangle of land between the railway lines and a spur was built connecting to the London & North Western line (as the Lancaster and Carlisle had become). The waste material was dumped on the shore and the tip is to be seen when doing walk 6. 1871 saw the company go into the production of steel which continued until 1889 when it ceased with 300 redundancies. The Iron Works continued in production until 1929. Now, the area is an industrial site.

In 1801 Warton with Lindeth had a population of 464 compared with only 219 for Carnforth. By 1901 the population of Carnforth had risen to 3,040. By that time, the town had been given Urban Status, this having been granted in 1894.

The nearest bus stops for this walk are on Scotland Road, before the traffic lights on entering Carnforth if coming from the north or through the traffic lights after turning left from the main shopping street if travelling from the south.

Walk along to the traffic lights and turn to the left up Kellet Road. Cross over the Lancaster Canal and straight on up the road, past the cemetery, and over the M6 motorway. After the M6 has been crossed, there is a good view over to Warton and Warton Crag on the left. Continue up the road to Over Kellet. (Unfortunately there is no footpath route, which is why the road has to be followed to here.)

Over Kellet is a village that was originally built round a village green. However, modern development has meant that it now expands out from there. The 'Kellet' element of the name is said to mean 'a slope on which there is a spring'. The village was part of the Bolton-le-Sands parish, where it was a chapelry. The church once also served Nether Kellet, which is why it is situated at the end of the village.

At The Green take the right-hand road towards Nether Kellet, passing the village store, which is also the Post Office. Pass the Eagle's Head and then just before reaching the building whose appearance shows it was the old village school, turn to the right up some steps leading to a kissing gate into the field above. Go up the field, quite close to the hedge on the right. At the top, see part of an old barn ahead, and pass to its right. Over Kellet church is to be seen across the field to the left. After passing the barn, the bottom corner of an adjoining field is reached, with a stile leading into it. From the stile, go straight up the field with the hedge and fence on the left towards a magnificent ash tree at the top.

Cross a stile by the ash tree and go towards the young woodland in front. The path continues along the edge of the woodland, having been diverted from its original route because of extensive quarry workings. In the springtime there is an abundance of flowers in this woodland, bluebells, early purple orchids, celandine, primroses, garlic, wood sorrel, arum lilies and others.

Chorleys Bridge, Lancaster Bridge

The path turns to the left on reaching a fence bordering onto a quarry road. Follow the path round at the very edge of the quarry area, dropping down first some ordinary steps and then some natural limestone steps. The path continues onwards by the fence, piles of building blocks being on the other side. It then goes up some steps and turns to the right with the road between Over Kellet and Nether Kellet a few yards to the left. Go through a gate, across the quarry entrance, watching out for lorries, and through another gate opposite and straight along the path, still parallel to the road.

A stile is crossed into a plantation and there go to the right by the hedge for a hundred or so yards. The path then goes to the left to pass an ash tree on its left and then continues straight along with the plantation to its left as it goes up the sloping ground. The path then goes over to the right to follow along the foot of that slope which is planted with young trees. The path runs close to the slope, overall bearing right until it swings round to the left towards a gate in front.

Go through the gate and up the field by the hedge on the left to the next gate, which is only a short distance in front. The gate leads out onto Laithbutts Lane, the end of the diversion caused by the extensive quarry workings that can be seen here. Follow the lane to its end at the top of Nether Kellet and then turn right onto the road down through the village, pass a road to the right for Carnforth (9) on the way.

Pass straight through Nether Kellet and cross the bridge over the motorway. Immediately it has been crossed, turn right for about twenty-five yards and then turn along the track to the left. Go along the track to its end where there is a stile into the field. Cross the field following the line of the old track, keeping by the hedge and fence on the right. At the bottom of the hill, in the right-hand corner of the field, a stile is crossed into the next field. Turn sharp left and cross this field to its far left corner where another stile by a field gate leads out onto a farm track.

Go to the left along the track. At a junction, cross over (Bolton-le-Sands is to the left and Carnforth to the right) the roadway and continue along the track in front leading into woodland. The track turns to the right above the Lancaster Canal. Continue straight along it and come out onto Thwaite Brow Lane. Go straight ahead along the lane, do not cross the canal bridge (8), and at the end of it is the driveway to The Linden Lea Christian Fellowship. To the left of the driveway is the path to be followed, its passing through a kissing gate and dropping down to the canal. This way down is clearly part of a very old road that ran from Bolton-le-Sands to Carnforth. Continue ahead along the canal bank and through a kissing gate ahead and then follow the path along until it meets the track from the earlier junction. On the way the path passes the remains of coke ovens, which were once very common on the banks of the canal.

Turn left along the track towards the bridge over the canal, which is crossed. Turn right and join the canal bank at a gate in the hedge. Turn left and follow the canal bank to Carnforth, pass the Marina on the way. Before reaching the next bridge there is a metal kissing gate leading to a path through a children's play area (10). Follow the path up to the road by the bridge, which is the one crossed at the start of the walk. Turn left down the road and then right at the traffic lights for the bus stops.

8. Walks 6 and 7 use the canal bank from this bridge.
9. Here, walk 7 is met on its way to Bolton-le-Sands via Thwaite Bridge.
10. Walk 10 goes straight along the canal towpath from this play area.

WALK 9, CARNFORTH, WARTON, WARTON CRAG, CARNFORTH.

Easy.
4.75 miles.
Allow 2.5 to 3 hours.

At Carnforth, leave the bus from the north at Scotland Road and then go ahead to the traffic lights where turn right to go down Market Street to the bottom. From the south, leave the bus at Carnforth station. From there, whether having approached from the north or the south, take the road past the station, cross over the main railway line and continue along the road until crossing the River Keer in about half a mile. Once over the river, there is a roadway to the right, passing in front of some houses. Follow it along, past the playing fields and, at the end, pass into a field at a kissing gate.

Cross over the grassy path to a second kissing gate and then follow the path along by the hedge on the right towards Warton. At the end of the path ahead there is an aluminium kissing gate onto a short lane, which leads onto a road. At the road, turn right and cross it to another path leading across The Weir to the main road by a telephone kiosk and bus shelter.

Cross the main road through Warton and go up Churchill Avenue straight in front. Where the road turns to the left there is a grassy path ahead between the houses, leading to a gate into a field. Go straight up the steep field, with the parish church over the wall on the right, to a tight squeeze stile onto a road at the top. On the way, note the limekiln to the left. It can easily be visited on reaching the road before continuing the walk.

(If the reader is not familiar with Warton village, it is suggested that before going up Churchill Avenue a diversion is made along the main street to the right to have a look at the village.)

The name 'Warton' may refer to the Weir, a green area close to the centre of the village, its being a version of 'Ware', a quite large stretch of water, the name being 'the township by the Ware'. Now, the area is drained, but the nearby fields still flood after heavy rainfall.

By The Weir is The Malt Shovel, an inn which housed the Manor Court after the Old Rectory fell into decay.

Stars and Stripes fly above Warton Crag

An Iron Age fort occupied the top of Warton Crag, probably covering the entire summit. This also may have given Warton its name, 'tun' meaning 'town' and 'weard' referring to a lookout.

In later times the Crag was used as a beacon, its light being able to be seen from Black Coombe across Morecambe Bay, from the Lakeland Fells, from the Pennines to the east and from the Lancashire plain. Following the Norman Conquest, Warton was in the Barony of Kendal.

The parish church is dedicated to St. Oswald, who was a Christian king of Northumbria and who was murdered in 650 A.D.. Carnforth, Borwick and Yealand were all part of the parish, as was Silverdale, which was a chapelry having its own chapel with the curate being paid by the Vicar of Warton. It is probable that the first stone built church in Warton was constructed in the fourteenth century, the south aisle dating from that time and being the oldest part of the building. Robert Washington, who died in 1483, had the tower built.

Across the road from St. Oswald's is the Old Rectory, which also dates from the fourteenth century. At the time it was built, the Rectory was also the Manor, courts being held there. The building had a large hall off which were a buttery and a pantry and a passage to the kitchen. Above them was the principle private room for the family. Quite a lot of restoration work has been done to preserve the remains of the building.

The village school on Back Lane is named after Matthew Hutton, who became the Archbishop of York. It replaces a building close to the church and which, in turn replaced the building he had erected in 1594 when he was the Bishop of Durham.

Back Lane was also a cattle route to pastures behind the village. A path from here leads to Senset Well, the name being a corruption of 'St. Oswald'.

Warton is famous for an ancestor of George Washington, Robert Washington, having lived in the village. On 4 July, American Independence Day, St. Oswald's Church flies the Stars and Stripes on the top of the tower. Down below, inside the tower at the back, is a weathered stone Coat of Arms of the Washington family, which was inserted in the wall there in the 1950's owing to deterioration from when it was outside. It is said that the Washington Coat of Arms, a design of mullets and bars, formed the basis of the American flag, the Stars and Stripes. On the village street is Washington House, the building being later than the date stone to the right, which relates to the Washington family.

Another Warton connection is with the Spencer-Churchill family and Sir Winston Churchill, via the Kitsons of Warton Hall. Churchill Avenue is named both in honour of the former Prime Minister and because the hill is by the church.

Warton parish commences at the River Keer, the area being named Millhead, a reminder of when a water-mill stood here, grinding the locally grown corn.

For the walk, cross the road and go through Ged's Gate, which is slightly to the left, into the woodland of the Warton Crag Nature Reserve. When through the gate, follow the path straight up over limestone rocks. Continue ahead on reaching a grassy area at the top, ignoring the path to the left (it leads over limestone pavement and by going right above the former quarry, eventually to the summit). Follow the path along by the wall with Warton over to the right. Ignore the various paths leading off to the left. The path goes ahead through a gap in a wall coming down the hillside from the left.

Towards the end, the path goes a little higher than the wall to the right and then comes to another gap leading out onto a track in front, known locally as the "Occupation Road". (By turning right you come to a road and by going right again come to the top end of Warton.) Turn left along the track, going up by the wall on the left. The track climbs upwards and then drops down. At the bottom of that drop there is a gate (Kate Breakell Gate) with a squeeze stile by it. Go through the stile and follow the path along through the woodland.

Keep to the main pathway and reach the summit plateau of Warton Crag. On the plateau is a metal basket for a beacon which is lit for commemorative purposes, the top of the Crag having been used for warning beacons in ancient times. Close by it there is an Ordnance Survey triangulation pillar. Pass straight over the plateau, keeping the beacon on the left. From the rocky outcrop in front there are very good views all round Morecambe Bay.

The path drops down at the left of the outcrop, going towards the Carnforth end of Morecambe Bay in front. Follow the path along, across another path, and then descend the cliff face over limestone rocks to a wooden stile at the bottom. The path then continues straight ahead and crosses another path before dropping down to come to the fence above the former quarry. Turn to the right, following the path along by the quarry fence. Shortly, the path goes ahead as the fence drops below and then the path, too, turns to the left. It is a grassy path to follow until it reaches a track in front. Here, turn to the right along the track. The track turns to the left and comes out at a gate leading onto the road. Here, turn to the left. Pass the first public footpath sign on the right, but continue to a second one, which is indicated by a Lancashire Coastal Way sign. (For those wishing to visit the former quarry, which is a Local Nature Reserve, the entrance is about 75 yards further along the road form here.) Cross into the field and drop straight down by the hedge on the left and at the bottom continue straight down a farm lane to the Silverdale road.

Turn right onto the road and go straight ahead on reaching a junction about a quarter of a mile in front. Cross the railway line and then turn sharp left to follow the roadway by it. At the end there is a wooden footbridge over the River Keer leading onto another roadway (11) where turn left. On reaching the Warton-Carnforth road in front, turn right for Carnforth and retrace your outward steps to the bus stops.

11. By turning right along this road, walk 6 can be joined at Galley Hall.

WALK 10, CARNFORTH, LANCASTER CANAL, CAPERNWRAY, WARTON, CARNFORTH.

Easy.
6 miles.
Allow 3 to 3.5 hours.

From the bus stops in Carnforth North Road, just to the north of the traffic lights, go down to the lights and then turn left up the road. On reaching the canal bridge in under a quarter of a mile, do not cross it, but go through the children's playground to the right and out onto the canal towpath at an aluminium gate (10). Turn to the left, pass under the bridge and follow the towpath. Pass under the motorway at two bridges between which the canal was rechannelled when the road was built.

Continue along the towpath for about a mile and a half from the motorway. See the arches of the Capernwray Viaduct over to the left, taking the railway line from Carnforth to Yorkshire. Less than five minutes after passing a bridge spanning the canal, there is the Capernwray Aqueduct taking the Lancaster Canal over the River Keer.

Capernwray Aqueduct is the last of John Rennie's 'Little Aqueducts' on the Lancaster Canal. It is very strongly buttressed. On the eastern side there are the remains of a windlass for raising a plug should the canal needed to be drained into the river for repair work to be undertaken.

Below the aqueduct, to the left of the river, is a former corn mill, which was powered by water from the river. Close by is an old packhorse bridge.

Stone was quarried at Capernwray, resulting in the quarry arm and the remains of a crane for loading barges at New England.

From the aqueduct, retrace your steps to the bridge (12) and go up the steps on the aqueduct side and out onto roadway. Go along the lane to where, by a turning to the right leading to the houses by the river, there is a stile leading into the field. There, go across to the railway arches, strictly you should pass beneath the left-hand one, and then turn left and through a gateway into the next field, which is crossed by going up it bearing right.

There is a regularly used alternative which is not the right of way. Go under the railway arches and straight along to the far corner of the

Along Capernwray Arches

small field where there is a stile by the river. Cross it and go along the field by the river. Part way along, the right of way meets this path.

Continue along the river-bank to the end of the field, cross over a stile and follow the river-bank across the next field. Cross the stile at the end of that field and follow the fence by the river-bank across the next field and then over a stile leading onto a road.

Cross the bridge and then cross the stile on the opposite side of the road to rejoin the river-bank. Keep following the river-bank, up to the M6 where there is an iron stile to cross and then pass under the motorway by the Keer. This stretch of river was re-channelled when the motorway was built, resulting in a diversion from the right of way as shown on the map. When the work was originally done, the area was devoid of wildlife and plant life but now, in summer, there is an abundance of both.

The path passes close to some of the chalets of Pine Lake, on the other side of a fence before reaching the exit road of the M6. There, the path turns to the right going along by the road. Keep on along the path by the fence until reaching the entrance to Pine Lake. Cross straight over the entrance and the path continues along between the A6 road on the left and a fence bordering Pine Lake on the right.

At the end of the path there is a stile leading onto the A6. Take care in crossing straight over this busy road to a lane opposite, Threagill Lane. Go along the lane, under the West Coast main line and continue up it to the road, Borwick Lane, where turn left. Go up the road towards the main road through Warton, but, opposite the Methodist Church, turn left onto Back Lane. Go along Back Lane and past the school. The roadway can be followed all the way to the Main Street and then turn left, but there is a rather nice little diversion that can be taken.

For the diversion, at the end of the school grounds, turn to the left and go straight over the grounds by the wall on the right, on the other side of which is the Old Rectory. Cross a stile into the next field and then pass just a few yards by the wall on the right before going through a squeeze stile into the following field. In that field, turn to the right, passing along by the wall, to its end where there is a wooden stile onto a lane in front.

Go along the lane, turning to the right and follow it to the Main Street. Turn left along the road to the bus shelter and telephone kiosk by the Malt Shovel. There, turn left along the path which shortly goes to the right at the back of the dwellings and then left onto the road. Cross the road and turn right for a few yards to where the footpath is indicated going off to the left by a fence. Pass along it, through a metal kissing gate and into a field. Cross the field by the hedge on the left.

At the end of the field, pass through another kissing gate and cross the next field to another gate and out onto an unsurfaced road. Follow the road to its end and turn left along the road from Warton to Carnforth. Go straight along it to Carnforth and then up the main street to the traffic lights where turn left for the bus stops on either side of the road.

10. Walk 8 leaves the towpath at the play area.
12. Walk 11 passes over this bridge in each direction when diverting to Capernwray Aqueduct on the way to Burton.

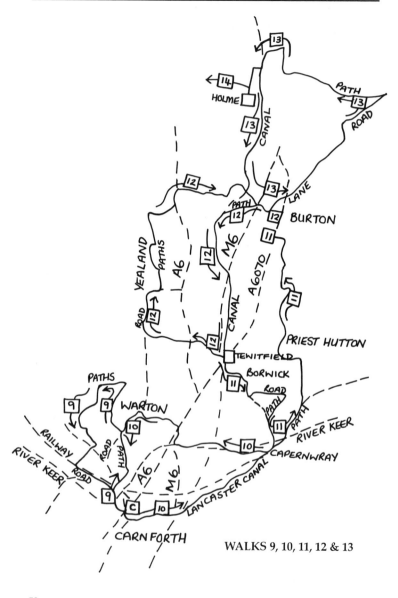

WALKS 9, 10, 11, 12 & 13

WALK 11, TEWITFIELD, CAPERNWRAY, PRIEST HUTTON, BURTON.

Easy.
5 miles.
Allow 3 to 3.5 hours plus extra time for looking exploring the villages.

Tewitfield probably refers to the marsh where the lapwing or pewit is found.

It was at Tewitfield that the Lancaster Canal originally terminated on its opening on 22nd November 1797. By 1805 the Westmorland proprietors were becoming increasingly annoyed at the lack of progress to take the canal the 14.5 miles through to Kendal. In August 1807 an Act of Parliament authorised changes to the line of the canal as originally proposed by John Rennie and on 7th February 1809 it was resolved that the work be commenced. However, the lack of funds and the Napoleonic Wars delayed the start of construction for another four years.

It was not until 14th April 1819 that the first boat sailed up the Lancaster Canal to the basin in Kendal. Originally, the official opening was to have been on 1st May, but this was postponed until 18th June owing to an embankment bursting.

Once again, Tewitfield is the head of navigation on the Lancaster Canal, the line to Kendal having been closed since 1944 when coal traffic for Kendal gasworks was transferred to road haulage. The canal became ponded, i.e. the water level was lowered, but the water channel remained intact, until the coming of the M6. The A6070 crosses the culverted canal at Tewitfield, replacing a skew bridge similar to the one seen at Holme. There is another culvert at Cinderbarrow near the Yealand road.

At Tewitfield there is a flight of eight locks which raise the canal by 76 feet in three quarters of a mile. In order that small sea-going vessels coming up from Glasson Dock could be accommodated, the locks were built as wide locks with two gates, as on the Glasson Arm. They were completed in 1818. Although not in use, they remained intact for many years, complete with the gates and the footbridges. Now, although the masonry is intact, the gates have been removed and they are all turned into weirs.

There are plans to re-open the canal through to Kendal. If this takes place, the top lock will be taken to the other side of the Cinderbarrow culvert so that the water channel can pass beneath the M6.

At Tewitfield, the former Turnpike road from Carnforth through to Heron Syke joins the modern road by the Longlands Hotel.

At Tewitfield the bus stops are on either side of the road at the northern end of the Longlands Hotel. The walk starts by passing along the roadway in front of the hotel, parallel to the main road, and straight down to the Lancaster Canal.

Turn left at the far side of the canal, by some picnic tables. Continue along the canal bank, pass under Tewitfield Turnpike Bridge and then under two more bridges which are very close to each other. Over to the left, before reaching the next bridge, some of the gardens of Borwick come down to the water's edge. On reaching the bridge, cross it and enter Borwick village, passing the entrance to Borwick Hall on the right.

The main feature of Borwick is the 16th century Borwick Hall, which is owned by the Lancashire County Council and only occasionally open to the public. It was once owned by the Bindloss family who were Roman Catholics and were loyal followers of King Charles II who was once their guest. The building is constructed round a central pele tower. The hall is said to be haunted by a White Lady. One room is shaped like a coffin and is known as 'The Coffin Room.' Legend has it that anyone sleeping in that room lengthwise never wakes up.

Round Borwick there are a number of old farms and farm buildings, showing that the village existed long before the coming of the Lancaster Canal.

After passing the Hall, the Green, which has a red telephone kiosk and a Victorian letter box in the wall opposite, is reached and there turn right along the road. Pass some attractive old dwellings, one house having a 1681 date stone. Pass the sign indicating the way to Hodgson's Bridge. About a quarter of a mile further on, after leaving the village, there is a stile in the wall on the right. Cross it and go over the field keeping close by the fence. Pass through another stile and just beyond a lovely old lime tree there is the next stile to cross. From it, bear diagonally left across the field towards where some caravans can be seen in the woodland. Cross the stile by them and turn right onto the path going through the wood. Note the quarried out area over to the left, now full of trees.

Shortly, the Capernwray Quarry Arm of the Lancaster Canal is reached, where barges were once loaded with stone from the quarry. Follow the path along, passing beneath the iron bridge carrying the railway line to Yorkshire over the canal.

A short diversion can be done at this point. Pass the remains of an overhead derrick at another small loading wharf. As the Keer Aqueduct is reached, there is a windlass close to the parapet, this once being used to draw a large plug from the bed of the canal to drain the section whenever repairs to the aqueduct had to be carried out. Cross the bridge (12) shortly in front onto the towpath and then turn to the right to look down on Capernwray Mill, which is now a house, and see the strong construction of the Keer Aqueduct with the river below.

By the railway bridge, having passed under it coming from the quarry arm (to the right, just in front of it if the diversion has been done), there is a farm track leading off to the left. Go along it and cross the stile by the gate. Go along the field path by the hedge on the left with the railway above until part way along the field there is a waymarker indicating that the path bears right to the right-hand corner ahead. Pass through the rather narrow squeeze stile and by the hedge on the right to the next stile. Cross into the field and then turn to the

left and follow the grassy farm track to the corner of the field.

The track passes over a small bridge and bears left to pass under the railway arch, where there is a field gate. Immediately after passing through that gate, look for a kissing gate in the fence to the right by the stream. The path follows the bank of the stream until a high ladder stile is reached. Continue across the field to cross the stream by a small footbridge. Immediately afterwards, the stream is re-crossed to the left by a second bridge leading into the adjoining field. Pass straight up the field by the fence on the left to a stile in the hedge leading out onto the road from Borwick.

Capernwray Quarry Arm, Lancaster Canal

Cross straight over the road, pass a cottage and go on towards a white gate. Just before reaching the gate, turn sharp left by the hedge to a box stile going into the field to the right. Pass up the field by the hedge on the right until another box stile is reached in a short stretch of fence, this dropping down into the field below. Turn left and follow the grassy path along, continuing straight ahead where the fence and hedge to the right bear away from the route.

The path reaches a squeeze stile in the top right-hand corner of the field. Go along by the hedge on the right to where another stile leads onto a short lane, in turn leading out onto a road at another stile by a gate. Turn left along the road and continue to the triangular village green of Priest Hutton, where there is a red telephone kiosk and an Edward VII post box in a wall.

Priest Hutton, along with Borwick, was a within the parish of Warton. The 'Hutton' part of the name refers to its being a township on a spur of land. 'Priest' refers to Matthew Hutton who, as Bishop of Durham, founded the original school in Warton. His parents lived in Priest Hutton (then called simply 'Hutton') from where he went to receive private lessons in Warton. The abilities of the boy came to the attention of a wealthy Yorkshireman who sent him to Ripon College and then on to Cambridge.

In 1825 Priest Hutton had a farrier's and a wheelwright's, but now there is no industry.

Turn along a very minor road to the right of the green, going northwards. Follow it for about a quarter of a mile to where, at a bend leading to the last of the houses, there is a track to the left. Go along the track, which is very overgrown with wild flowers in summer, pass a signpost for the Lunesdale Ramble, and at the end there is a stile to cross into a field. Go to the right round the edge of the field to avoid growing crops. Reach a pair of gates with an adjacent stile to cross. Follow the path along by the hedge on the right and then into the next field.

With this next field, the right of way is straight over towards where a hedge can be seen leading away from the field boundary and past Coat Green Farm buildings. Again to avoid growing crops, go to the right and round the edge of the field until a stile is reached on the right. Cross it and then across the field with the hedge past the farm on the left.

At the end of the hedge, the path turns left to pass through a gate and onto a track passing in front of the farm buildings. Immediately after passing the farm there is a signpost indicating the track to Burton to the right. The first part of this track is well used by animals and can be very muddy until the gateway they use has been passed. Follow the track along, through a field gate and then close to the bottom of the sloping ground to the left.

On reaching the end of the sloping ground, turn diagonally left, cross a farm track, and go through a gate into the next field. There, go diagonally left towards the top left corner of the field. Cross the stile there and follow the path at the edge of the small but dense cluster of trees and come out onto a road. Turn to the left for a few hundred yards to the main road at the southern end of Burton. There are bus stops on either side of the road by the corner on the right. Alternatively, turn right and go into Burton village and the bus can be caught from the square.

12. Walk 10 leaves the canal for Warton and Carnforth from by this bridge.

WALK 12, BURTON, TEWITFIELD, THE YEALANDS, BURTON.

Easy, but can be very muddy in parts.
7.25 miles.
Allow 4 to 4.5 hours.

On visiting Burton today it is hard to believe that it was once a bustling market town with the largest corn market in the county of Westmorland, its Market Charter having been granted in 1661. The Market was held every Tuesday and farm hands came here for hire. The coming of the Lancaster Canal and the railway led to the market's ultimate demise. In addition to the market, Burton had a wide variety of businesses in the square and the main street, including the postmaster, a dressmaker, grocers, a butcher, a plumber, a draper, a tailor, a blacksmith and several others. The Market Cross in Burton Square still has the remains of leg irons where prisoners were held fast in the stocks.

On either side of the Market Square are several picturesque old houses, some with pillared and overhanging upper storeys. The Royal Hotel, on the north-eastern side of the Square, is a fine old coaching inn. Just beyond the Square to the north is the very pretty Cocking Yard, its old cottages having undergone much restoration over the years.

On the eastern side of the road, to the south of the square, is the Manor House. The ancient Manor Courts, which were presided over by the Lord of the Manor, were held in the Green Dragon, a former inn at the south end of the village.

To the south of Burton village is Heron Syke, formerly on the county boundary between Lancashire and Westmorland, but this was moved to the south in 1896. It was to here the Garstang and Heron Syke Trust turnpike road terminated and the Heron Syke and Eamont Bridge Turnpike Trust road started. The old turnpike road lies in front of the cottages, below the modern road.

With the coming of the Lancaster and Carlisle Railway one station served both Burton & Holme, but it was closed with the Beeching Axe.

From Burton Square, go a short distance northwards along the main street to Neddy Hill, which leads off on the left. Turn down there and come to Station Lane, which is by an old fashioned signpost. Turn left down Station Lane and cross the M6. Immediately it has been crossed there is a wooden stile to the left, which is crossed into the field. A few yards further on there is a kissing gate to pass through and the path is then followed across the field by the M6. At the end of the field there is a gate, but do not pass through it. Instead, turn up the hillside, Hanging Hill, by the hedge, keeping it on the left.

As the top of the hill is crossed an extremely narrow squeeze stile comes into view in front. From it, cross straight over the field to a stile in the fence opposite and then turn diagonally leftwards towards Moss Bridge, which can be seen spanning the Lancaster Canal. At the bridge go through the gate, across the bridge and then right down the lane until steps leading to another squeeze stile and the canal bank are reached. Turn right along the canal bank, passing under Moss Bridge.

At the next bridge, Yealand Road Bridge, an interesting diversion can be taken. Go under the bridge and then onto the road and turn left down it. Cross the railway, pass a minor road and a bungalow and then a gate is reached on the right. Pass through it onto Cinderbarrow, where there is a picnic site and a model railway on which trains run on certain days in the summer season.

Returning to the canal, continue down the towpath and at the end of it, by a culvert under the M6 is a kissing gate leading onto the road. Turn left along the road and cross the M6 and then turn right down the service roadway to where the canal bank is rejoined on the left. From here, the top lock of the Tewitfield flight of locks can be seen in front.

On passing down the locks, a pair of old gates, which were in use from 1890 to 1942 are passed. Shortly after leaving the bottom lock there is the road bridge at Tewitfield in front. There are steps leading up to it from the towpath (13). Once on the road, turn right over the bridge over the M6 and then right again onto the track past the farm.

Follow the lane along towards Tewitfield Farm. There is a turning to the right and then shortly before reaching the farm buildings there is a gate leading to another lane on the left. Go up that lane and into the field at its end. Here, turn to the right and go over the field to the far right-hand corner by the railway. Cross the stile, pass under the railway bridge and pass through a squeeze stile onto the busy A6.

Turn left along the grass verge until the beginning of the dual carriageway is reached. Cross over the A6 and go straight up the minor road opposite to Yealand Conyers. This is Snapes Lane. So as to see the village, do not turn along the bridleway to the right but continue straight up to St. Mary's Catholic Church at the top of the road. Here, turn right and pass through the village. Besides the attractive buildings of the village, note the pump on the right. Come to Yealand Old School, beside which is the driveway to the Friend's Meeting House. To the left of the driveway is an old mounting block to help worshippers get on their horses. Pass the converted Manor Farm Barn.

There are three Yealands, Yealand Conyers, Yealand Redmayne and Yealand Storrs. 'Yealand' refers to the Anglo-Saxon for high land whilst both 'Conyers' and 'Redmayne' refer to the names of landowners. 'Storrs' refers to woodland belonging to the Yealands. Formerly, the Yealands were townships within Warton parish.

Most of the older houses in the Yealands date back to the 17th century and originally each had its own barn for sheltering animals in the winter and for the storage of fodder. It was during that century that George Fox, who founded the Quaker movement, preached there, the event taking place in 1652. A local man, Richard Hubberstone, became a friend and one of Fox's strongest adherents and organised secret meetings in the villages. At that time, the Quakers were heavily persecuted. The Quaker Meeting House in Yealand Conyers was built in 1652 and is still in use today.

Flax and hemp were produced at the flax mill of Waitham & Co at Yealand Conyers, production there ceasing in 1860 and ending a tradition of several centuries.

Quaker Meeting House, Yealand Conyers

In 1825 Yealand Conyers had a boarding school that was run by Mrs. E. B. Creek.

To the east of Yealand Redmayne the fields form part of a medieval field-system. At the time of the Domesday survey there was an open field-system and land was measured in carcurates. These fields were split into unfenced strips, each worked by a peasant, plus common land for use by all. Each family had a number of strips a furrow long (furlong). During the early 18th century, Parliamentary Enclosures saw much change to this system and the old multi-strip fields were changed for new compact field units that varied in size according to the number of people they had to support, these being enclosed by stone-walling and hedging. Below Yealand Redmayne is a section of the old medieval field system with enclosures on either side of each house. At the bottom of the fields is the old Back Lane from the village well, which forms part of the path followed for the walk.

Shortly after passing the New Inn there is a road to the right, with an old-fashioned signpost at the corner. Turn down the road until a junction is reached. The road to the right passes the Anglican Church. To the left is Well Lane, the track to be followed. At the end of the lane there is a gated stile into the field in front. Turn right from the stile and then pass through a similar stile to the right of the field gate in front. Turn left across this second field, keeping by the hedge on the left. At the end of the field cross a wooden stile, which is by a squeeze stile, into the next field.

Cross over the field to another squeeze stile by a gateway. On crossing this field, a very reedy and overgrown pond is to be seen to the left. This is an old drovers' pond, where cattle following the drove road from the north would stop to drink.

The following field is crossed by bearing to the left and over a stile close to a field gate onto a farm track. Cross the track and go through another squeeze stile on the right, by a curved wall on the other side of which is a pump. The stile leads out onto a road, a few yards along which you turn right onto the bridleway leading to Nineteen Acre Lane, its still being part of the drovers' road. Go through a metal gateway and then straight across the next field. From here, continue along the path at the bottom of a number of very narrow fields until a road, Nineteen Acre Lane is reached. These fields are part of the medieval field system.

Turn right onto Nineteen Acre Lane and in about 100 yards turn left along the track, which is the bridleway, and part of the old drove route, to White Moss. At the end of the track, pass through a gate leading onto another track, where turn right. Over to the left is the Moss. Pass over two stiles by wooden field gates. Pass along the lane, which has a variety of trees growing by it, including hazel, elder, ash and hawthorn. Pass through a gate at a corner where there are several gates and fields joining up. There is another gate immediately to the left with a stile by it to cross.

Turn right down the field, fairly close to the hedge. Pass a field gate and, at the bottom of the field, cross a stile into the next field. At the time of writing, the way across this field to the road was not at all clear and can be very muddy. Basically, continue across the field bearing left towards a gateway through which traffic can be seen on the A6. A few yards to the left of the gateway there is a stile leading onto the road.

Cross the A6 and then turn left along the grassy verge. A dwelling house is seen ahead to the left of the road. On reaching it, there is a bridleway to the right. Follow the bridleway until it comes out onto a road where turn left.

At the junction at the end of the road, turn right and pass under the railway bridge. Continue straight up the road, under the aqueduct (14) carrying the Lancaster Canal, pass over the M6 bridge and then straight up to Burton and turn right for the Square. From the M6 the route is the start of the walk in reverse.

13. By going straight under this bridge walk 11 can be joined.
14. From here, walk 13 can be followed to Holme.

WALK 13, HOLME, BURTON, HOLME.

Easy
6 miles
Allow three hours.

Until 1939, when Holy Trinity Church was erected, Holme was part of Burton Parish. Close by is Pinder's Farm, a reminder of when Pinders were the keepers of the pinfold.

Holme Mills, now an industrial site, originated in the 13th century since when there has been a succession of mills on the site because of the abundant supply of water. Until demolition in 1983 the mills had a chimney. At one time, linen, flax and hemp from Holme Mills were transported to the south along the Lancaster Canal.

The limestone bridge over the Lancaster Canal taking the road from Burton into Holme is a skew bridge, something not common on the canal. It is known as Holme Turnpike Bridge owing to this being on the former turnpike road from Burton to Eamont Bridge.

At Holme leave the bus at the Smithy Inn. From the north, go along the road a few yards further towards Lancaster, from the south turn back a few yards and then turn left up North Road.

Holme Turnpike Bridge, Lancaster Canal

Follow North Road to Park Lane on the right and turn down it. A gap on the left on reaching a bridge over the Lancaster Canal leads down a flight of steps and onto the canal bank where turn right and pass under the bridge. Follow the canal towpath along, noting the skew Holme Turnpike Bridge taking the main road into Holme. About half a mile further on the Holme Mills industrial area is over to the right. In front of the former mills is a large millpond.

Three-quarters of a mile further on there is a house on the far side of the canal by Burton Wharf (15). Just before reaching there steps and a pathway drop down to the right from the towpath to a road at the bottom. There, turn right and pass under the aqueduct (14) and go up the road to a junction where take the left-hand road, Tanpits Lane.

At the top of Tanpits Lane cross straight over the main road through Burton and then go up Vicarage Lane. About two hundred yards up the road, on the left, there is a track with a signpost indicating Burton Fell. Turn onto the track and follow it along, its being Slape Lane. The track winds its way along between two hedges. Along the way, to the left, there is the twisted trunk of an ancient small-leafed lime tree. This tree is believed to be well over a thousand years old.

The lane itself ends at a large field gate, which is passed through into the Hutton Roof Crags Nature Reserve. After leaving the gate come to a junction where take the left-hand path. It continues along by the wall on its left, until a field gate is reached. An arrow indicates that the path is through this gate and from there follow the main path along, ignoring a small one to the left.

Go through a wooden gate into a field and then straight across the field towards the wall opposite. Pass through a large gap in the wall and at the end of the next field go through a green metal gate by a field gate and out onto a road. Turn right along the road for about two thirds of a mile.

On reaching a corner of the road where there is a ladder stile to the right for Hutton Roof and a sign showing Limestone Link, Holme Park to the left, go through the metal field gate to the left. Follow the track as it bears off left up the field. It is a grassy track as it makes its way towards a limestone outcrop in front and then go onto another grassy path going over to the left. Over to the right, at the time of writing, a large pile of old tyres is passed.

The path goes to the right of a limestone outcrop and also to the right of the pylon line. A good field track is reached and crossed straight

The double gates on the sea lock at LancasterCanal at Glasson
The Lune Aquaduct at Lancaster..

Across the Lune to the site of Halton Hall..
Looking up the Lancaster Canal at Hest Bank.

Bolton Church Bridge, Bolton-le-Sands.
Hawthorn bushes near Bolton-le-Sands.

Raven on the Lancaster Canal near Carnforth.
Tewitfield Locks, Lancaster Canal

over towards a wall in front. There, pass through a wooden gate as the stile to its right is disused. Cross over the field bearing to the right to where a field gate is seen in front.

Cross the stone stile by the field gate and go straight ahead along the bridleway, the large Holme Park quarry being clearly visible in front.

The clear, grassy path goes towards the quarry and then to its right. It is good limestone country all around here. Pass through a metal field gate and go straight ahead, ignoring a path to the right. Note an old limekiln over to the right as the path drops downwards, still with the quarry over a fence to the left. The pit on the old kiln is not now in very good condition.

The quarry is left behind and a metal field gate passed through and a farm lane followed. Pass by part of the farm buildings, through another field gate, and along the last stretch of track and out onto a road.

Turn right along the road and pass an 1826 milepost for Burton 2 miles, Kendal 9 miles. On reaching a road junction, turn left for Holme. On reaching the Lancaster Canal, which is culverted under the road, turn left and cross a small wooden stile onto the towpath.

Pass under a bridge and at the next bridge go up the steps that were descended at the beginning of the walk. Turn right for North Road and on reaching it turn left down to the main road and the bus stops by the Smithy Inn. On the way, a footpath leading off to the right is passed. This is at the beginning of the following walk and the two can be linked to make a longer walk.

14. Walk 12 also passes under the aqueduct.
15. By continuing straight along the canal bank the next bridge, Moss Bridge, which is used in walk 12 is reached.

WALK 14, HOLME, HALE, BEETHAM FELL, MILNTHORPE plus MILNTHORPE to HEVERSHAM

Easy
6 miles
Allow 3 to 3.5 hours.

At Holme leave the bus at the Smithy Inn. From the north, go along the road a few yards further towards Lancaster, from the south turn back a few yards and then turn left up North Road.

About a third of a mile up North Road there is a signpost on the left indicating the footpath to Pye's Bridge. Go through a small wooden gate by Paddock Lodge and straight across the yard to another small wooden gate by a field gate. Cross a very short stretch of field to a wooden stile in the fence. Drop straight down that field towards a fence that curves round in front. Part way along that fence, in a straight line from the way already walked, is the next stile to cross.

Go down the field to the next stile, which is by a stone slab spanning a stream. Cross over the field by the wall and hedge, passing a gate into the field to the right. Pass through a rather narrow squeeze stile into the next field and go over it by the fence on the left.

Cross an easy wooden stile into the next field and continue straight ahead by the hedge on the left to the end of the field, which is left by a small wooden gate by a squeeze stile. There, cross the road from Holme to Milnthorpe.

Enter the field at the signpost and bear right towards the footbridge over the railway. The bridge was constructed in 1999 and is one of several replacing old foot crossings along the main line. Once over the bridge, go ahead over the next field towards a gateway in the hedge opposite, passing ponds to the left and the right. Cross the wooden stile to the right of the gateway and then immediately turn left into the adjacent field. In that field, turn right to go up it by the fence on the right. WARNING, there could be an electric fence in this field.

On reaching the top of the field, go over a stile by the field gate into the next field and up it by the hedge on the right. Leave that field at a field gate and turn left along the very minor road so as to cross Pye's Bridge. The road is followed past the farm and goes straight on to Hale.

Hale could refer either to the nearby Beetham Hall but more likely refer to a corner or a slope, which fit in with its location.

Prior to the construction of the turnpike road from Carnforth to Ulverston in 1820, there were only bridleways and footpaths linking Hale with Beetham. With the coming of what is now the A6, the Kings Arms was built and it was here that the horses on the mail coach were changed. Hale was an agricultural area and had its own tithebarn, this having now been converted into a cottage.

About half a mile south of Hale, by the A6, is the Lakeland Wildlife Oasis where there are some of the world's threatened creatures, a number of which can range with the public if they so wish, both indoors and outdoors. Also, there are interactive displays.

At Hale, cross the A6 and go straight up the road in front towards the line of houses strung along the hillside (but a diversion down the A6 to the Lakeland Wildlife Oasis is well worthwhile before continuing with the walk). As this road turns to the left, there is a signposted lane for Slackhead and Beetham going to the right behind some of the houses. Follow this lane along and at its end pass through a squeeze style and then straight along by the wall on the left. To the right is a path coming up from the A6.

At the end of the field there is another squeeze stile to go through and then turn left at the signpost, taking the path for Slackhead via Marble Quarry. Follow the track upwards and cross a stile by a field gate. It is a good limestone path to follow, but can be slippery after rain, and it is waymarked. Shortly, on reaching a crossroads of paths, go straight across into some woodland.

A few yards further on there is a junction where take the right-hand path for Slackhead. Go along this path towards some limestone rock in front and there turn right. At the end of the rock, turn left to go up above the limestone and then follow the path along. In another few yards another waymarker shows

Limestone pavement at Hale

that the path is straight ahead by the wall on the right and not along a good path, which is private.

Cross a low wall and immediately beyond it turn to the left, passing through the trees. On reaching another path junction, turn to the right along a nice woodland path. At the end of that stretch, still in woodland, bear left at another waymarker to follow the path over the clints and grikes of the limestone pavement. The clints are the projecting rocks whilst the grikes are the spaces in between. Limestone pavement was formed during the ice age.

Comparatively speaking, it is quite a long stretch of pavement to be crossed before another waymarker shows that the path is to the left, leading off the pavement. There, the path enters woodland, passing a many-stemmed lime tree growing amongst rocks. Continue along the path to another junction where turn to the right. This path is followed along and comes out onto a road.

Turn right along the road for Fairy Steps and the Limestone Link. Pass a road junction and come to some houses on the left of the road. There, a signpost indicates the track for Fairy Steps and Storth going to the left by some of the houses. At a junction at the beginning of the track, go left, to the right being private. Pass straight in front of a white-painted house and follow the track into woodland.

Go through a gap in a wall and come to an indicator cairn (16) where turn left towards Fairy Steps. Shortly there is a junction where take the right-hand path for Beetham Fell. This path soon comes out into a more open area with a lot of silver birch around. On reaching another waymarker cairn it shows two paths going right for Cockshott Lane. Go straight ahead along the right-hand path that is followed for a little less than half a mile to where it comes out onto the road.

Turn right along the road for about 350 yards to where a lane leads off to the left and a signpost indicates it is the footpath for Haverbrack. Follow the lane along with woodland to the left and an open field to the right. Come to a junction and continue along the main track round to the right and onto a tarred surface. This roadway comes out onto a minor road, which is crossed straight over, and then go through a wooden gateway and down some steps into a field. Drop straight down the field towards another gateway to be seen by a line of trees which border a very minor road.

Go through a metal kissing gate and cross the road bearing left to another metal kissing gate leading into Dallam Park. The footpath goes ahead towards a line of trees in front, passes them, and then skirts round the left-hand side of the hillside in front and passes a large old oak tree. An indicator cairn is passed and the way followed for Milnthorpe to be seen in front.

Keep going across Dallam Park, bearing to the right and reach the bridge over the River Bela. Cross it and come out through a metal gate onto the road where turn right for Milnthorpe. Cross the A6 road and go up to Market Square for the buses northwards and southwards, the stops being on the Burton road adjacent to the Square and opposite the offices of a firm of financial advisers. See the beginning of the next walk for more about Milnthorpe.

16. Walk 16 goes a short way towards Fairy Steps from here.

MILNTHORPE TO HEVERSHAM.

About 1.75 miles.

Allow three quarters of an hour for the walk from Milnthorpe to Heversham.

For the continuation on to Heversham, from the bus stops adjacent to the Market Square, pass the office of the financial advisers and turn northwards into Police Square. Cross over Police Square to its top right corner and from there follow the minor road to the right. Pass straight over the junction at a crossroads for about two hundred yards towards the dwellings at Lower Haverflatts and before reaching them a signpost indicates a footpath in the field to the left. Go about half way along the field to a field gate on the right, through it and then curve round the field to the right to pass behind the buildings of Low Haverflatts.

Continue round to the top right-hand corner of the field based on where it was entered (not the corner by the Haverflatts dwellings). Go through the squeeze stile by the gate and cross the next field by the hedge on the right. At the end of it, cross the stile on the right, go down by the hedge on the left and just round the corner there is a squeeze stile to pass through and there turn along the field by the hedge on the right. (This arrangement is rather odd as it is a complicated way from one field to the next.)

The field comes to a point at its far end where there is a stone slab stile into the following field. Follow the hedge on the left to where it turns left at a corner. Turn to the left and bear a little way right from the hedge towards a squeeze stile in the hedge in front. Actually, there are two stiles together to pass over as a wooden stile has also to be crossed to enter the field.

Go straight across the field, over a wooden stile into the following field and bear down it to the right towards a gateway. To the right of the gateway there is a wooden ladder stile leading out onto a minor road. Turn left down the road to Heversham Church and the bus stops.

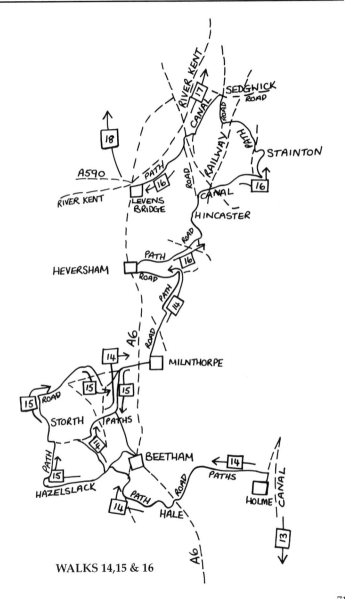

WALKS 14, 15 & 16

WALK 15, MILNTHORPE, BEETHAM, KENT ESTUARY, MILNTHORPE.

Easy
6.5 to 7 miles
Allow 4 to 4.5 hours.

Milnthorpe does not appear in the Domesday Book although Beetham Heversham and Levens do. In the 10th and 11th centuries the area was on the borders of the Kingdom of Strathclyde. Its name refers to a mill and a village.

Until 1837, with the consecration of St. Thomas' Church, Milnthorpe did not have a church and was part of the joint township of Heversham within the parish of Heversham until 1896. It was not until 1924 that it became separate from the ecclesiastical parish of Heversham.

Edward Wilson of Nether Levens purchased the Manor of Heversham in 1614. Edward's step son-in-law, Thomas Wilson, inherited Edward's estates and his descendants moved the family into Dallam Tower, which had newly been rebuilt, in 1720. The building was extended in around 1826 when the side pavilions and the porch of Tuscan columns were added. The Wilson's owned the lands for very many years and Dallam Tower has since been regarded as the manor house of Milnthorpe although it lies in Beetham Parish.

Opposite Dallam Tower, where the Bela turns to flow north, is Dallam Wheel where there were timber and ship building yards. These were cleared around 1813 when the present bridge and road from Milnthorpe to Sandside were built. Previously the road had been to the south of the river and passed close by the tower. The hamlet of Scout Bank, which stood above the northern bank of the river, was cleared over the following years to improve the view for the Wilson's of Dallam Tower.

The old road bridge over the Bela remains and is crossed when entering Dallam Park from Milnthorpe. The wooden slats hanging below it are a deer fence.

The only sea-port in Westmorland was at Milnthorpe, but it was never of major significance, unlike Lancaster, as it lacked a stone-built quay although there was a wharf at Dixies. The various warehouses were not all in one area but were scattered around the village and along the shore of the estuary of the River Bela. The port had its own customs officer to ensure that taxes had been paid on incoming cargoes and to levy Excise Duty on the export of salt.

Milnthorpe's market was granted to the Manor of Heversham by a Charter of 1334 and this is still operative. Originally it was held on a Wednesday, but it has since been transferred to every Friday. Today, it is a thriving market, but almost vanished during the First World War with no weekly markets being held and only stalls selling surplus produce appearing from time to time. Other traders visited and traded from the Market Cross, resulting in its never quite dying out and the market rights lapsing. The Market Cross was used for proclamations, as well as other things, and there is a photograph from May 1910 showing the proclamation of George V as Monarch. The Market Cross was Milnthorpe's first listed building.

The Turnpike Road from Beetham, authorised in 1818, reached the Main Street at the Cross Keys. At that time, no attempt was made to widen the road as it passed between the Old Bull's Head and a row of cottages on the Beetham road, leaving a gap of less than twelve feet.

Overlooking Milnthorpe is St. Anthony's Tower on St. Anthony's Hill, a Victorian Folly built to commemorate the Reform Bill of 1832. This land formed part of an endowment left by William Shepherd for a priest serving a Chantry dedicated to St. Anthony in Kendal Church.

Buses stop by the Square in Milnthorpe, opposite to (northbound) and adjacent to (southbound) the financial advisers' office. Go down the road, past the shops, to the traffic lights and pedestrian crossings on the main road, which is crossed. Pass along the road ahead, past the Post Office, until to the left there is a bridge spanning the River Bela. Cross the bridge and go straight up the hillside in front, passing some trees on the left.

After passing the summit of the hillside, bear left, passing a clump of trees on the right. On looking towards the skyline in front, there is a short row of trees, a gap and then a longer row of trees to the left. The path is to the left of the left-hand row, fairly close to the A6 road at the other side of the river Bela. There is a stile to cross and then go straight ahead between two lines of trees which are quite newly planted, with Beetham to be seen in front.

At the end of the field, pass through the stile by the gate. Over to the left is the Heron Corn Mill and paper museum. The walk is straight ahead along the roadway into Beetham village. At the Wheatsheaf, turn right along the road, pass the Church with its avenue of roses, and at the end of the houses there is a squeeze stile to the left and a signpost indicating Fairy Steps and Hazelslack Tower.

Beetham church, dedicated to St. Michael and All Angels, has evolved over the centuries, having its origins in Saxon times. The pergola of roses, beloved by brides, was erected in 1893 to commemorate the marriage of the then Duke of York to Princess Mary of Teck. Prior to the late 19th century, neither Silverdale nor Arnside had chapels where people could be buried. Until then, the way over Fairy Steps was part of a coffin route to Beetham, the coffins being hauled up the rock face by way of ropes.

Thomas de Betham obtained a charter from Edward II in 1311 for a weekly market that has long gone.

Before the building of the Turnpike Road, which was to become the A6, the route from Carnforth to Milnthorpe was via Warton, the Yealands, Leighton Furnace, over Slackhead and then dropped down to the Wheatsheaf at Beetham. There were then two ways to Milnthorpe, one via Dallam Park and the other close to the route of the A6.

There have long been mills at Beetham using the waters of the River Bela, the Heron Mill now being a museum where corn can still be ground. By it is a museum to paper making. Close by are the large paper mills of Henry Cooke.

Heron Mill, a fine example of a manorial mill, was rebuilt in the 18th century using timbers from the port of Milnthorpe in its construction. The mill is a lowder mill, a type of construction where the wheel is inside the mill walls. Above the wheel there is the lowder, a stone platform, where the corn is ground, which supports four pairs of grinding wheels. The waterwheel supplies over 15 h.p. and when one stands on the lowder platform there is a feeling of that power.

The path up the field is grassy and at the top there is a stile into the woodland. Turn right along the woodland path and at a junction turn right. At the next junction again turn right. At the following junction of paths turn left, a sign indicates that the path to the right is private. A few yards along the path there is a small cairn at a crossroads of paths. The route to Fairy Steps is straight ahead, ignoring a path shortly passed on the right (16).

Go straight ahead at the next junction and shortly come to the limestone pavement with a path crossing over the top. Cross the path to where a fissure is seen leading down through the rock face. This is Fairy Steps. Tradition has it that the fairies will grant the wish of anyone climbing the steps without touching the sides. The steps are actually so narrow that this could not be done. At the bottom of the steps, turn right and come to a junction with a signpost. Continue straight ahead for Hazelslack, passing through the woodland.

Morecambe Bay near Sandside

A good view is had across Morecambe Bay and to Arnside Knott from the top of another stretch of limestone pavement. Turn right here, passing between two parts of the rock to drop down to the path below, going over some steps on the way. At the bottom, the path turns left beneath the cliff face before dropping down to the right again. From here, follow the limestone path ahead to a wooden field gate. Go straight across the field by the wall on the left and continue straight across the following field. Stone steps lead across the wall at the end and onto the road. Cross straight over the road and pass Hazelslack Farm.

As the farm is passed, there are the ruins of Hazelslack Tower, a former pele tower. Just beyond this there is a stone step stile to cross into the field on the right and then go diagonally to the left to the wall opposite where another stone steps stile in the wall leads into the next field. Bear hard left across the field to another steps stile leading onto a minor road. Cross the road and to another stile by an aluminium gate. Follow the farm track along for a few yards and then, before reaching the next gate, go left to the wall beyond which is a plantation of trees. In the wall by the corner of the plantation there are some stone steps and a stile through the wall. Once over the wall, turn left to follow the wall bordering the plantation. At the end of the field there is a rather quaint little stile that serves no useful purpose as the field gate has been removed.

As the end of this field is reached the path turns to the right, following the wall, towards a fence. On reaching the fence, there is a squeeze stile to the left onto a short track. At the end of the track pass through another squeeze stile and go straight across the field by the wall on the left. At the end of the field there is a stile out onto a road.

Turn left along the road until a junction is reached and then turn right along Throughs Lane. This comes out onto Yans Lane, where turn left to go through part of Storth. Go right down the road to the Post Office and The Green and War Memorial, where turn right. (Actually, you can turn right just before reaching the Post Office since this part of Storth is triangular.) Go straight along the road and come out onto the road from Arnside skirting the top of Morecambe Bay, where turn right for Sandside.

Storth, and Sandside run into each other. Sandside was sometimes known as 'Milnthorpe Sandside' and looks out over the Kent Estuary, an area noted for sea birds and quicksands. Also there is the tidal bore which can be seen, but this is larger at Arnside where it can be spectacular. Much of the port activity of Milnthorpe was in this area.

The Furness Branch railway line from Arnside to Hincaster was only 5.25 miles long, but passed through difficult terrain. There were deep limestone cuttings at Sandside, Hawbarrow and Dug Hill at Heversham. The Bela was crossed by a beautiful viaduct of local limestone and had red sandstone pediments and copings. There were three open box girder arches over the river. Sadly, the viaduct was demolished in 1966. The line opened on 26 June 1876, when there were only three passenger trains a day. The main traffic on the line was iron and coke trains running between the North-east and Barrow via Tebay, leaving the main line at a junction at Hincaster. Passenger traffic ceased during the Second World War and freight traffic was a victim of the Beeching Axe.

The main industries of Sandside today are the large quarry and tourism.

It depends on the state of the tide whether a path below the road can be followed at the top of the shore.

At the eastern end of Sandside, the road goes upwards and at the top there is a footpath leading off to the left. The path passes along by the site of the old railway line, which was to its right, and then crosses a stile onto the track bed itself. Continue along here until a path on the left, dropping down to the beach below, is reached.

Go to the right, along by the beach, and as a corner is turned pass close to the fence bounding a field. Continue along by the fence, passing near to the mouth of the River Bela, and then through a gate into the field. Pass straight up the field by the river until reaching a weir. Here, bear a little to the right towards a wooden gate leading onto the road to the right of the bridge spanning the river.

Cross straight over the road and onto a minor, fenced, road through Dallam Park. At a bend in the River Bela there is a large metal kissing gate into the park to the left. Go straight over Dallam Park, close to the river, until reaching the gate and bridge at the start of the walk. Go straight up the road retracing your earlier steps to the Square and bus stop.

16. Walk 14 from Holme joins this walk from the cairn and leaves at the path to the right.

WALK 16, HEVERSHAM, STAINTON, SEDGWICK, LEVENS.

Easy
6 miles
Allow 3 to 3.5 hours

Heversham is dominated by St. Peter's Church, which not only claims to be the oldest church in the former county of Westmorland but also one of the three oldest Christian sites in Cumbria. It is probable that around this site there was the only Anglian monastery in the north-west established in the 7th century. The name 'Heversham' is Anglian, probably from the Anglian Chief Haefar together with the Anglian suffix "ham" meaning a farmstead, village or estate. There is an Anglian cross-shaft in the church porch.

St. Peter's became a parish church in 1180, serving Levens, Milnthorpe, Sedgwick and Stainton as well as Heversham. A fire, apparently caused by a careless plumber, destroyed the building in 1601 resulting in its being largely rebuilt. The tower and the north arcade date from 1868. The lych gate was built in 1794.

The rather narrow road from Heversham, through Leasgill and down to near Levens Park was part of the main road north prior to the opening of Princes Way on 1st July, 1927. The following year Levens Bridge was widened to over double its previous width. The old Toll Bar House from the days of the Turnpike road was demolished, this having stood at the end of Ninezergh Lane, at the corner of the Levens Hall garden wall.

Heversham is known for its school which was founded and endowed by Edward Wilson, an ancestor of the Dallam Tower Wilson's, of Nether Levens in 1613. He also made provision for two scholars who did not otherwise have the means to be able to continue with their education at universities. The chosen colleges were Queen's College, Oxford and Trinity College, Cambridge. The grammar school was exclusively for boys. The original school was built on Heversham Head, but replaced by a new building at the southern end of the village in 1878. In 1984 the Grammar School and Milnthorpe Modern School were merged to become Dallam School.

In the early 1800's there was much land in the Heversham and Levens area that was Common, Mosses or Waste Grounds. It was of very little value and the Enclosure Acts of the time were to encourage agriculture by enclosing the lands and exonerating them from tithes. The Master, Fellows and Scholars of Trinity College, Cambridge were owners of some of the Commons rights and accepted an allotment of the enclosed lands in lieu of the Corn Tithes belonging to them.

Heversham railway station, being situated at the end of the cutting bridged by the main road before entering Heversham, was actually nearer to Milnthorpe than its own station, and used by Milnthorpe people. The Furness Railway ran the line and one engine became popularly known as "Kendal Tommy". The station had its own Station Master for many years. He was Thomas Walker who also became Chairman of Milnthorpe Parish Council.

To commemorate the millennium, a topograf was erected on Heversham Head. Monies for it were raised from the residents of the parish and local bodies and they can be justifiably proud of the finished structure, which shows many of the Lakeland Fells and local landmarks around Morecambe Bay. It was unveiled on Midsummer Day 2000 by Mrs. Susan Bagot of Levens Hall.

The bus stops for this walk are by Heversham Church. The path to follow starts by going through the churchyard, passing to the right of the church building, and leaves through a metal gate in the wall surrounding the churchyard. Follow the grassy path on straight up the field. Go through a squeeze stile by a field gate and then up by the wall on the right to a metal kissing gate.

After passing through that kissing gate, go up by the wall on the left and then bear to the right, passing a seat, towards a line of trees. This is a large field and there is no real indication of the line to follow. On reaching the trees, there is a waymarker and another seat. Bear to the right at the trees and continue along the field, passing another waymarker, and go towards the far left-hand corner. On reaching it there are some stone steps leading into the next field. Go over that field bearing left towards the far left corner by Heversham Head Plantation.

(For a diversion to the topograf, go straight up the field to the wall in front, instead of bearing right, passing quite close to the plantation over the wall on the left. A kissing gate leading into the following field is reached and the topograf is up the hillside ahead. Return by the same route to pick up the path for the walk.)

On reaching the wall, a few yards before a field gate, there is a squeeze stile to go through to the right. Cross the farm track in front and continue along by the wall on the right. The wall becomes a hedge as the grassy path is followed and then a squeeze stile leads out onto Mabbin Hall Lane where turn to the right along the road.

No more than 100 yards along the road there are some steps into the field on the left. Go across the field bearing right to its right-hand corner and then cross a stile and drop down onto a road. (This stretch of path cuts off a corner in the road and does not have to be followed.) Follow the road ahead for half a mile to Hincaster.

Hincaster appears as Hennecastre in the Domesday Book. Its name suggests that it was a castle or camp in Roman times. No Roman remains have been found in the township, but it could have been that a Roman road between Carnforth and Watercrook passed through here.

A major works of the Lancaster Canal is the 378 yards long Hincaster Tunnel taking the canal through Hincaster Hill. The Canal Committee favoured the use of stone for the lining of the tunnel, considering brick to be an inferior material. To have used stone would have involved considerable expense and it was eventually agreed to use brick apart from the first few yards at the portals where stone was to be used. The bricks were made below Moss Side Farm at Heversham. The change from stone to brick can be seen by looking into the portals. Also to be seen at the West Portal is one of the iron hoops that held the fixed rope for pulling the boats through the tunnel by hand.

Horses crossed Hincaster Hill by the horsepath, which is unique as it is not connected to any road and is sunken. Low bridges take the path under the railway line and farm access tracks. By the west portal are converted canal cottages and stabling. It was from the wharf here that Lyth Valley damsons were transported to the south.

From the Green in Hincaster, take the road to the left, passing straight through the village. Come to a junction where there is a road off to the left and the one that has been followed to here bears left. On the right a signpost indicates the path, which passes in front of a house. Turn along the path and follow it upwards. (A path behind the house leads to the West Portal of Hincaster Tunnel.)

Follow the path ahead, its being the horsepath over Hincaster Hill. Where there are farm access gates to the left and right the path turns to the right and starts to drop down again. This stretch of path is particularly sunken, making it unique, and passes under two low bridges. The first (built in 1846) carries the West Coast Main Line over the path and the second is an original accommodation bridge from 1817 for the farmland above.

On coming off the horsepath the East Portal of Hincaster Tunnel is to the left. A flight of stone steps leads down to the viewpoint or the path can be followed down to the canal towpath.

Follow the towpath past a picnic area on the site of the de-watered Lancaster Canal and on to a wooden gate out onto a road. There, turn left to pass under the A590 and then cross a wooden stile on the right by a field gate. Follow the grassy path to the right from there to join the former towpath by the old water channel to the left. Pass under a now very overgrown Sellet Hall Bridge.

At the next bridge, Stainton Crossing Bridge, the Lancaster Canal becomes watered again. Whilst one can turn left onto the road after passing under the bridge, it is more interesting to turn up the steps to the right and cross the bridge for its view down the canal. Turn to the right at the road junction on the far side of the bridge and then follow the road to Stainton, about a third of a mile ahead.

At Stainton there is a very old non-conformist church. The United Reformed Church dates from 1698 and is now linked with the one in Kendal. The township appears in the Domesday Book as Steintun and straddles Stainton Beck.

In the middle of Stainton there is a sycamore in a circular bed. The proper road goes ahead, but to the left it crosses Stainton Beck by a ford. To the left of the ford is a narrow, stone footbridge to be crossed.

From the bridge, turn left along the very minor road and turn right at a corner just ahead. Look at the hedge on the left and notice it goes a short way from the road at a point shortly reached, the road itself bearing a little to the right. In that corner of the hedge there is a not very conspicuous stile leading into a field. From the stile, go up to the top right corner of the field and come out onto a minor road, this being the road coming up from by Stainton Crossing Bridge.

Cross the road and go through the large aluminium field gate and then straight ahead with the hedge on the right. At the end of the field there is quite a high wooden ladder stile to cross. From there, continue by the hedge to its end a few yards ahead and then bear diagonally right across the field, as indicated by a waymarker. Halfway along the hedge in front there is a wooden ladder stile to cross into the next field.

Bear leftwards to the gate to be seen, pass through it and then cross the following field bearing to the right and towards the railway line. On reaching the railway, there is a wooden stile to cross onto a new track leading to the bridge to the right, its being erected in 2000 and replacing the old 'Well Heads Crossing' over the track. From the bridge, follow the track to its end where there is a stile leading into the adjoining field. Go up the field by the hedge on the left. Cross a stone slab stile into the next field and go up it quite close to the hedge on the left until at the top, there is a stile in the hedge opposite leading out onto Well Heads Lane. (If it is not desired to go to Sedgwick, there is a path up the field in front and then dropping down to a bridge, which is just out of sight at the left of the trees, crossing the bed of the Lancaster Canal.) Turn right along Well Heads Lane for a little over a quarter of a mile into Sedgwick.

Sedgwick, its name coming from the Norse for a dairy farm, is split in two by the aqueduct taking the now empty water channel of the Lancaster Canal over the main village street. This very strongly buttressed aqueduct is unusual in that it is skew to the roadway it crossed. There used to be a small school in the village and a smithy near the aqueduct.

The village owes much of its existence to the Wakefield family, who were Quakers. John Wakefield was a Kendal banker. In 1764 he opened his first gunpowder works in a former corn mill on the east bank of the River Kent, the river providing the necessary waterpower. The business expanded and was moved to a larger mill at Bassingill, which is below Force Bridge. In 1850 he opened a mill at Gatebeck. 1857 saw a new Sedgwick gunpowder works opened on the West side of the Kent at Low Park Wood, gunpowder being produced there until 1920. A number of those employed at the works came from Natland.

Another member of the family was Mary Wakefield who lived in Sedgwick House, which was rebuilt by 1869, having been inherited by her father in 1866. She was a talented singer and sang in concerts around the country. In 1885 she held the first of her famous musical festivals on the tennis court at Sedgwick House. There were more events the following year and the competition was transferred to St. George's Hall in Kendal. Following the death of Mary's father in 1891, the event became the Wakefield Choral Competition. Mary died in 1910, but the competition lived on.

On joining the main road through Sedgwick village, turn left to go under the aqueduct carrying the bed of the Lancaster Canal over the roadway. Having passed under it, turn right up the steps onto the towpath and there turn right to cross the aqueduct. Follow the towpath along by the drained water channel, which is now full of trees and other growth, and pass under Sedgwick Hall Bridge, where the path

mentioned earlier joins. Pass through a kissing gate and then straight ahead along the grassy path. It reaches a point where there is a fence close by to the left and trees over to the right. Drop down the field here to a kissing gate leading onto the road.

Turn left to pass over the A590 and about 100 yards along there is a signpost indicating the path to

Sedgwick Aqueduct, Lancaster Canal

follow to the right for Levens Bridge. Go into Levens Park at a stone step stile and turn left down the avenue of oak trees. Follow the path along the avenue until a marker indicates that the line to be followed is to the right, above the River Kent. Continue along the path and come to a flight of stone steps leading up to the road.

The bus stop for the south is a few yards to the left. The bus stop for the north is across the road, cross the bridge and turn left along the road for Grange-over-Sands for a few yards.

WALK 17 LEVENS BRIDGE TO KENDAL VIA RIVER KENT.

Easy
6 miles
Allow 3 hours.

Levens Hall, which stands on the south bank of the River Kent by Levens Bridge, dates back to around 1250 to 1300. It is a fortified structure with a pele tower as well as a hall. The South Wing and Brewhouse were added later. In the Hall is some fine oak panelling and a visit is well worthwhile. The Hall was used for some of the scenes in the BBC production of Mrs. Gaskell's "Wives and Daughters". It was formerly owned by the Bellinghams, one of whom was said to have been determined to outdo Walter Strickland, his contemporary at Sizergh Castle, in the variety of ornaments, figures and emblems featured on the Hall.

During the times of James II the Hall was acquired by Colonel James Graham, Allan, the last of the Bellingham's being forced to sell to pay gambling debts. Colonel Graham brought with him Monsieur Guillaume Beaumont, who had been a gardener to the king and had trained at Versailles. It was Beaumont who laid out the famous gardens and started the magnificent Topiary Garden. Some of the trees and bushes in the garden are 300 years old and they are formed into a wide variety of designs, including peacocks, chess pieces and a judge's wig. The topiary is clipped only once a year, this being during late August and September, a task which takes several weeks to complete.

Also in the garden is a Ha-Ha, the first one to be recorded in Britain. The Ha-Ha is a sunken ditch that kept out animals but allowed for a view from the main garden which is uninterrupted by a wall or fence.

Levens Park, to the east of the A6, was also laid out by Beaumont and here is the famous herd of Black Fallow Deer and the herd of black and white Bagot Goats. (The Bagot family are the present owners of Levens Hall.) It is amazing to think that in the 1960's it was planned to build a dual carriageway road through the park. If that had been done, the road would have cut through the mile long avenue of oaks, which once formed the carriage drive to the Hall. The Avenue is well maintained and when any tree dies it is replaced with a new sapling. In various places in the park are limestone seats dating from the 19th Century.

Before the link road was constructed, Levens Bridge was a notorious bottleneck for traffic. Now, vehicles northwards all first follow the road round to the left and only southbound traffic uses the road ahead on its way down to cross the bridge.

Levens Village, as it is now known, was formerly called Beathwaite Green, a name showing it had once been a woody area all around with the township being in a clearing, "Thwaite" means clearing. In the Domesday Book the area is shown as 'Lefuenes' and it was held in 1066 by Tosti, Earl of Northumberland, from whom it passed to Roger Poictu. The parish of Levens included part of Leasgill, Beathwaite Green and part of Brigsteer. Levens church, a chapelry, in the parish of Heversham, was erected in 1828 at a cost of £2,000, this being met by the Hon. And Mrs. F.G. Howard.

This walk can be linked straight onto the previous walk by crossing Levens Bridge. By the north-eastern end of the bridge there is a little gate in the wall leading into the Park. At first the grassy path follows the river, but it soon curves to the left and makes its way up the grassy hillside. It becomes two grassy paths, the one to follow being the right-hand one, it still bearing to the left of the river. Go up some stone steps, through a metal gate and down into a field. There, turn to the right and follow the path along by the wall.

At the end of the field go over stone steps into the next field and follow the grassy track ahead to a stone stile. This stile leads out onto a road where turn right up to its end. There, a path leads under the A590 and back onto a minor road. Follow this road along, passing the Sedgwick falls on the way.

At the end of this road, which it will have been seen is a former road that was cut with the coming of the A590, come out onto a proper

road and go straight ahead for about 150 yards to where there is a turning to the right onto a minor road. Go straight along that road, ignore a junction to the left, and come to a footbridge spanning the River Kent on the right. Cross it and turn left along the bank of the river.

Follow the grassy path along to a field gate, pass

Bridge over River Kent, Wilson Place

through it and then follow the track from there. Across the river is Low Park Wood, now a caravan site. Around a quarter of a mile further on the track starts to leave the river-bank and just after that there is a gap in the wall on the left. Go through the gap and into the field and follow the clear path along quite close to the river. Cross a stile and then take the right-hand path at a junction, continuing to follow the good stony path along above the river, crossing another stile on the way.

Another stile is crossed and the path followed along by the river-bank and into an open field. Follow the path to a wooden stile leading out onto the road by Hawes Bridge (17). Turn right along the road for a few yards and then turn left to pass round the end of a large field gate and onto the path for Kendal.

Go through a gap in the wall into the next field and continue straight on quite close to the river. Pass over a stile that has been rebuilt using a mixture of concrete and stone. Come to a narrow gap in a wall and keep on going over the following field to a wooden stile. Continue following the grassy field path close to the river with Kendal to be seen ahead.

On reaching a point where the Kent comes down from the left, continue straight along the path, leaving the river behind. Go over the grassy path, passing through a small squeeze stile on the way. Close to Watercrook Farm cross a stile onto the roadway. where turn right to a motor road, cross it and turn to the left (18).

A line of trees on the other side of the fence indicates the line of the Lancaster Canal. At a sign, go onto the cycleway and footpath for Canal Head. Follow the path along, pass under an old canal bridge and follow the path along the line of the old water channel. Go up to a busy road, cross it and then drop down onto the path again.

Pass under a turnover bridge, where the towpath changed sides on the canal for the last half-mile stretch into Kendal, and come to a further road to cross. Another road is passed under (19) and then continue along the cycleway as it passes beneath Kendal Castle after which it joins a road at Canal Head. Turn left along the road to its end by the Kent, coming off Canal Head North at Little Aynam. Turn right along the riverside road to where it turns to the right. There, turn left to follow the footpath leading to a footbridge over the Kent. Having crossed the bridge, turn left to the pedestrian crossing, cross it and go straight up the road in front for the 555 bus stands just below the shopping precinct and car park.

17. Walk 21 crosses walk 17 here.
18. Walk 21 uses the same route to Kendal from here.
19. Walk 19 passes over this bridge going into Kendal.

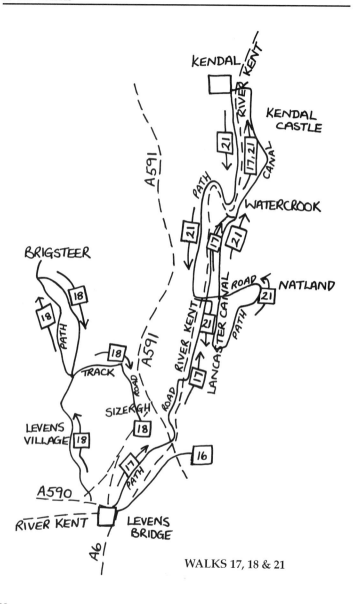

WALKS 17, 18 & 21

WALK 18 LEVENS BRIDGE, LEVENS VILLAGE, BRIGSTEER WOOD, SIZERGH

Easy
5.5 miles
Allow 2.5 hours plus time to look round Sizergh Castle, if it is open.
Also allow extra time for if looking round Brigsteer village.

The bus stop from the north is roughly opposite the entrance to Levens Hall whilst that from the south is across the bridge and round the corner on the Grange road.

The walk starts at a footpath close to the bridge and is by the road junction. Follow the footpath along the river-bank, with Levens Hall across the water. Come out onto the Grange road, cross it, go left and then and take the turning to the right for Levens Village. Go under the by-pass on what was part of the roadway before the road above was built. At the junction, cross straight over, and continue along the road into Levens Village.

Follow the main street straight through the village, passing a bus stop for local buses, and come to a junction. Here, take the left-hand road, pass Levens Methodist Church, and cross straight over the junction ahead to go down Hutton Lane. Keep on following the road, noting a stone archway and studded door to one house on the right.

The road continues through Cinderbarrow and comes to where it swings to the right. Here there is a signpost indicating the footpath straight ahead for Brigsteer Wood. Leave the road and go through the squeeze stile and then straight ahead over a farm track towards the wood in front. Come out at a kissing gate onto the road and immediately turn left into the woodland. Brigsteer Woods are famed for their wild daffodils in spring.

Go down the path to a wooden kissing gate by a field gate. Follow the main path ahead from the gates, past an information board, and come to where the path splits. Take the path dropping down to the left. This path joins another path, where turn to the right. Follow this path along and come to a wooden kissing gate into a field. The way generally followed from here is not quite the right of way according to the map. Go up the field by the wall on the right and then see a grassy path going off to the left towards the farm buildings seen ahead. On reaching Park End Farm, go through a wooden gate by a field gate

Brigsteer

and out onto the road, where turn left. Follow the road to the beginning of Brigsteer village where there is a footpath going to the right across a field, it is signposted. (Brigsteer is an attractive village and worth a look around before following the path.)

Brigsteer is first mentioned in a record dated 1227, when it was spelt 'Bryggstere'. The name is suggested to refer to a bullock and a bridge. The bridge may actually have been the causeway over the marshy land below the village, which is a part of Levens Moss in the Lyth Valley. The area was part of the Moss lands mentioned regarding the Enclosure Act for the Heversham area. The straight roads along the valley bottom and following the rectangular field boundaries are typical of Enclosed lands.

At the signpost at the beginning of the village, pass through a small wooden gate in a wall and then go up the following field going steadily upwards and bearing diagonally right, towards a hedge. At the bottom of the hedge there is a field gate. Do not go through it but, instead, pass straight up the field keeping the hedge on the right. In the wall at the top there is a gap leading out onto a lane, where turn right.

Follow the lane along, going to the left at a junction, the way to the right being to a farm. Pass in front of Heather Bank House and then through a large wooden field gate spanning the track. Follow the farm track ahead as it crosses over a field. The track to follow becomes grassy as it goes up the field to a very good track at the top.

Follow the good track to the right for a few yards to where it turns left. A signpost indicates that the field gate in front leads onto the Brigsteer Park path. Go over the grassy field path, which is very vague in places, and ignore a small path dropping down to the right. Continue along the path and through a field gate and at first go straight ahead. Shortly, the path bears right to pass through a line of lime trees and then goes steadily ahead and down the field. Sizergh Castle is to be seen over to the left.

Bear right down the field towards Brigsteer Wood over to the right. On reaching the far right corner of the field there is a wooden gate out onto the road. This is directly opposite the point where Brigsteer Wood was entered earlier.

On reaching the road, turn sharp left onto a field track. Go through a field gate and straight along the track, coming to a pair of gates. Go through the right-hand gate and onto a farm lane. Pass through a wooden kissing gate by a field gate and before long another field gate with a gate by it is reached. Straight in front is Sizergh Castle, the car park and pay box being on the right.

At the Castle, turn right and go straight down the drive and through a gate by a cattle grid. Continue straight down the drive and at the bottom, where there is a junction, turn right onto the road. Leave the castle grounds and come out onto a public road, pass the Strickland Arms, and out onto the A591. The bus stops in each direction are about 100 yards to the left.

If it is not wished to visit the Castle because of its being closed, there is another footpath that can be followed. On reaching the gate before the Castle, turn right and go straight across the car park, keeping close to the hedge on the right. (This is not strictly the line of the right of way, but is the easiest way to follow.) At the end there are two field gates with a kissing gate by the one on the right. Go through the kissing gate and across the field keeping by the wall on the left. At its end there is another kissing gate to pass through and there bear right to another such gate a few yards away, leading into the field in front and dropping down to the left. Go down that field, which can be rather wet, and come out at another kissing gate onto a track. Follow the track down to the road and turn right along it, passing the Strickland Arms.

Sizergh Castle is now a National Trust property and is well worth a visit. This is another building that has developed around a fourteenth century pele tower. In 1239 Sir William Strickland was married to Elizabeth Deincourt, the then owner of the property, thus bringing the Strickland name to Sizergh, the family having come from Great Strickland which is near Appleby.

The present pele tower dates from about 1350 and has a projecting turret (the Deincourt Tower) rising from it on the south side. Much of the rest of the building is 16th century apart from the Great Hall, which is now the entrance hall, dating from the 15th century.

In 1464, Sir Thomas Strickland married Agnes Parre, the daughter of Sir Thomas Parre of Kendal, who was the grandfather of Catherine Parre (Parr).

Sir Gerald Strickland acquired the estate, which was in financial difficulties, from his cousin in 1896. He married twice, but had no male heirs, and settled the estate on his eldest daughter and her husband in 1931. The Hon. Mrs. Hornroyd-Strickland and her husband, Henry, together with their son Lieutenant-Commander T. Hornroyd-Strickland, gifted the estate to the National Trust in 1951. Mrs. T. Hornroyd-Strickland still resides at Sizergh Castle.

WALK 19 KENDAL, CASTLE GREEN AREA, KENDAL CASTLE, KENDAL

Easy/moderate
5.5 miles
Allow 2.5 hours plus time at Kendal Castle.

Kendal is the most northerly town to appear in the Domesday Book. In 1086, Westmorland was not a county, but the lands recorded were classed as being part of Yorkshire. The land to the north was considered to be part of the dominion of the Scottish king, Malcolm Canmore. It was not until 1092, when William Rufus, the Conqueror's son, drove the Scots back to the Solway and claimed Carlisle that the present boundary between England and Scotland was established. From the time of the survey, the only thing known about Kendal was that it had a church as the Domesday surveyors recorded it as 'Cherchebi' or 'churchtown'. Later, it became known as 'Kirkby Kendal'.

Kendal is known as 'The Gateway to the Lakes' and is famed for Kendal Mint Cake. However, there is much more to the town than that. The town's motto is 'Pannis mihi panis', meaning 'Wool is my bread'.

Flemish weavers came to the town in the 1300's, but the wool trade was established before that. Wool was spun and woven in all the Kendal townships. After weaving, it was dyed and then fulled to restore its strength, this process in early times being done manually in long troughs of soapy water. In due course, fulling mills took over from the fullers. After that, the cloth was washed in clear water to remove the soap and then hung to dry and shrink, its already having shrunk from its original size during the earlier processes.

The cloth was hung to dry on tenter frames, to which it was fixed by tenter-hooks, the origin of the well-known expression. These frames were outdoors and supervised by a tenterer. Old maps show several areas around Kendal as having tenter fields, and some had to be moved on the coming of the Lancaster Canal. Once the cloth had dried out, it was treated either to enhance the fluffy effect or the fluff was removed. There is a reminder of the old woollen industry in the Woolpack Yard leading off Stricklandgate, close to the library. Formerly, the Woolpack Inn had stood there since its rebuilding in 1781, but only part of the inn building now remains following modern development.

The Romans came to Kendal and established their camp at Watercrook, which was an ideal site as a crook in the River Kent surrounds three sides of the camp. This camp was on the road from Burrow in Lonsdale to Ambleside and also on the road to Low Borrow Bridge.

The next fortified site in Kendal is the motte and bailey on Castle Howe to the west and would probably have originally been established by the Romans. Later, the Normans would convert it to the motte and bailey structure.

To the east of the Kent stand the remains of Kendal Castle, which have been the subject of a good deal of restoration and display work. The building is Norman, but is not the first fortification to occupy the site, which is a drumlin left behind by a retreating glacier at the end of the Ice Age. It is not known who built the castle or when it was built, but it is probable that the edifice had been constructed by 1241. At that time, King Henry III returned a castle, which had previously been surrendered, to William de Lancaster.

In 1383 Kendal Castle passed into the hands of the locally influential Parr family, its coming into the possession of William Parr through his marriage to Elizabeth de Roos. Around a hundred years later, the then head of the Parr family, also William Parr, left Kendal and it is said that this was the last time that the family head lived in Kendal, the castle from then on being in the care of a steward. William's daughter was Kathryn Parr, the sixth wife of Henry VIII and the only one to survive him.

A local tradition has it that Kathryn was born in Kendal Castle, but it is not certain that she even visited Kendal. However, it is a nice, romantic story, as is the tale that Henry VIII stayed at Cunswick Hall whilst courting Kathryn. Actually, it is believed that he never came further north than Warwick. It is certain that Kathryn was one of the Parr family of Kendal.

Kendal Castle looks down onto the former basins and terminus of the Lancaster Canal, an area it is hoped to restore in the future. On 18 June, 1819 Castle Hill saw an estimated crowd of 10,000 people gathered on the side of it to witness a flotilla of sixteen boats arriving at the basin at 5.00 p.m. This was at the opening of the canal from Tewitfield through to Kendal, thus completing the line through from Preston. Following this, there was a dinner for a hundred and twenty at the Town Hall, where the mayor presided.

That Town Hall was not the present one but the Moot Hall, which stood at the south-west corner of the market place. It was burned down by vandals in the 1960's. The present Town Hall was formerly the White Hall Assembly Rooms and built in 1825. It was altered in 1861 and altered again and extended in 1893/94. The latter alterations were the result of a donation from Alderman Binloss and his wife and included £3,000 to replace the tower and include a carillon in it. The bells paid for by the Binloss's still play tunes every three hours during daylight hours.

Part of Kendal Castle and moat

Richard I granted Kendal a weekly market by a charter granted on 9th December 1189, its being held on a Saturday. In 1310 Edward II granted the right to hold a fair as well. The tolls from the markets and fairs provided income for the successive Barons of Kendal. As the markets and fairs were not restricted to the Market Place, Kendal was no doubt colourful and noisy with the stalls selling produce and livestock. In fact, the noise made by the cattle was such that complaints from shopkeepers led to their being removed to New Road in 1851.

Now, there are both outdoor and indoor markets in Kendal, selling a wide range of goods and produce. In addition, there are the occasional Farmers' Markets, but no longer with live animals.

Holy Trinity is the parish church of Kendal. Until the 1540's Kendal was in the diocese of York, next Henry VIII incorporated it in the diocese of Chester and it is now in the diocese of Carlisle. Prior to the Reformation, the parish included all the various townships up to and including Grasmere.

At 140 feet long and 103 feet wide, the church is the second widest church in the country. Being so large, the roof is supported by thirty-two pillars and has two aisles on either side of the nave. It is not known when the church was first established on the site. A fragment of a cross shaft dating from Anglian times was found under the foundations of the present building, which has been much altered and extended over the years. The only Norman remains are the base of the tower. There are three chapels within the church, Bellingham Chapel, Strickland Chapel and Parr Chapel, all three named after formerly eminent local families.

The early Quaker movement was strong in Kendal, the annual meeting of Friends from around the north of England being held in the town in the eighteenth century. However, numbers were falling when the large new Meeting House was built in 1815. Besides being used for worship, this building houses the Quaker Tapestry, a large number of individual tapestry panels which all link together much as the Bayeux Tapestry, which was its inspiration, and which were worked by Quakers all over the world.

Kendal used to have a House of Correction on Windermere Road, it becoming known as Kendal Prison following the passing of the Prisons Act in 1877. It ceased to be a civilian prison in 1894, but was used for military prisoners until after the Boer War. The site was sold by auction in 1907 for £1,000 to Mr. W. F. Pennington, who took 20 years over the demolition of the buildings.

On 22 September 1846 the railway line from Lancaster to Kendal was opened and the passenger service on the Lancaster Canal from the town ceased. The following year the line was opened through to Windermere. Seeing the unmanned station today, with just a single line, it is hard to believe how much railway traffic there was until comparatively recent times. There were local passenger trains, to places such as Grange, Morecambe and Preston and express trains to London. To the north of the station was the goods yard, two pick-up goods trains a day being dispatched from there. Another important train was the early evening parcel train to Euston, which carried parcels from K Shoes, Gilkes and other Kendal businesses. Several of the circuses visiting the town came by rail. In addition, excursion trains to Windermere passed through Kendal. Now, with just a single track, between Windermere and Oxenholme, there can only by one train at a time on the line.

In 1920 a number of ex-servicemen set up the Kendal Motor Bus Company to transport workers from Kendal and Endmoor to the Burneside paper mills. The service expanded to take in all South Westmorland and crossed into the north of Lancashire. By 1930, when the company was taken over by Ribble Motor Services, it owned 32 buses. Ribble Motor Services ran buses for many years, the Company later becoming part of the National Bus Company. Following privatisation, the former Ribble services in Lakeland are operated under Stagecoach in Cumbria.

From the bus stands on Blackhall Road, go down the road to its end and cross the pedestrian crossing. Turn left to follow the road round and across the River Kent. Continue along the road on its right-hand side, passing under the railway line close to Kendal station. Continue

Jensons Bridge, Lancaster Canal, Holme.
Dallam Park in Autumn

Looking up Fairy Steps, Beetham.

Avenue of oaks, Levens Park.
Hawes Bridge over River Kent, near Natland.

Stramongate Bridge and Kent, Kendal.
Daffodils and Cowan Head complex.

along the road on the right-hand side, Appleby Road, for about a further quarter of a mile until Fowl Ing Lane (the third road on the right from the railway bridge) is reached.

Turn up Fowl Ing Lane and at the top, as the tarred road turns to the left, go straight up the roadway in front. This roadway becomes a proper tarred road as it is followed along. Continue along the road as it climbs steadily upwards, crossing a stile round a cattle grid. There are good views over Kendal from up here. The road turns to the left and passes a small former quarry to the right.

The road passes between two drystone walls towards Jenkincrag Farm in front. Pass the farm and the track then becomes unsurfaced. Keep following it along, crossing a bridge over the main West Coast railway line after which the track becomes rougher.

Go through a small stile by a field gate and then turn right to cross a channelled stream. From the stream, go straight up the field by the wall on the right. At the top right-hand corner of the field a stile leads out onto Paddy Lane, where turn right.

Paddy Lane is followed for about a mile, crossing a road down to Kendal by Greyhound Farm on the way. Pass North Lodge on the right and, shortly before reaching the next farm, there is a concrete slab stile leading over the wall on the right and into a field. Cross over the field and in the wall at the bottom, to the right of a field gate, there is another stile to cross.

Go straight across this next field to a gateway into another field and then bear to the left down this field to the gate into the following field. Cross the stile by the gate and then follow the hedge/fence on the left. On reaching the end of it the path drops down a grassy slope with a stream over to the right. The stream is forded at the bottom of the slope which has been followed down the field.

Continue following the path to two gates where pass through the one on the right and follow the grassy way along by the wall on the left. Shortly a bridge is reached taking the path and farm track over the main railway line again. Follow the farm track to a field gate where there is a stile to the left. Go through the stile and then down a path between two quite high walls densely covered with moss.

The path comes out onto a road at a junction by Castle Green Hotel. Cross over the road and go down Park Side Road in front. Pass over the railway line for Kendal and Windermere and come to a housing estate on the right. Follow the road to the end of the estate. Just before reaching a football field, turn to the right to follow a path behind a row of garages.

Continue along the pathway which turns to the left towards Kendal Castle in front. Go along the path until it is left to turn up a grassy path to the castle. At the top of this path there is a path going round the top of the former moat. Turn right and follow this path round to the main entrance of the Castle. After having looked round the Castle, resume following the path above the moat to where a grassy path drops down to the right.

Turn down this grassy path, reach some railings by a paved area of path and then go through a kissing gate onto a road. Pass straight down Sunnyside, which becomes Parr Street, (19) to where it joins the main road to the south by the River Kent. Cross the road at a pedestrian crossing to the right and then over a footbridge spanning the Kent. Turn right from the bridge and go along beside the river. Cross the road before reaching Miller Bridge (it is easier to cross here) and then follow the riverside road on its left. Turn left at the next junction to go up Blackhall Road for the bus stands for buses north or south.

19. Walks 17 and 21 pass under the bridge over the former Lancaster Canal on their way into Kendal.

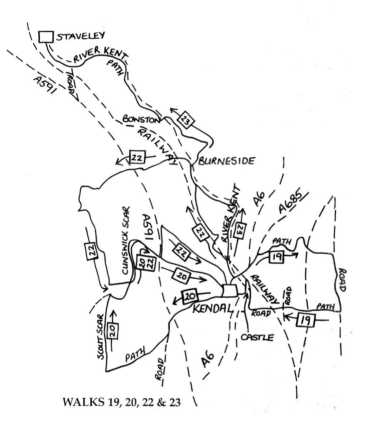

WALKS 19, 20, 22 & 23

WALK 20, KENDAL, UNDERBARROW, CUNSWICK FELL, KENDAL

Easy / moderate
6.5 to 7 miles
Allow 3.5 to 4 hours.

If coming from the north, leave the bus at the bus station, go down Blackhall Road to the road junction by the pedestrian crossing and then turn right up Finkle Street to the top and then left to the Town Hall. If travelling from the south, leave the bus at Kendal Town Hall. Walk back south on the Western side of the street, i.e. the opposite side from the Town Hall, to the road to the right, Gillingate, a sign indicating it is the way to Underbarrow. Go up it to the green and there take the Brigsteer Road leading off to the left.

Pass along the road, up the hill and come to the by-pass road, which is crossed. Pass a signpost for a path to Scout Scar and a few yards further on, by a milepost of 1900 indicating that it is 1 mile from Kendal, there is a signpost for Scout Scar and Barrowfield. The path from here is grassy and bears diagonally left over Kendal racecourse to a kissing gate in the wall opposite.

The racecourse dates from 1821. It was used on and off until 1923, from when no races were held until the 1990's.

A stony path leads upwards from the gate, passing over limestone country. A stile in a wall is crossed and the path continues straight up the hillside. At the top of Underbarrow there are a

Along Scout Scar, Kendal

number of paths to the left and right but, for this walk, continue straight ahead to the edge of the Scar, where there is a view to Barrowfield down below. This view is from by a cairn. At this point there is one path to the left and another to the right. Take the right-hand path.

Continue along this path, which follows the top of the Scar, until a kissing-gate is reached at the end, leading out onto a road. Turn to the right, round a corner, and by a car park there is the start of a permissive path to Cunswick Scar, which passes close to the TV relay mast.

Shortly after passing the TV mast a kissing gate is passed through and the path followed close by the wall on the left. Near the next wall, shortly reached, a post indicates the path turns right, again by a wall. It continues on to where a track crosses it (20). From here, the path ahead is a right of way to Cunswick Fell.

The path bears diagonally to the left and then continues quite close to the wall to the left, crossing a stile on the way. At the next signpost, turn sharp right up the gentle slope of the hillside, Cunswick Fell. There are a number of paths up here, which are crossed. There is a wall ahead, enclosing fields from the open country of the Fell. Pass along the wall with it on the right to where there is a stile by a bush, not noticeable until it is reached (21).

Cross into the field and follow the path, first just to the left of the wall and then continuing straight ahead as the wall drops away to the right. The path is going towards a bridge which can be seen spanning the by-pass road ahead. Once across the by-pass, go straight up the hillside ahead (22).

On reaching the wall, there is another stile to pass through and continue by the wall to the left to yet another stile, this one leading onto Kendal Golf Course.

There is a well-marked path up the golf course, leading to a wall. On reaching the corner of the wall, there is a sign indicating the path going to the left, its being on the immediate right of the wall. It is a clear path to follow, with Kendal spread out below. Do remember golfers and take care not to spoil their game.

On reaching the end of the path, which has dropped steadily downwards turn right, go down the road for a few yards to where another road drops down to the left. Just by this road are some steps leading down to the roadway, and then turn right. Drop down Sepulchre Lane, *which lies on the boundary of a medieval chapel close from which the burial ground passed was purchased. It was bought in 1656 by Kendal Quakers for £9 3s. 0d.* At the end of the lane turn right to the road ahead and then left down it, Allhallows Lane, to Highgate, coming out opposite the Town Hall.

20. Walk 22 crosses walk 20 here.
21. Walk 22 rejoins here.
22. Walk 22 uses the path to the left.

WALK 21, KENDAL, RIVER KENT, NATLAND, LANCASTER CANAL, KENDAL

Easy
8.5 miles
Allow 3.75 to 4 hours

From the bus stands in Blackhall Road, go straight down the road and at the bottom turn to the right without crossing the road. Cross over the bottom of Lowther Street and then over to the riverside path which starts by the end of Miller Bridge, which is not crossed. The path passes at the back of Kendal Parish Church and at the back of Abbott Hall Art Gallery and Museum. At the end of the path, cross the road at the end of the bridge over the Kent and continue along South Road, again by the river. On the far side of the Kent is 'K' Village. Where the road goes round to the right there is a pathway continuing along the riverbank, passing behind some houses.

The pathway comes to an end by Romney Bridge and there cross straight over the road. Drop down to the riverside walk and follow the path along again. The path becomes a gravelly riverside path. As the Kent swings sharply round to the right Watercrook Farm is to be seen on the other side of it. The field in front of the farm is the site of the Roman Fort.

The path continues along above the river as it goes round to the left, circling the site of the fort. To the right are the backs of some of the houses of Kendal. The path ends at a broad squeeze stile leading out onto a minor road. Turn left, cross the bridge and then pass through a small metal gate leading into the field on the right. Pass along the middle of the field and at the end come to a bend in the river. A small bridge is crossed, and then go straight along the grassy path over the next field. At the far left corner of the field the Kent is rejoined. There, cross a small wooden stile into the next field and pass over it close to the river down below.

A squeeze stile to the left of a field gate leads into the next field and from there continue along the riverside path to a stone stile into the following field and on to another stone stile into another field. At the end of this field there is a wooden stile to the left of a field gate leading out onto a road where turn to the left and cross the bridge (17).

Continue along the road to where it is seen to cross a bridge ahead (Crowpark Bridge). On the left, before reaching the bridge, there is a metal gate to pass through and there turn right to go under the bridge, which formerly spanned the Lancaster Canal. Follow the grassy path along by the wall and hedge on the right, this being the former towpath. Cross a wooden stile into the next field where the curve of the former water channel is passed above. After the next wall is crossed the water channel is filled in again. Continue along the line of the towpath, passing over a roadway to a farm, until Larkrigg Hall Bridge is reached.

Pass under the bridge, where the full former depth of the canal can be seen, go over a stile on the right and then cross the bridge. Go along the track to the left, this being a bridleway. Come out onto the roadway down to the farm, which was crossed earlier when on the towpath, and turn right along it. Where the farm track swings round to the right the bridleway goes straight ahead, following a clear, grassy path over the field. At the end, go through a large metal field gate and along the lane in front. This comes out onto a roadway where turn right to the road. On reaching the road, turn left to Natland Village.

After passing Smithy Close, either go straight ahead along the road or turn right to have a look at the large, attractive village green with the Parish Church at the head. If you have been round the Green, go down the road on the far side to the Post Office and shop and pass it and turn round the corner to the right. (If going straight along the road and not to the Green, turn left at the Post Office.)

Natland Green and Church

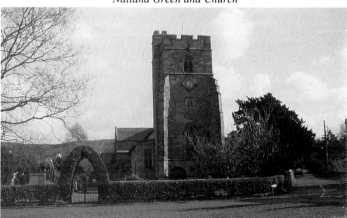

The name 'Natland' could come from the bondmen who were placed there as attendants to the lord living at Kendal Castle. Also, it could come from the Norse for a wood with a very uncertain first element. St. Mark's church, which is by Natland Green, only dates from 1910, but is the fourth to be built on or near the site, the first being in 1246. Prior to 1872 it was a chapelry to Kendal church. Near to it was a tithebarn for the storage of tithed produce.

A few yards along the road from the junction by the Post Office there is a turning on the left, Hawes Lane. Go down Hawes Lane for about a third of a mile to where Crowpark Bridge is crossed. Turn through the metal gate onto the canal towpath again, but this time turn left and follow the grassy path along the field. Cross a stile to the left of a field gate on the way to a bridge seen ahead.

From the bridge, continue straight ahead by the hedge on the left, crossing stiles into other fields on the way, partly with a fence on the right. The canal water channel has been filled in, but at one point it can be seen how there was a cutting in the ground on the right. The towpath comes out onto the Natland Road where turn left (18). Cross the road to the line of trees opposite and then go left along by the fence until the cycleway along the former towpath and canal bed can be joined.

Follow the path along, passing some gardens, which now spread over the site of the canal, and under a former canal bridge. Come to a busy road to cross and then rejoin the cycleway on the other side. The next bridge that the track passes beneath is Kendal Change Bridge, a turnover bridge where the towpath changed from being on the left of the water channel to being on its right.

The path goes along by a roadway and then another road has to be crossed. Pass under the next bridge (19) and continue along the path beneath Kendal Castle. The path comes out at roads at Canal Head, where turn down the road to the left. At little Aynam turn right along the road, cross it and turn left into a parkland area. From there, cross the footbridge over the River Kent and turn left to the pedestrian crossing. Go over it and up Blackhall Road to the bus stands.

17. Walk 17 crosses walk 21 here.
18. Walk 17 uses the same route into Kendal from here.
19. Walk 19 passes over this bridge.

WALK 22, KENDAL, BURNESIDE, CUNSWICK SCAR, KENDAL.

Easy / moderate
8.5 miles
Allow 5 to 5.5 hours.

From Kendal bus station, walk back to Sandes Avenue and turn right after having crossed the road. Immediately before the bridge over the Kent there is a pathway to the left. Follow the path along by the river, pass beneath the railway bridge and then turn left following it close to the railway line. The path reaches a point where it turns sharply to the left and then right again before passing a row of cottages and coming out onto the Burneside road. Here, turn left, pass under the railway and then turn right again to go along Sparrowmire Lane.

Follow the road to the next junction where turn right onto Low Mead. About twenty yards along here, turn right down the track and follow it over the railway line and round a demolished farmhouse. (From by the former farm buildings there are actually two paths quite close to each other and the following instructions apply to whichever one is taken.) Circle round the farm buildings and then turn right through a field that is full of buttercups in spring. Reach a farm track and follow it to its end. Go diagonally left towards the railway at the far left of the field then entered. (This route is the way people follow and is not the same as the right of way shown on the OS map.)

By the railway bridge, go over the stile up the wall, cross the track, and drop down the opposite wall at another stile. Walk along the grassy path with the railway to the left. Towards the end of the field there is a good view over Burneside and towards the Kentmere Fells. A stile is crossed over a wall and the path followed to where a farm track comes in from a railway bridge to the left. Turn right onto this track, which then swings leftwards towards a corner of the field. Pass a field gate to the right and then at the end of the field the farm track passes between the hedges. At the end there is a stile by a gate. From there, the grassy path bears diagonally right up the hillside until it comes out at a kissing gate leading to the nearby Burneside road. Turn left along the road and pass straight through Burneside (23).

Burneside is famous for the James Cropper plc paper mill, situated here because of the abundant water supplies. James Cropper took over the mill in 1845, its being established as a paper mill in 1833, having earlier been first a cotton mill and then a woollen mill. The firm thrived and expanded until today it is a leading manufacturer of coloured, strong paper. It was through Croppers that much of Burneside village came to be built.

The paper mills needed a good supply of water under pressure and, in 1901 James Cropper built a concrete dam to reform the Old Potter Tarn on Potter Fell. Lower down the water was joined by the stream from Gurnal Dubs and entered Ghyll Pool. From there, high-pressure water pipes were laid, taking the water down to Burneside Mill. Potter Tarn and Gurnal Dubs are passed in walk 26.

Cornelius Nicholson, who sold the mill to James Cropper, was one of the promoters of the Kendal and Windermere Railway and it was he who cut the first sod on 16 July, 1845 ready for work to commence on constructing the line beyond Kendal.

Charles James Cropper was a director of the London and North Western Railway, who took over the line, which enabled him to have extensive private sidings at Burneside to serve their mills at Cowan Head, Bowston and Burneside. In addition, they had first tramways and then standard gauge lines to the mills, these running partly by the roadsides. The line to Cowan Head closed in 1970. Now, Burneside station is an un-manned request halt.

The village consists of two townships, Strickland Roger and Strickland Ketel, where the larger part of the village is situated. Strickland Roger is more rural and has land on the fells above, including round Low Taggleshaw (see walk 26) where there is a four acre area which was awarded in perpetuity to the village and neighbouring parishes for recreation by the 1838 Enclosure Act.

Burneside Hall, a farm, is another with a former fourteenth century pele tower. There has been a building on the site since 1290 when Gilbert Burneshead (an earlier spelling of Burneside), Under-Sheriff of Westmorland, lived there. The present hall was built later than his times. Later it was owned first by the Bellingham and then by the Braithwaite families. Eventually, the Hall came into the hands of the Cropper family.

Towards the end of the village there is a roadway to the left leading to the station. Go to the right of the station buildings and cross the level crossing. On the other side of the line the driveway is followed for the few yards to where there is a kissing gate by a field gate on the right. From here, go up the field bearing right towards some trees, but not as far right as the barn to be seen. At the top, pass to the right of the trees, which have a stone retaining wall below them. On reaching a fence by an oak tree there is a stile to cross. Continue on up this field by the fence and then, towards the top, turn to the right towards to a metal gate in the fence in front.

Go straight across the field to a kissing gate by a field gate and pass through it into the next field. Go up this field to a gap in the wall in front, its being rather hidden by a hawthorn bush, and then pass up the hillside to the right of the wall by a plantation. At the top there is a squeeze stile made of two large slabs of stone to pass through into the next field. Cross this field to a stone slab stile over the wall and into the following field.

This field is crossed diagonally to the right to the field gate in front, the route now being followed avoiding the farmyard. Pass through that gate and then bear slightly left up the field to the wall in front where there is another stone slab stile to cross. From it, go up by the wall on the left and come out at a metal kissing gate to the right of the farm and by the A591.

Here there is an interesting geological detour that can be made. By turning right along the verge by the A591 a rock face is soon reached on the right. This face is carboniferous stone, and has an anticline (ridge of stratified rock) from when it met with the Silurian rock. Continue along the verge for another few yards to the next rock face, which is Silurian, the southern end of the main rock of South Lakeland. This is the point where the two rock plates met millions of years ago.

For the walk, on coming out onto the road from the kissing gate, turn left for a few yards towards the farm and then cross the busy A591 to a wooden kissing gate into a field. Once in the field, follow the farm track to the right as it goes to the wall on the opposite side of the field. Follow the wall, still going right, and go round a corner. From that corner turn right to go ahead over the rather long field, bearing steadily up towards the wall to the left. Before reaching the far end of the field the wall turns left as a farm track is reached, leading to Bank End. Go through a kissing gate in the fence and then round the house to the front to a large gate leading out onto a tarmac roadway. This section of the path is through a private garden.

Once on the roadway, turn right and follow it to the road for Crook. Turn right along the Crook Road for about a quarter of a mile. Pass a very attractive garden at Low Bunrigg where the rocky outcrop is a feature. This is about half way along the road towards the field gate on the left, which has to be passed through and the path followed diagonally to the right. Continue across the field until a corner to the left is seen with a farm track beyond. Go to this corner and cross a small stream by a stone slab bridge and come to a stile through the drystone wall leading out onto the farm track.

Turn left along the track to the farm and then follow the arrows through the farmyard, passing the farmhouse, and then turning left at some buildings in front and onto a farm track. Follow the track into a field and then straight up it. As the left-hand corner of the field is reached, there is a large wooden gate to go through and then cross a tiny corner of a field to another gate into the next field. It is waymarked.

Go straight along this field, the first part of which can be very muddy, bearing to the left to a gate at a fence splitting the original

field in two. Pass along the hedge to the left to a Lakeland stone squeeze stile. Pass through it and turn right by the hedge. This field, too, has been split and there is a stile to cross. A short way beyond the path bears up to the left. Go towards the wall at the end of the field and then turn left, still going upwards. On reaching a farm track, opposite the

To the Lake District from Cunswick Fell

kissing gate onto it, there are arrows painted for both directions on the wall. Turn right down the track towards Cunswick Hall.

Before reaching the Hall there is a kissing gate to the left from which the path is followed close to the wall on the right, passing a short way from the Hall on its far side. Keep along the field, ignoring a stile to the right, and towards its end there is another kissing gate back onto the track. Turn left along the track to its end and then left along another track. This is part of Gamblesmire Lane.

Follow the lane, from where there are good views back. It swings round to the right and passes below Cunswick Scar. At the end of some woodland, over on the left there is an old limekiln with a fence on top to stop people falling into the pit. A gateway is reached with a signpost by it (20). Go a few yards ahead from the signpost and turn to the left. Shortly, another signpost is reached showing the way down the hillside. Pass this post, continuing along the track, not turning down the hillside. The field's right-hand boundary wall comes up closer to the path. By looking left the opposite boundary wall is to be seen, by which is the path used in walk 20.

At the narrowest point of the field there is a stile in a fence, but there is no need to cross it as it is by a gateway with no gate. The path continues along quite close to the wall on the right. Continue following the wall up the slope of the hillside until a stile is reached by a hawthorn bush which has hidden it from view (21). Cross the stile and go by the wall and then straight ahead towards the by-pass road as the wall drops to the right.

The grassy path is followed to a ladder stile leading into the corner of a field and then over another stile and cross the bridge over the by-pass. Cross into the next field (22) where turn sharp left, following the wall above the roadway. Cross two more ladder stiles and then, at the end of the by-pass cutting, the grassy path drops down quite steeply and then bears to the right. Go in front of a double barn and turn right to go through a squeeze stile into the next field. Cross straight over it close to the wall on the left, ignoring a gate. At the end of the field go over a stile into the next field where the very clear grass path bears right. It then skirts along above the wall and fence bounding the next field. On coming to a junction at a field gate, cross the stile leading onto the left-hand path. There are good views of Kendal to be had as the path is followed over the field towards the left.

Carry straight on along the path, through a kissing gate, and at the next junction, near a former building, take the right-hand path. It goes along above a wall and then drops to the left as it crosses an open field towards a gateway in the corner. Continue on along the path, skirting the next field with traffic on the Windermere road to be seen over to the left. Go through another gateway and along the track above the fence at the left of the field. At the end, go through a gate out onto a roadway and turn right to a main road.

Cross the road to Low Fellside, a minor road, and go straight down it. At the end of the road, turn left for Kendal Town Hall. Turn left to pass the Town Hall and then pass down Finkle Street to its junction with Blackhall Road, where turn left to the bus stands for the 555 buses either way.

20. Walk 20 crosses walk 22 here.
21. Walk 20 rejoins here.
22. Walk 20 uses the path ahead.
23. Walk 23 goes through Burneside to a staggered road junction before reaching Ivy Cottages.

WALK 23, KENDAL BURNESIDE, BOWSTON, STAVELEY VIA DALES WAY

Easy
6.5 miles
Allow 3 to 3.5 hours.

Go back up Blackhall Road from Kendal bus station, down which the bus had turned, to Sandes Avenue. Here, cross the main road and turn right towards the River Kent. Do not cross the river, but take the footpath to the left. It is a tarred path, passing by the river and under the railway. Ignore Dockray Bridge, the footbridge leading to the Shap road, but continue on by the Kent.

The path swings round left and then a kissing gate is reached. Go through it and turn right. Pass in front of a row of cottages and the come out onto the Burneside road. Turn right along the road for 100 yards or so to Kentrigg Walk. Here, do not cross the road, but turn right going by the fence and down to the river. The path then turns to the left and passes the gardens of the houses on the left. Across the River Kent is the industrial estate at Mintsfeet. A rather rough few yards of path going up to a higher level is reached. Here, the path joins another path. Turn to the right and along the grassy path by the river. Note the River Mint joining the River Kent by the factory opposite.

At this point, the path swings round left, over a stile, following the Kent. Go through a narrow stile into a narrow field, the path continuing by the river to the next stile, still keeping to the river-bank. On the opposite side of the Kent there is part of a golf course. Go through a gate and again along by the river. This is part of the same golf course, which is linked by the private footbridge seen ahead. Continue straight along the path, which crosses the golf course roadway, and comes to a gateway onto the Burneside road. By turning left for a few yards, there is a footpath, which can be joined on the opposite side of the road, avoiding the traffic. The footpath goes to the right and comes out onto the road again at the end of Burneside.

Pass along the main street of Burneside (23). Before reaching the Post Office, and just before Ivy Cottages, there is a staggered road junction, the right hand road, which passes a Spar shop, being for Long Sleddale and the A6. Follow this road for about a quarter of a mile as it passes over the Kent and by Cropper's paper mills. A footpath

Bridge over Kent, Bowston

leading off to the left is reached, a sign indicating it is for Bowston. The path, which is part of the Dales Way, is well used and can be very muddy as it circles round Cropper's mill until it comes to a stile which is crossed into a field. Follow the path along above the River Kent. To the left is a weir and a view across to Burneside. The path bears right and drops down to a stile by a stream, which is crossed by stepping-stones.

Once over the stile, go straight across the field towards the trees lining the river-bank and then continue straight along by the river, over another stile and along another field until an attractive bridge is reached at Bowston. Here, go up to the road, cross the bridge, and then up to the Burneside to Staveley road. Turn right at the road junction and follow the road for a few hundred yards to where, after crossing Kent Close, there is a signpost indicating the path to Staveley. At Winstanley Cottage, which is part of Winstanley Row and lies at the beginning of the path the garden is full of gnomes that, according to a notice, love to be photographed. This path comes out onto a very minor road by the river, and besides which the railway line ran.

Follow the minor road straight ahead up the Kent to Cowan Head, where the main building was the mill.

Cowan Head Mill dating back to around 1750, was acquired by Croppers in 1845. The mill was closed and was only used for storage from 1982. From

1984 various schemes for its use were put forward, the local papers revealing that they were very controversial. Now, the former mill is a private housing complex.

Pass the Cowan Head buildings and the weir and continue along by the river, passing through a gate. A bridge is passed, but it is not a right of way and there is no public access across the river. A few yards beyond the bridge there are two gates to pass through within yards of each other. In between is a large Lakeland stone barn. The path continues on by the Kent.

A wall is crossed by using pieces of stone jutting out. Across it, in spring, there are wild daffodils blooming. Keep on close to the river, crossing walls and stiles. A stile is crossed into a short stretch of woodland and then another one back into an open field. The path follows the river as it bends sharply round to the left. Pass through a gateway into a narrow field and then through another gateway into the next field. Continue along this field a short way to the left of the wall on the other side of which is a very narrow field bordering the river. A stretch of farm track is reached. Go through a kissing gate and then diagonally left following the path to another kissing gate for the path to Staveley.

Turn right, going close to the wall on the right as it zigzags to another kissing gate. Here, there is a path junction (24). Go to the right and in a few yards there is a gate onto the road for Staveley. Turn right along the road and in a few yards there are bus stops, southbound before reaching Stock Bridge Farm and northbound by the farm. Continue straight down the road for the Staveley shops, pubs, businesses and Abbey Square. At the Square there are the main Staveley bus stops, by the River Gowan northbound and on the opposite side of the square southbound.

※ ※ ※

An alternative ending for this walk or for those wanting to continue straight along the Dales Way to Windermere is to cross the road at Stock Bridge Farm. The Dales Way passes the farm and continues along the track beneath the railway bridge. The path then turns right through a kissing gate by the railway before following a wall on the right. It reaches a kissing gate into another field where continue by the wall, with some cottages over it to the right. The route then to follow is indicated as it crosses the wall into a private garden. Pass through a courtyard and onto a lane leading to the Crook road. (At the road, turn left and over the by-pass for the Dales Way, walk 24.) For Staveley village, turn right and pass under the railway by the station, from where it becomes Station Road. Continue straight along the road to Abbey Square.

This easy ending is about a mile from Stock Bridge Farm, allow about 20 minutes to half an hour.

23. Walk 22 continues along the main street through Burneside.
24. Walk 28 joins here.

WALK 24, STAVELEY, DALES WAY, BOWNESS, WINDERMERE.

Easy / moderate
8 miles
Allow 4.5 hours.

Staveley is an industrious village with a number of businesses. Its name comes from the Old English for 'the clearing where staves are cut'. The area around used to have two Lords of the Manor besides the King, these being Hugill-with-Staveley and Kentmere, but they mainly lived elsewhere leaving the area to be run by yeomen. The yeomen took turns to act as constable and other duties and they sat on juries, collected rates and turned out to defend the border, this area of land being subject to border raids by the Scots.

Until the union of crowns in 1603 the yeomen were expected to have their weapons ready and be able to use them. In 1619, Prince Charles, to whom King James I had given his northern manors, tried to increase the 'entry fines', premiums which a customary tenant had to pay on taking over land from his father. The tenants resisted this and persuaded the prince's lawyers to continue with the traditional system whereby the incoming tenant paid a 'fine' of three years rent. Other lords put on pressure for more to be paid and January 1621 saw a meeting of over 100 people from all over the Barony being held in Staveley chapel to organise opposition to this. Samuel Knipe, a leader, drew up a petition to the king.

July of 1621 saw King James making a proclamation that as the border danger was gone there was no need for border service and all land to be let on up to date leases. Two years later Samuel Knipe and others were brought before the Court of Star Chamber where they were accused of holding an unlawful assembly and of libelling the king by their protests. In turn, they argued that customary rights had nothing to do with border service, and they produced evidence to satisfy the judge that they were right. This decision gave Knipe and the other tenants secure possession of their customary lands. This event is referred to in a plaque on the tower that is all that remains of St. Margaret's Church, which was founded in 1388 and the main part demolished in 1865. The present church is St. James', a short up the Kentmere valley.

The Abbey in Abbey Square was built in the 1844 as an hotel by J. H. Wilson of the Grange in Sussex and who held considerable property in the area. At one time it was a home for orphans and run by the Kendal Guardians of the Poor Law Union. It never had any religious connections and is now a retirement home.

Owing to its being on two rivers, the Kent and the Gowan, Staveley had a number of mills, both for textiles and bobbins as well as corn. Barley Mill was formerly a textile mill, but is now used by Kentmere Ltd., famous for the manufacture of photographic paper.

Staveley was on part of the turnpike road from Kendal to Cockermouth, authorised in 1761. A tollhouse stood close to the Eagle and Child Inn. By 1875 the era of the turnpike was over and the trust was abolished, the road being taken over first by the Kendal Road Board and then in 1888 by Westmorland County Council.

Tuesday, 20 April 1847 saw the opening of the railway line from Kendal to Windermere. Slate for the late Victorian houses was brought here by rail, as was coal for the Staveley Gas Company, which was founded in 1865. There was a goods yard from which the products of Staveley Wood Turnings, Kentmere Ltd. and Cape Asbestos were dispatched. Coal for the two coal merchants was received and there was a cattle dock. Now, the station is an un-manned halt on the singled track.

In 1900, Staveley had several shops, four pubs, and a bank, amongst other facilities. There is still a reminder of the bank in the house called 'Martins Bank' on Kendal Road. Many villages had either or both of a Martins Bank or a District Bank, their becoming Barclays and National Westminster respectively, but a lot of these rural branches have now been closed.

The A591 now by-passes Staveley, making for a much quieter village. It was opened in December 1988, having first been discussed in 1937.

This walk starts from Abbey Square in Staveley. Cross the river by the bridge which is to the right of the northbound bus stop. Go straight up the road, under the railway and across the by-pass road. Shortly after leaving the by-pass there is a roadway on the right leading to private houses. Turn left up the roadway which, as the last houses are left behind, becomes a grassy lane. A wooden field gate just ahead is passed through and then follow the path across the field towards another field gate by which there is a kissing gate. Go through it and straight across the field towards the farmhouse opposite.

Before reaching the farmhouse there is a tarred roadway that is actually a very minor public road. Turn right along the road. Pass through a field gate that spans the road and continue along it.

On reaching another very minor road, turn right along it, passing Fell Plain. A little over a third of a mile along the road there is a bend to the right with a track going off to the left. Go down the track, which is a bridleway. Just before the end of the track there is a large metal field gate on the right to go through. Turn left and follow the grassy path along, fairly close to the wall. Pass through a gateway and follow the path along to the end of the plantation on the right and then turn right to go behind the plantation. The path becomes stony along there. At a corner of the plantation there is a junction where the path going ahead is followed and not the one to the right.

The path comes to a wooden field gate and then passes on, turns a little right, straightens again and then turns well right to go towards Crag House. In the wall just before the path turns right, note the filled in hog hole for sheep to pass through from one field to another. Continue along the path and over a stone step stile by a gate and follow the clear track along towards the farm.

Just before reaching the farm, go through a field gate and turn sharp right along the farm track. Keep straight along by the wall on the right and go through another field gate as the track is followed along. The path next swings round to the left and comes to a kissing gate by Outrun Nook. Turn to the right along the road for a hundred or so yards and then, at a bend to the right, there is a good stony farm track going to the left. Follow the track along to Hag End, where the Way goes straight through the farmyard.

On reaching buildings in front, the path turns right to pass in front of them and at their end there is a field gate to go through on the left. Go by the farm and then turn left again and onto the track, which is the Dales Way. Follow the track along and over a stone step stile into a field. Follow the grassy path up the field and through a gap in the drystone wall in front. Continue straight ahead to a waymarker where the path swings round to the right. From up here there is suddenly a good view across to the Langdales, which are seen just as a section of old drystone wall is crossed.

Once over that wall, do not follow the next wall but turn to the left, there is a waymarker, following the grassy path over the field. Note the outcrops of Silurian rock. Drop diagonally to the left going down the field to where a gateway can be seen by some larches in the left-hand corner of the field. There is a kissing gate to pass through and then turn sharply to the left (25) to go along by the wall to another field gate with a kissing gate by it. Once through there it is a proper cart track to follow. A stream is forded and the track drops down to join another track.

Turn left onto this new track and continue along it for about half a mile, passing through field gates on the way, the last one leading onto a roadway. Follow the roadway, past some houses, to come out onto the Crook road. By the road, turn right and pass over a stone step stile onto a permitted path that avoids walking by the road itself.

At the end of the path, drop down to the road and turn right for a few yards to the next path, which is for Low Cleabarrow. There are two lanes side by side, the left-hand one being the one to follow. Just before reaching the farm, turn to the left and pass through a small wooden gate by a field gate and then turn right to follow the grassy field path by the wall on the right.

After this, pass through three kissing gates in very quick succession and after the last one follow the grassy path over the field, going over to the right. The path is reasonably straight to follow before dropping down to a kissing gate in the wall, this having been partially obscured from view by an oak tree in front of it. After leaving the gate, go straight along the path, passing a fenced off area where various plants are regenerating. Come to another kissing gate and then cross the road to another one, after which pass along by the fence on the left.

Two more kissing gates take the path over another roadway and then bear left towards another kissing gate in the wall, close to some trees. The path goes straight along by the trees and then comes to another kissing gate to pass through. On reaching another roadway, turn right for a few yards (26) to where the Dales Way goes off by the fence on the left. Go through an iron gateway and then follow the grassy path straight across the field in front.

The path passes a stone seat on its way to the next field where it continues by the wall on the left. Go through another kissing gate by a field gate that leads onto a proper farm track with walls on either side. Cross straight over the track and at last Lake Windermere, about half a mile ahead, can be seen, just before reaching another wooden gate by a field gate.

Cross the field quite close to the wall and then through a metal kissing gate, across a track and through a wooden kissing gate (27). Drop down the track and have a good view of Windermere on the

Up Windermere from above Bowness

way. Pass through an iron gate and out onto a road where drop down to Bowness, coming out near the parish church.

For a walk continuing on to Windermere, turn right on reaching Bowness and go straight up the main road and then turn left onto Rayrigg Road, which passes the World of Beatrix Potter at the Old Laundry. Continue along the road and shortly before the Steamboat Museum there is a road with no access for cars or motorcycles to the right. Go straight up there, passing some old cottages. Cross a roadway and then continue along the woodland path, which is Sheriff's Walk. Come out onto the road from Bowness near the clock tower and turn left for Windermere. Go up Windermere following the main roads leading up to Booths Supermarket and the railway station. Buses to the north and the south are caught from by the station.

25. Walk 31 joins here from the right.
26. Walk 31 turns left along the road.
27. Walk 31 comes down the track from the left.

WALK 25 STAVELEY, KENTMERE, GARBURN PASS, TROUTBECK, BROCKHOLES

Moderate
10 miles
Allow 5.5 hours.

From Abbey Square in Staveley, cross the pedestrian crossing by 'The Abbey' retirement home and turn left onto the road for Kentmere. Go straight up the road, passing a road junction and weir on the right. On reaching the next road junction turn right to cross the bridge and then left to continue following the main valley road up the Kentmere Valley.

Pass the turning from where the path can be followed to Kentmere Pottery and just after that Kentmere village comes into view. Take the left-hand road towards the church on reaching a junction in the village. Pass by St. Cuthbert's Church (28) and follow the road to a junction, where ahead is the way to Larkrigg Farm, through a gate which may or may not be shut. Ignore the way towards the farm and, instead, follow the road round to the left and follow it to its end.

Kentmere Hall, which is now a farm, has the only pele tower within the National Park, showing that it was once considered necessary to have a defensive structure. The tower dates from the 14th century but the house could date from the following century.

Now, the Kentmere valley is generally quiet apart from tourists and walkers. However, this was not always so as it lay on one of the drove roads from Scotland and other parts of Cumbria to the south of England. The drove road would be in use from around 1500, when drovers would bring their cattle to Troutbeck and then over the Garburn Pass, through Kentmere and Stile End and on towards Longsleddale and Old Town in the Lune valley. The roads were not generally in good condition. In 1730 Benjamin Browne, who was the High Constable of Kendal Ward, wrote that the Garburn Road was in such bad condition that neither man nor horse could travel over it "without danger of being bogged in moss or lamed among the stones".

St. Cuthbert's church stands on a hillside overlooking the valley. The present church dates from the 16th century whilst the tower was built to its present height in 1866. However, it is reasonably certain that there would be a church on the site several centuries earlier. The burial ground was consecrated in 1701. Within the church there is a memorial tablet to Bernard Gilpin.

Bernard Gilpin was born in Kentmere Hall in 1517. He went to Queen's College Oxford in 1534 and transferred from there to become one of the first scholars of what is now Christ Church College. Queen Elizabeth, following the death of Bishop Oglethorpe, offered the Bishopric of Carlisle to Gilpin, but he refused it.

There is the story that when Bernard was a small boy a begging friar came to Kentmere Hall one Saturday evening and was treated very hospitably. On the Sunday morning the friar preached against debauchery and, in particular, drunkenness. Bernard heard this and at length could stand it no more before crying out that he wondered how the friar could 'preach against drunkenness when he himself had been drunk' the previous night.

Kentmere also achieved notoriety for a court case following the refusal of the Brewster Sessions to renew the licence of Low Bridge Inn. Although the premises had been licensed for around 30 years, the Licensing Justices felt that the inn was too remote from police jurisdiction and that it was not required in a neighbourhood with such a low population. Jane and Susannah Sharpe, the owners, took the case to the Quarter Sessions, Queen's Bench, and the Court of Appeal on 15 December 1888, where it remained for several days. By then the case had become a matter of importance throughout the country as it concerned the right of the Brewster Sessions magistrates to withdraw the licence of any outlying public house if they deemed it proper. The case went on to the House of Lords, who decided in favour of the magistrates. This resulted in Sharpe v Wakefield going on the statute books, Mr. W. Wakefield being the chairman of the magistrates at the time. The outcome of the case was classed as of such importance that the Scottish Temperance league published a leaflet on it.

Kentmere Tarn was formed by the glacier coming down the valley in the last Ice Age and scooping out the ground. It was drained in the 1830's, its being hoped it would become fertile farmland, however it became only sour, marshy ground. Another attempt was made in the 1870's, but this one fared little better. Later, it was found that the waters of the Tarn had been a breeding ground for microscopic organs. These had fossilized on the bed of the tarn to become the mineral diatomite, used in various industrial processes, including explosives.

The diatomite was extracted at first by a dragline and later by a dredger. An aerial ropeway took the materials to the processing site, now Hepworth Air Filtration. Mining took place from 1929 to 1985. As a result, the present tarn was formed, and is now being used by anglers.

At the dwellings at the end of the road a sign indicates the bridleway for Troutbeck going to the right. Follow the ancient, stony track along, passing through the right-hand one of two gates side by side. Kentmere village drops steadily behind. Over to the left can be seen Kentmere itself, and below is Kentmere Hall. On looking up to the Garburn Pass ahead, a wall can be seen crossing over the top. Although not visible from this point, the track is by that wall on its right.

The track is very clear to follow as it climbs steadily upwards. At the top there is a wooden gate to pass through as the Kentmere Valley is left behind. The track shortly passes over the summit of the pass and the Troutbeck valley comes into view in front. Pass through another field gate and start approaching the Troutbeck Valley. Another field gate is passed through and then the main descent to Troutbeck starts.

Descend the stony track, passing old quarry workings on the way. Go through a wooden gate by a field gate, just beyond which there is a junction. At the junction (29) go to the right   Continue downwards and at the next junction in the tracks (30) again go right. This track drops down, through a gate and then left for the main road up the Troutbeck valley.

Turn right and follow the road along, past a road junction on the left for Troutbeck village, and come to Troutbeck church. Immediately after passing the church there is a bridleway to the left. Follow this path along, passing a gate leading from the churchyard. Pass a path to the right shortly after leaving the church and then come to another junction. Here, take the right-hand path and go along by the wall on the left.

The path becomes rather sunken as it goes towards a wooden field gate. From there, follow the track ahead between two low walls and, as the houses of Troutbeck are reached, turn left along another track for a few yards before turning right onto another bridleway. Go along the side of Rose Mount and out onto the main street of Troutbeck, where turn left.

Troutbeck has a division of three hundreds. In the past, locals boasted of it having three hundred constables, three hundred bulls and three hundred bridges, this being because each of the hundreds had a constable, a bull and a bridge. Hundreds were an ancient division of land and there is still Hundred

Road, a track leading off from Robin Lane and The Hundreds below Wansfell on the Troutbeck side.

Anciently, Troutbeck was in the Archdeaconry of Richmond in the Diocese of York and transferred to the Bishopric of Chester in 1541, where it remained until 1856. The Parish Church is Jesus Church and was a chapelry within Windermere Parish, when it was known as Jesus Chapel. It was rebuilt in 1763, altered in 1861 and had the clock added in 1897. There are footpaths from each of the Hundreds leading to the church.

Between 1827 and 1869 the Incumbent was the Reverend William Sewell, a character of whom many tales were told. One day he was dressed as a workman and helping to build a wall when the Bishop called. The Bishop told him that the work he was doing was not suitable for a clergyman, to which Rev. Sewell replied, 'Then you give me a better job, my lord'. Besides his work as vicar, Rev. Sewell also kept cattle and was to be seen driving them to pasture before going on to take his Sunday service.

Troutbeck was in a royal deer forest and subject to forest laws until it was 'disparked' in 1552. Town End, a National Trust property, was rebuilt in 1623 on the site of an earlier building and is at the south end of the mile and a half long village. From 1626 right through until 1943 it was occupied by the Browne family, yeomen farmers, who accumulated many of its contents. No doubt T. Browne

Troutbeck

was one of this family. He, according to the school log, fell into the stream.

The public houses are at Town Head, the north end. There used to be a sign at the Mortal Man where he had a very ruddy nose. There was a jingle about him which ran:

> *"O mortal man that liv'st on bread,*
> *How come thy nose to be so red?*
> *Thou silly ass, that looks't so pale,*
> *It comes from Sally Birkett's ale."*

Around Troutbeck it will be noticed that the packhorse and drove roads have sunk so that they are lower than the fields and tend to have high hedgerows. Farm labourers for Troutbeck were hired at the annual Kendal hiring fair. An entry in the school log reveals that 'Many children absent – Sheepshearing – only three boys attended.

Follow the road left from Rose Mount, passing the road from near the church coming up into the village, and come to Troutbeck Post Office. Continue along the road passing first Robin Lane (31) and then Town Head, after which take the right-hand road. A quarter of a mile along the road, on passing round a bend to the right, Wain Lane (32) is passed.

Come to a farm about a quarter of a mile further on from the bend and there leave the road and follow the lane between the farm buildings. Cross a stile by a wooden field gate and continue dropping down the lane, seeing Windermere over to the left. Go through a field gate and onto a roadway leading past some houses.

Follow the roadway to the end of the grounds for the houses. There, a sign indicates the path going to the right from the roadway. Pass straight along the path, through a large field gate and straight down, pass Merewood Lodge and onto the A591 at Brockholes where there are the bus stops either side of the road. The southbound stop is at the end of the roadway that has been followed, the northbound stop being reached by using a crossing place which has been constructed to aid the crossing of this busy road.

Brockholes comes from the Old English meaning 'badger's hollow'. It was formerly the home of William Henry Gaddum, but is now the National Park Visitor Centre. Thomas H. Mawson, who became well known for his work as a garden architect, designed the grounds. He started in business with premises between Windermere and Bowness and later moved to Hest Bank, from where he opened an office in Lancaster. Mawson's work took account of the natural views and it is typical of his work that a view towards the Langdales from the terrace round the house is incorporated in his design of the grounds at Brockholes.

Brockholes grounds are open all year but the exhibitions are not and enquiries should be made when wishing to see them out of season to ascertain times of opening.

28. By going down the lane opposite the church, nearly to Kentmere Hall, walk 29 can be taken back to Staveley.
29. Walk 30 is joined here.
30. Walk 30 is left again.
31. Walks 33 and 34 meet walk 25 at the Post Office.
32. Walk 34 comes up Wain Lane.

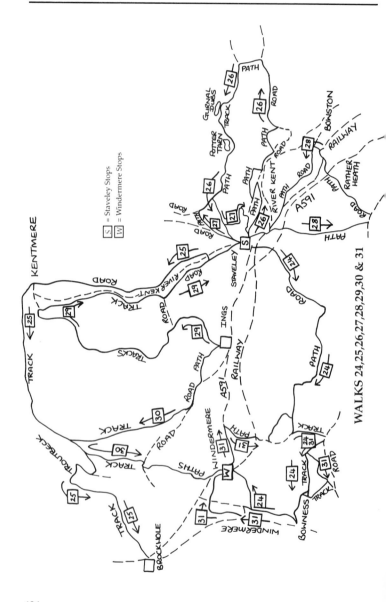

WALKS 24,25,26,27,28,29,30 & 31

S = Staveley Stops
W = Windermere Stops

WALK 26, STAVELEY, GURNAL DUBS, POTTER TARN, STAVELEY

Moderate.
9.5 to 10 miles.
Allow 4.5 hours.

From the bus stops on either side of the road at Abbey Square, go south-eastwards along Main Street to St. Margaret's chapel tower, which is on the left-hand side of the road. Immediately to the left of the tower there is a footpath to take, leading to a footbridge spanning the River Kent. After crossing the river, turn right along the path to a kissing gate by a field gate (33). Go through the kissing gate and bear left up the field towards the farm and then follow the farm track between some of the buildings.

Continue along the track for another few hundred yards to a kissing gate by a field gate. In the field, bear to the left of the pond and towards the left of a line of trees beyond it. To the left of the trees there is a wall to pass through and then go along by the wall on the left to a ladder stile, which is crossed.

Cross over this next field by the grassy path a little to the right of the wall. The path bears round a little to the left, still following the wall. At a corner of the wall the path bends round more to the left to cross over the field, cutting off a corner of the field over to the left, to the River Kent. The path then goes by the fence on the left and over a stone step stile. Beyond this it crosses a small wooden bridge and then goes on to a field gate in front, a sewage works being over to the right. By the field gate there is a stone slab stile leading out onto a road.

Turn left along the road (by turning right the road can be followed instead of the footpaths as it is the same road all the way) for less than a quarter of a mile to where the road has gone up hill and there is a stone slab stile to the right of a field gate on the right. There is a signpost there. Go along the path by the wall on the right and shortly cross a ladder stile to the left of a field gate. Beyond this the path fords a stream and then forks, where take the left-hand path.

Go up through woodland along a good, woodland path and ford another stream. Follow the path to the left to pass behind Spring Hag. Shortly, a track comes down from the left and the path joins it. Continue along the track, which comes out onto a roadway. Go straight along the roadway, which, in a quarter of a mile, comes to another roadway where turn right. Drop down to the road and turn left.

Follow the road for about half a mile, passing a path for Side House on the left and another at Hagg Foot Farm on the right. At the next turning to the left, which is for High Hundhowe, go up it, its being the start of a bridleway for Mirefoot. Go straight up and pass to the left of some farm buildings, ignoring the way to the dwellings. At the end of the buildings the track swings right but the bridleway goes straight ahead through a wooden gate. It passes between low walls and then fencing to come out at another wooden gate at a junction of paths.

Take the path bearing to the right and, just after passing a farm, see a small wooden stile into the field on the left. Cross it and drop down to the stream at the bottom of the field. Cross the footbridge there and follow the path to the right. The path comes to a track where turn to the left for a few yards to a small gateway on the right, leading into a field. This is just at the end of a garden.

Pass straight over the field, bearing slightly right of Godmond Hall to be seen in front. See two field gates ahead and by the right-hand one there is a small wooden gate leading out onto the road. Turn to the left and follow Potter Fell Road for about a mile and a quarter. Two public footpaths to the right are passed. On reaching the third there is also a footpath to the left. Go through the field gate onto the path to the left and up the grassy track for a few yards. There, the track turns to the right towards a wall. On reaching the wall, the track turns left to go up by it.

Go over the following field, still with the wall on the right and at the top there is a field gate leading onto a lane. Up here there are good views all around, including to the Howgills. Turn left to go up the track. It is crossed by a wooden field gate, to the right of which there is a kissing gate to pass through. (A few yards before reaching the gate there is a stile to the right leading to Low Taggleshaw, which includes the marshy pond to the left. There, the area bounded by four boundary stones is public and was awarded to the parish of Strickland Roger by the Enclosure Act of 1838.) Shortly, the track comes to a point where the tarn named Gurnal Dubs is seen in front and there is a path leading off to the left. A signpost indicates that the path to the left is for Potter Tarn.

Looking up the Garburn Pass, Kentmere.
Gurnal Dubs, near Stavely.

Up the Kentmere Valley from above Kentmere Hall.
Across the Troutbeck valley from Dubs Road.

Winter sunset from Cockshotts, Bowness.
Autumn at Town End, Troutbeck

Bluebells, Dora's Field, Rydal.
To Waterhead, Windermere, from above Clappersgate.

Along the dam, Gurnal Dubs

Turn along the path with Gurnal Dubs over to the right. At the end of the tarn there is a dam to cross. (Whilst there is a path going basically round Gurnal Dubs, it is not a right of way.) From the dam, follow the grassy path up the hillside ahead and come to a ladder stile over a wall. Once at the top of the stile, Potter Tarn is seen below and in front with the Lakeland Fells beyond.

From the stile, follow the sometimes grassy and sometimes gravelly path as it winds its way down the hillside towards the dam of Potter Tarn. Ford a stream and then follow the raised path over an old outlet of the tarn towards a wall in front. There, cross the stone slab stile and drop down to the stream in front of the dam. Ford the stream and then follow the path up the field just below the dam. At the top of the field there is a ladder stile to cross to the open ground beyond.

Bear to the right to follow the grassy path, which shortly starts to curve to the left round the hillside in front, away from the tarn. There are waymarkers. As the grassy path drops down the hillside there are good views to Cowan Head to the left, Staveley in front and the Kentmere valley to the right.

A field gate is reached and, once through it, turn right towards a gap in the wall leading into the next field. There, turn left along the clear path skirting along the hillside and going downwards in the Staveley direction. On reaching a farm track turn right along it for a few yards to where there is a field gate on the left. Go through it and follow the grassy path down by the wall on the left, passing over the way down to Frost Hole on the way. Pass through another field gate and continue along the grassy path by the fence on the left. It then swings round to go along by a stream on the way to Birkfield Farm.

At the end of the field go through a wooden field gate and follow the track round to the left, across a stream and to the farmyard, which is reached by crossing a stile by a field gate. Pass the farmhouse and through another field gate and then go along the roadway in front. After leaving the farm buildings there is another gate to pass through and then follow the roadway to where it comes out onto a very minor road. Turn right up this road, which has grass growing in the middle.

Pass through a gate spanning the roadway just before reaching Littlewood Farm (34). At the farm, turn left to go through the farmyard and then through the gate into the field in front. Go by the wall on the left, but do not enter the adjacent field. Follow the wall and come to a field gate with a ladder stile to the right. From it, follow the grassy field path by the wall on the right to the next ladder stile and then straight over the following field to another ladder stile in the wall in front. Cross this next stile and go down the field towards another ladder stile in a wall, to the right of a gap. From that stile go straight ahead (35) down the field, close to the wall on the right.

At the end of the field, pass over another stile dropping down into the field below and again continue by the wall on the right. At the end of the field there is a steep drop down to a wooden stile by the field gate and then drop down the following field, through a field gate and across another field. There, pass through a kissing gate to the left of the field gate and onto the roadway in front, where turn right. Follow this roadway, pass Barley Bridge Farm, and onto a road where turn right and immediately after turn left to cross over Barley Bridge. From the bridge, turn left for Abbey Square and the bus stops of Staveley.

33. Walk 27 comes down this path going into Staveley.
34. Walk 27 is joined here.
35. Walk 27 goes to the left here.

WALK 27, STAVELEY, CRAGGY PLANTATION.

Easy/moderate
3.25 miles
Allow 2 hours.

Starting from Abbey Square, pass The Abbey, taking the Kentmere Road to its left. Pass the Methodist Church, the War Memorial and the Kentmere factory, where photographic paper is manufactured. By a weir in the Kent there is a road junction with a road to the right crossing the river. Take this road and cross the bridge, which is Barley Bridge. Once over the bridge, follow the road to the left for about a quarter of a mile until a quite high stile is reached on the right. Cross it into the field and then go up the field keeping close to the wall as it bears round to the left. There are distinct signs that the path is an old roadway.

At the end of that field, which is quite a way above the valley floor, the old roadway goes through a gateway in the wall and then runs ahead with the wall on the left. Pass through another gateway and the path then turns right before crossing a stile into the next field. Continue straight along this field, with the wall on the left, and come to a stile leading onto a very minor roadway. Turn right along the road for a little over a quarter of a mile to where Littlewood Farm is reached (34). Here, there is a signpost indicating the way straight through the farmyard and through the gate in front.

Go up the field by the wall on the left and then cross a ladder stile into the next field. The path continues straight ahead, with the wall on the right, to another ladder stile. Cross it into the next field, from where there are good views up the Kentmere Valley, and on to another stile. From the next field, the area around Barley Bridge is seen. There is another ladder stile and, to its left, a farm track is seen passing through a gap in the wall (35). Once in that next field, turn left crossing

In Craggy Plantation, Staveley

over the farm track and close to the corner there is a small sign indicating a pathway. Cross the wall by the sign and into Craggy Plantation.

Once in the plantation, there is a typical woodland path that goes up to the left. There is quite a mixture of trees in the plantation, birch, oak, hazel, holly, sycamore, etc. some of the trees having been coppiced in the past. It is a clear path to follow as it continues through the woodland, passing through a gap in a wall and onwards over a hollowed area. Continue on bearing leftwards and then the path goes up some steps up the hillside. It then goes left, quite close to the boundary wall with views across the fields. At the summit of the path there is some more recent pine planting.

From the summit, the path bends round to the right as it starts its descent close to the boundary wall, passing through some larches on the way. As the path, part of which is stepped, winds down the hillside, a road comes into view below. Before reaching the road, the path turns to the right, not towards the gate seen in the wall by the road, and continues onwards more or less parallel to it. At the end of this section, the path zigzags down, over some more steps, and comes out at a gate onto the road.

Once on the road, go straight ahead along it, its shortly turning sharply to the right. At a junction, take the road to the right. Ahead, where the road turns right, a gate is to be seen. By that gate there is a kissing gate to pass through. Go along the path, pass through another kissing gate and over the yard at some dwellings to yet another kissing gate. The path then goes towards the river. At a junction of paths (33), turn right and then cross the river using a footbridge and then go down the last few yards into Staveley village, coming out by St. Margaret's Churchyard and the shops. (Instead of crossing the bridge, the path can be followed straight ahead, coming out onto the Burneside road, which leads on to Barley Bridge.)

33. Walk 26 uses the path to the left.
34. Walk 26 is joined here.
35. Walk 26 goes straight on to Staveley.

WALK 28, STAVELEY, RATHER HEATH TARN, STAVELEY.

Easy
6 miles
Allow 3 hours.

From the bus stops in Abbey Square, go southwards straight through Staveley village, passing all the main shops on the way. Stock Bridge Farm, which is by a bus stop, is reached on the right of the road. Here, turn along the track in front of the farm and pass under the railway bridge and immediately turn to the left, the signpost indicating 'The Ashes'. Go through a kissing gate by a field gate a few yards along the track.

Once through the gate, follow the track along the field by the wall on the right, its quickly becoming a grassy path. At the end of the field a stile is crossed onto the A591. Cross the busy road and at the other side cross two stiles by each other. Go by the wall to the left for a few yards to a kissing gate and pass through it. From there, go up the field by the wall on the left. The wall comes to an end at a corner, where carry straight on across the field, it is not a clear path to follow. On reaching a wall with a gateway in front, about twenty yards to the left of the gateway there is a stone slab stile over the wall to cross. Beneath the stile there is a hog hole through the wall.

Go up this field, bearing over to being quite close to the wall on the right, and then come to a signpost. Here, bear a little to the right across the field to a kissing gate by a field gate, where there is another signpost. Go straight along the field by the wall on the right to a stone slab stile into the next field. There, bear diagonally to the right over the field towards the wall. On reaching the wall, go left by it to the corner of the field where a stone slab stile by a field gate leads into Ashes Coppice.

Once in the coppice, follow the path ahead for about two hundred yards to where the path forks, the main path going to the left and a minor one to the right. (The trees are not thick to the right of the path and if it is noticed through them that the wall at the end of a field is being reached, the fork is just ahead.) Follow the minor path to the right towards a ladder stile and over a wall. Pass along by the wall on the left, its being the boundary of the plantation, and at its end bear diagonally to the left towards the wall in front. Continue along, quite close to the wall and then pass a small, new plantation.

Once past the plantation the way to follow is a little to the right. On approaching the wall in front two field gates are to be seen, one in front and one over to the right. Pass through the gate in front and then go straight up the field, just to the left of the hillside in front. On reaching a wall, turn left to go by it to the left-hand corner of the field where there is a stone slab stile to cross. Cross it and go straight along by the wall on the left. Keep going along by this wall, crossing over three fields in all and then cross a stone slab stile out onto the road from Kendal to Bowness via Crook.

Turn left along the road for about two hundred yards to a junction with a road to the left in front of the farm. Turn down the road, which is Rather Heath Lane, for about a quarter of a mile, passing a caravan and camping park on the way and just after it pass a stile into a field on the left. On reaching the beginning of the following field on the left there is a stone slab stile over the wall. There is a signpost. Bear right over the field, catching sight of Rather Heath Tarn over to the right. Reach the wall on the right and before coming to the fence bounding a plantation there is a wooden slab stile over the wall. From the stile, go over the field bearing leftwards towards the plantation fence. On reaching the fence there is a proper path to follow, starting at the end of Ratherheath Tarn. Follow the path along from the tarn to two wooden gates and go through the left-hand one, the one to the right being for anglers only. The path goes through the plantation and comes to a field gate leading onto a road. The Bronte sisters visited Ratherheath and were very impressed with the area.

Cross straight over the road and continue along the path on the other side. Follow the path over a wooden footbridge and come out onto another minor road. Turn left down the road for about fifty yards to where there is a stile to cross on the right, its being by a field gate. Go up the field by the wall on the right and come to a wooden stile leading out onto the A591. Cross the busy road and then go down the lane in front. The lane passes in front of a row of cottages and then round the corner at the end of them for a few yards before turning right to go through a metal field gate and onto a farm lane.

Follow the lane along, the Howgills being seen ahead. A bridge crosses the railway line and the track then turns right by the railway towards Bowston Farm. On reaching the far end of the field on the

Ratherheath Tarn

left, and before reaching the farm buildings, go through the gate and straight across the field towards a stone slab stile in the wall in front. Cross it and continue the straight line across the next field towards a gate seen in front. By the gate there is a stile leading onto Winter Lane. Turn left down the road for about half a mile, passing a junction to Cowan Head on the right (by going down that road to its end and turning left, walk 24 can be joined).

On reaching some dwellings there is a turning to the right for Crag Farm, this being a private road but part of a public footpath. Go through a metal gate by a cattle grid and just beyond it the roadway forks. Take the left-hand roadway. On reaching a point where the main track swings to the right towards a plantation there is a grassy track dropping down to the left towards a wall, which is at the very bottom of the line of trees that form the plantation ahead. At its end the plantation is very narrow, coming to a point.

At the bottom of the track, by the end of the plantation, there is a field gate to the left of which is a stone slab stile to cross. Pass over the clear, grassy field path in front with the wall on the left. In the left-hand corner of the field there is a stone slab stile leading onto a lane, which can be muddy. Follow this lane straight along, passing a signpost (24) where the lane bends to the left. Go through the field gate at the end of the lane and turn right along the road into Staveley.

Buses can be caught at the Stock Bridge Farm stops, the Eagle and Child stops or in Abbey Square, the start of the walk, the northbound stop being on the left of the square and the southbound stop opposite it on the right of the square.

24. Walk 23 uses the path from the right.

WALK 29, INGS, KENTMERE, KENTMERE TARN, STAVELEY,

Easy
8.5 miles
Allow 4.25 to 4.5 hours.

Ings is now by-passed by the A591, the original by-pass dating from 1914,when it cost £2,780. The old road passed through the village and had a dangerous corner as it passed round the church.

St. Anne's' church at Ings was founded in 1511. The present building is the second on the site, dating from 1743. The money for the rebuilding came from Robert Bateman, a local lad who had gone to London and prospered. He should have returned to live at Reston House, between Ings and Staveley, but was murdered by the captain of one of his own ships.

There was further restoration to the church in the 19th century, which was partly funded by £20 given by Queen Adelaide. It was not until 1751 that there was the first burial on the site.

Originally, the area around Ings would have a lot of tree cover and probably be marshy following on from the last Ice Age. Man would clear the area for his own farms and there are the remains of the ancient settlement of Hugill on the hillside near High House Farm. It is believed that these are Iron Age and date to around 200 to 300 B.C. Ings is part of the civil parish of Hugill.

There was a corn mill at Ings by 1272. Other mills followed, but now none are left working. However, one has been converted to a well-known restaurant, 'The Watermill Inn'.

During the Second World War the garage was closed, the proprietors having left to serve in the forces. From 1940 a small munitions factory was evacuated from Kendal to the garage.

The bus stops at Ings are by the road junction on the Windermere side of The Watermill Inn, which is after the church if coming from the Kendal direction.

The walk starts by going up the minor road at the opposite side of the A591 from The Watermill, a sign indicating that it is not a through road. This road is followed, passing a seat commemorating the 1953 Coronation, and shortly afterwards coming to a track going off to the right. Turn onto this bridleway and follow it to a fork just after passing through a metal field gate.

Take the left-hand track and pass the farm at Hugill Hall and then come out onto a minor road where turn left. The tarred road finishes at the next farm, The Heights, where go to the left to join the very good track, which is the bridleway. Go straight along the bridleway, from which there are good views around, and cross straight over the end of a tarred road coming up from the right, it is the end of a road used later on the way to Staveley.

The track comes out onto another track where turn right. Two field gates are reached where pass through the one on the right of the track. (Ahead is another track, but it does not go as far as the view of the site of the ancient settlement, the right of way going to the left. The settlement can be seen by going ahead, through a gap in the wall, up the field and looking over the wall on the left into the field with sheep pens. However, it must be emphasised that this is private land and not a right of way.) The bridleway for Kentmere is a grassy field track passing by the wall on the left.

Follow this track for about a mile, first by the wall on the left and later, after passing through a field gate, by the wall on the right. Pass through another field gate and there the track bears to the right away from the wall. It is a grassy one to follow and goes over some peaty ground. Walkers have diverted round some damp stretches. At one point the path swings to the left going round a boggy patch and then returns to the right. After that, a narrow stream is crossed and the path then continues ahead on the left bank of a stream, crossing some minor tributaries to it on the way.

Shortly, the main stream is forded and at the far side go up to the field gate in front. Once past the field gate, follow the good track as it passes along by the wall on the right. The track continues by the wall as it curves round to the right, with a good view down Park Beck and to the Kentmere Valley. Go through a field gate where a fence comes down the hillside and continue along the track, fording a stream on the way. Pass through another field gate and shortly after look across to the Green Quarter area of Kentmere.

Kentmere Tarn comes into view down below and the main part of Kentmere village is seen ahead. The track passes through two more field gates before reaching Kentmere Hall with its pele tower. By the Hall, turn right onto a lane. Follow the lane for about 45 yards (28) to a field gate on the right and pass through it and follow the track in front, its having been seen below on the descent to Kentmere Hall. At the end of the field, pass through another field gate, over a concrete bridge spanning a stream, and then through another field gate just ahead. The track goes up to and then by woodland. Another field gate

leads the path into the woodland. Shortly, the track forks and there take the lower left-hand one. Leave the woodland at another field gate, the top end of Kentmere Tarn being below and to the left. The grassy track, which has been cut through the slope of a hillside, reaches a wooden stile by a field gate and after that becomes fenced on either side.

Looking up Kentmere Tarn

The bottom end of Kentmere Tarn is passed and shortly the track becomes a concrete roadway. Pass along the roadway, the buildings of Hepworth Air Filtration being on either side. At the end of the buildings follow the roadway, which goes slightly to the right, its being the way to Kentmere Pottery. The roadway terminates at Sawmill Cottage, where there is the pottery and studio.

To the left of the buildings, between two iron fences, is the path to be followed. Pass over a footbridge over **Park Beck**, which is about to join the River Kent. Go through a field gate and follow the track along. It comes out at another track, where turn left (to the right leads to the ford crossed on the way to Kentmere). After passing some dwellings, the lane is tarred with grass growing in the middle. Shortly come to a turning where go to the right, ahead being for the main road up the valley. Pass through a field gate onto a good stony track and follow it along close to the River Kent.

The track leaves the Kent to turn up to Browfoot, where it passes to the right of Browfoot Dale and to the left of the next building and then to the left of a stream until a road is reached. This road is the one where its end was crossed after leaving The Heights. Turn left to go down the road for a mile and a quarter to where the main road along the Kentmere Valley is joined. Follow the road straight down to Abbey

Square in Staveley, where the bus stops are to the right, the one for northbound buses being across the road.

28. Walk 25 is reached by going straight ahead to Kentmere Church.

WALK 30, INGS, DUBBS ROAD, LONGMIRE ROAD, FAR ORREST, WINDERMERE.

Easy/moderate
7 miles
Allow 4 hours.

The bus stops at Ings are by the road junction on the Windermere side of The Watermill Inn, which is after the church if coming from the Kendal direction.

The walk starts by going up the minor road at the opposite side of the A591 from The Watermill, a sign indicating that it is not a through road. This road is followed for about half a mile to Grassgarth where, as the road swings to the right, go straight ahead along the footpath, over a piece of track and down to a stream which is crossed using a footbridge. Go through a kissing gate by the bridge and a few yards further on through a wooden field gate. There, pass along by the wall on the left.

A small stream is crossed to a stile by a field gate at the end of the field. From the stile, follow the grassy track straight ahead over the field. When the track swings to the right the path carries straight on ahead towards a footbridge spanning the stream again. Go up the path bearing right towards a wall. At the top right of the field there is a stile by a gateway leading into the next field.

Go up the field by the wall on the right and towards the farm coming into view ahead. At the top of the field a double stile, the first being wooden and the second a stone slab stile, leads out onto the road. Turn right along the road, passing Broadgate Farm, for a mile. On the way, two road junctions to the left are passed, the second leading back to a road joining the one from the first junction.

On reaching a point where the tarred road swings to the left there is an untarred roadway going off to the right, its being Dubbs Road. About three quarters of a mile along Dubbs Road there is Dubbs reservoir on the other side of the wall to the left. Vehicles come along the roadway to here.

After leaving the reservoir, pass through a wooden gate by a field gate. The ground is open along the following stretch of road and there are very good views to be had of Troutbeck and part of Lake Windermere. (After this, a short cut can be taken by crossing the ladder stile to the left and then dropping down to the Garburn Road.) A small plantation on the left is passed and then Dubbs Road terminates at the Garburn Road (29). Turn left down the Garburn Road and drop down it until reaching a junction (30) where take the track to the left, which is Longmire Road.

As Longmire Road is followed, there are again good views over to Troutbeck and up the Troutbeck valley. Pass through a wooden gate by a field gate and follow the track along, its becoming tarred. Longmire Road ends on its joining the road which was left earlier to go up Dubbs Road. On reaching the road, turn right for about a hundred yards to where there is a kissing gate by a field gate on the left and a sign indicating Far Orrest.

Once through the kissing gate, follow the grassy track over the open field. Pass through a gap in the wall in front and then by a wall on the right, skirting the foot of Allen Knott. Pass a stile on the right (36) and continue along the track to a wooden kissing gate by a field gate. Continue along the track until close to Far Orrest Farm there is a field gate on the right with a signpost indicating Crosses Farm and Windermere (37).

Go through the field gate and then by the fence on the left of the field to where there is a wooden ladder stile to cross onto a farm track. Go over the track and then through a kissing gate and continue straight ahead across another farm track after which go to the right of some farm buildings at Far Orrest and over a stile. Next, turn left by an old farmhouse to pass over a small section of track and through a field gate. Follow the farm track along to another wooden ladder stile by another field gate.

From that stile, follow the farm track over the field to the wall in front and then turn left, continuing to follow the farm track and not passing through the gate in front. The track goes towards another field gate, to the left of which there is a stone slab stile to cross. From there, continue along the grassy path close by the wall. The path goes straight ahead as the wall leaves it to the right before rejoining the path.

At the next field gate in front there is a wooden ladder stile to cross to its left. From there, cross the grassy farm track over the field. Go through another field gate and then by the buildings of Crosses Farm to a road, where turn to the left.

Towards High House, Ings

Follow the road for about a quarter of a mile to The Causeway Farm. Turn right through a field gate and onto a farm track opposite the farm. The first part of the track has walls either side, but the one to the left soon ends. Continue by the wall on the right. Next, cross a wooden stile leading into a fenced off lane in front. Follow the path along, passing a gate into woodland that is not entered. A fence in front is reached with a stile to cross and then continue by the wall on the right, its being the boundary to the plantation. A good view down Windermere is reached.

The path then drops down fairly steeply, still with High Hay Wood on the right, until a little to the left of the bottom right corner of the field there is a stone slab stile over the wall to be crossed. From there, drop down through the wood and out onto a good track in front.

Turn left along the track and pass some of the houses of Windermere. On coming out onto a tarred roadway, cross over it and continue straight along the path in front. It at first passes between two metal fences, these becoming a fence and a wall. At a driveway by a house, go straight on to its left to pass behind the house.

Pass a path on the left for Orrest Head. The path then comes out onto a tarred road where turn right for the few yards down to the A591 close to an entrance to the Windermere Hotel. Cross the road to the National Westminster Bank in front and turn left and cross over

143

that road towards the Tourist Information Office. Pass the Tourist Information and pass Booths to reach the bus stops in either direction by the railway station.

29. Walk 25 is joined here.
30. Walk 25 is left again here.
36. Walk 33 to Waterhead passes through this stile.
37. Walk 33 passes here on the way to Troutbeck.

WALK 31, WINDERMERE, SCHOOL KNOTT, DALES WAY, BOWNESS, WINDERMERE

Easy / moderate
7 miles
Allow 4 hours.

Transport from between Windermere and Keswick has long gone from by the station or across the road from opposite the Windermere Hotel. Rigg's mail coach ran from the station to Keswick and was one of the last routes in the country where the Royal Mail was taken by coach and horses.

It was the coming of the railway that brought the town of Windermere into existence. Prior to then, there was the hamlet of Birthwaite, which is now a part of Windermere. Nobody would have know the location of Birthwaite when buying a ticket, hence the name change. Otherwise, the area around was farmland, several of the farms still being in existence. Bowness was the nearest village, nearly two miles distant.

Rigg's Windermere Hotel, as the hotel was originally known, opened with the arrival of the railway and the rest of the building of Windermere followed on with the shops, hotels and many of the residences.

William Wordsworth did not like the idea of a railway line entering the Lake District, particularly as it was originally proposed in 1844 that the line would terminate at Low Wood, only a mile from Ambleside. He did not like the idea of the area being filled with "droves of working people", who would not benefit either morally or mentally, but it should be for the educated people's enjoyment. However, in spite of all his protestations in the newspapers of the day and a letter to Mr. Gladstone, the line was built. Various local landowners also objected to the intrusion of their privacy.

In November 1844 it was decided to abandon the proposal to take the line the extra three and a quarter miles to Low Wood as it would prove too costly crossing Trout Beck and cut into valuable property. Once this had happened, the landowners beyond Birthwaite were largely satisfied and many withdrew their support of Wordsworth, who kept up his campaign. On 30th June 1845 the Kendal and Windermere Railway Act received Royal Assent and work on constructing the line could begin. On 20th April 1847 the line was opened through to Windermere.

The Kendal and Windermere Railway was not long lived as such. In 1858 it was leased in perpetuity to the Lancaster and Carlisle Railway, which in turn was leased in perpetuity to the London and North Western Railway the following year and bought outright by them in 1862.

In its heyday, Windermere had a covered station with three lines, an engine shed, turntables and a warehouse and sidings for coal traffic. There used to be local trains and express trains to London and other destinations, one being a famous one, the elegant 'Club Train' to Manchester. Now, the trains run to Oxenholme or Manchester Airport. The station itself is small and the buffers are in front of what was the trainshed (the covered platforms), which has been converted into Booth's supermarket. The site of the lines is now under the shop floor and the original main entrance has been filled in. It was to the right of the Victorian letterbox in the front wall.

During the Second World War Windermere was host to a flying-boat factory, complete with hangars and housing for the workers. The base for the Sunderland flying-boats is now White Cross Bay Caravan Park. The buildings of the factory were removed in the 1950's and The Lakes School and modern housing now occupy the site.

Another hamlet, now part of Windermere, is Applethwaite, the parish church being St. Mary, Appplethwaite.

On 26ᵗʰ July 1840 Queen Adelaide landed on the shore of Windermere and ascended Rayrigg Bank, which is now known as 'Queen Adelaide's Hill and is National Trust property.

Below the hill is Low Millerground, formerly a landing place for Applethwaite, and named after the mill that stood on Wynlass Beck. The building at Millerground is one of the oldest in the area, dating from around 1612. Tradition has it, but there is apparently no documentary evidence, that a foot ferry across the lake to Belle Grange operated from here and that the bell tower on the building was for summoning the boat to come across the water. Such a ferry makes sense as, although it is the widest part of the lake, the journey on foot to Hawkshead crossing Claiffe Heights would be around half of that via the main ferry. However, the sixteenth edition of 'The English Lake District', originally compiled by M. J. B. Baddeley, does refer to there being a ferry with a one shilling fare "between Millerground and Belle Grange (but not in the reverse direction)".

The Baddeley Clock Tower on the road down to Bowness is in memory of the writer of the guidebooks.

From the bus stops by the railway station, go along to the main road and turn right towards Kendal. Follow the road for about a third of a mile, passing a footpath at Orrest Head Farm, and reach the top of a hill. Just over the top there is a wooden kissing gate on the right to pass through. Follow the farm track round and go through a wooden field gate and continue straight along the track. Just before reaching another field gate there is wooden ladder stile on the left to cross. From there, go across the field close to the wall on the right.

Turn to the right at the end of the wall to go down towards the railway. A stile is reached and there drop down to the track, cross it, taking care that there are no trains coming, and at the far side cross another stile. Follow the path along by the fence on the left, through a small plantation, cross another wooden stile and over a stone bridge right by Gill Droomer Stile, a house with an interesting garden. There, turn right down the roadway.

There are a number a new houses down here, more being built at the time of writing, and pass to the right of them. Come to where the road crosses the stream at a little bridge. Do not cross the bridge but continue straight ahead by the new dwellings. There is a signpost for School Knott. Go straight ahead, over a very minor piece of roadway. There is a wooden

Down path to School Tarn

kissing gate by a field gate to pass through and continue along the roadway.

Just before reaching the next gateway turn left up the field at the signpost for School Knott. Follow the grassy path up the field and as it reaches the next wall there is a wooden kissing gate in the corner. The path from the gate is quite a clear one to follow as it goes to the right.

The path becomes grassy and rather indistinct as it is followed up School Knott. It goes between two peaks, which give the Knott the shape of a saddle, and then towards the highest peak, which is slightly to the left of centre. Pass a pile of stones forming a cairn. At the top of School Knott there are good views across Windermere and to the Langdales. Cross over the top of the Knott to see School Knott Tarn less than a quarter of a mile ahead.

Drop straight down the grassy path towards the tarn, passing through a wooden kissing gate by a field gate on the way. As it reaches the tarn, the path swings round to the right and then passes along by the stream. Cross the stream and continue along to its left. A gateway on the left (25) is passed on the way to a kissing gate by a field gate in the wall in front.

Follow the track down, fording a stream and come to a junction with another track below. Here, turn left and follow this track along, passing through a number of gates to its end at the Crook road. Here, cross the stone slab stile to the right and follow the permissive path above the road.

On coming out onto the road again, immediately turn off it to the right and go up the roadway for Low Cleabarrow, its being the left-hand one. As the house is reached, the path to follow is through a wooden gate by a field gate and once through it turn right down the field to another kissing gate seen in front.

Go through the kissing gate and another two in quick succession and then bear right up the field. Follow the grassy path to a wooden kissing gate in the wall in front. From there, go straight ahead along the path and come to a wooden kissing gate leading onto a road (26). Turn left down the road to a junction at the end of which there is a metal kissing gate on the right. Whilst it is possible to go straight down the road, it is more pleasant to go through the kissing gate and follow the path along, skirting the trees.

The path becomes a grassy one as it goes towards a wall in front. Just before reaching a gate in the wall, turn left to go along by another wall, one which terminates for no apparent reason. Follow the grassy path with the wall on the right and come out onto the road left earlier at a wooden kissing gate by a metal field gate.

Turn right along the road and cross over a stream a few yards along. There, turn right to pass over a stone slab stile by a metal field gate. Follow the track along and as Brant Fell Farm is reached turn to the left to follow the grassy path by the wall above the farm. Go over a wooden stile by the wall and then follow the path with a fence on the left bordering a plantation and the wall on the right. The path comes to a very easy stone slab stile over a wall and then goes diagonally left over the open ground in front. It bears up the hillside of Post Knott to the viewpoint on top. There is a good view all along Windermere and to the Langdales. In front is Cockshotts Point with Belle Isle beyond.

From the top of the viewpoint, do not cross over it but turn to the right near the seat and go down the hillside from there. Aim towards a kissing gate by a field gate in the wall in front. Once through that gate, turn left to follow the good stony track. Continue along the track until a gateway is reached, to the right and left of which are kissing gates (27). Go through the kissing gate on the left and drop down the Dales Way. Go through the gate at the end onto the roadway and drop down the road towards St. Martin's Church.

The story of Bowness is dealt with in walk 32.

On reaching the main road opposite the church, turn right up that road to a mini roundabout where take the road to the left. Pass the World of Beatrix Potter at the Old Laundry. Continue along the road, passing the Steamboat Museum and on reaching the first open field on the left after the Museum, go through the wooden gate by the field gate into it and cross straight over the grassy path to a metal gate.

Turn right from the gate to pass along by the shore of Windermere. On reaching a junction, take the lower path to the left and keep on by the lakeshore. Go through a wooden field gate and then along by the wall on the other side of which are the wooden buildings of the Windermere Sea Scouts. On coming to a wooden kissing gate in the wall, close to a large stone-built boathouse, go through it and cross the stream to the right by a stone slab bridge. Follow the path along to Low Miller Ground, where turn left to follow the path up by the building. Cross a bridge close to a small waterfall and then come out onto the road.

Cross the road and turn left for a few yards and then go through the metal gate on the right and follow the path straight up to St. Mary's Church and the A591. On reaching the top of the path, turn right along the main road, passing the lych gate by the church, and continue along the road, ignoring Old College Lane to the right. On reaching the road down to Bowness, by the National Westminster Bank, cross over it and pass the Tourist Information Offices to Booth's supermarket. Pass along by the buildings to the bus stands by the railway station and the start of this walk.

25. Walk 24 joins here from the left.
26. Walk 24 leaves here.
27. Walk 24 joins again here.

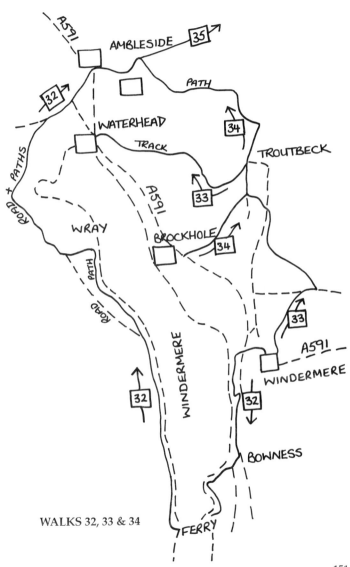

WALKS 32, 33 & 34

WALK 32, WINDERMERE, BOWNESS, CLAIFFE SHORE, WRAY CASTLE, AMBLESIDE

Easy
11 miles
5.75 to 6 hours

The first part of this walk through to Bowness is largely walk 31 in reverse.

At Windermere, leave the bus by the railway station. Go along to the road, cross it opposite the bank and continue northwards along the main road for Ambleside. On reaching the Parish Church of St. Mary, Applethwaite (actually, there are bus stops on both sides of the road here), cross over the road to the left, St. Mary's Parade, and come to a public footpath on the left, this being for Queen Adelaide's Hill and Millerground. Turn down the track, which is between two walls. At the end of this track, do not go along the roadway to the left but straight ahead to the gate in front.

The gate leads out onto a road, which is crossed. To the left there is a gate leading into the field, which is part of Queen Adelaide's Hill. Follow the track through the gate and then turn up the hillside. From up here there are excellent views to the top of Windermere and the Langdales.

Go along the hillside to the left, with a wall on the other side of which are trees over to the right. On reaching a point where the wall bends round to the left, rather than being a corner, there is a stone step stile to cross to the path below. There, turn left to follow the path along by the lakeshore. On reaching a rather large rock, note the plaque indicating that this is where Queen Adelaide landed in1840. Continue along the path until a gate is reached in the wall on the left. Turn through here and follow the grassy path over the field and out onto the road.

Turn right along the road and pass the Steamboat Museum. Continue following the road until reaching a junction where take the road to the right, Fallbarrow Road. Pass down it and go right at the next junction to pass the Old England Hotel. On reaching the main road ahead, turn right and pass the Bowness Bay Piers.

Bowness and Windermere are joined together so that when descending the main road between the two it is not possible to know where one ends and the other begins.

In the centre of Bowness stands St. Martins Church, the Parish church of Windermere. Formerly, the next parish to the north was Grasmere and to the south was Kendal. The present building, which underwent much work in 1999, dates from 1483 and replaced an older building that had been destroyed by fire.

Bowness refers to the bull's headland. As there is more than one place with a similar name, the 'on-Windermere' has been added. The village lies within the township of Undermillbeck, one of four townships making up the parish of Windermere. Windermere is Old Norse plus Old English for Vinandr's lake. Its name was written as 'Wynandremer' around 1180. In the churchyard are yews, which it is estimated could be 700 years old.

Prior to the development of tourism in the Lake District over the last 200 years, the main industry of Bowness was fishing. One species of fish, the char, is thought to be a survivor of the last Ice Age, and it has long been considered a special delicacy.

The principal piers for sailings on the lake are at Bowness as the steamers and waterbuses depart from here, both south to Lakeside and north to Ambleside, with some extra services in the summer months.

Passenger sailings started on Windermere before the age of steam, barges being oar propelled. 1845 saw the Windermere Steam Yacht Company being formed. In 1848 The Windermere Iron Steam Boat Company was formed, resulting in competition between the two companies. However, they united in 1858 and, in turn, the combined company was taken over by the Furness Railway in 1872, its having extended its railway line through to Lakeside. In 1891 the Railway Company launched the Tern and this vessel is still in service, but now diesel powered, together with the Swan and the Teal. The two latter vessels were always diesel powered. Formerly, all three vessels had two classes, but are now one class throughout, and there has been much refurbishment and some constructional alteration over the years.

Many of the wealthy merchants who owned houses on the shores of the lake had their own steam yachts. A number of these vessels are to be found at the Steamboat Museum along with the Raven, which was a cargo vessel built by the Furness Railway in 1871.

November 1911 saw the first British Hydro-aeroplane practising over Windermere. The Lakes Flying Company was based at Cockshott and had designed and constructed a biplane "Water Hen". Their leaflet stated that the safest and easiest way of learning to fly was on one of their waterplanes, a biplane costing £880 and a monoplane from £750. They did passenger flights from £2.

Bowness formerly had a laundry, this having been converted into "The World of Beatrix Potter". Beatrix Potter lived at Hilltop, Near Sawrey, a property that is open in the summer months, its being owned by the National Trust. As Mrs. Heelis, Beatrix Potter became a wealthy farmer and gave her land to the National Trust.

The Windermere Ferry crosses the lake at its narrowest point, where there are promontories on either side and only 560 yards of water separating them.

At the Steamboat Museum

The Bowness side is known as Ferry Nab. There has certainly been a ferry there for nearly 550 years, the first written mention being dated 1454 when John Idyll and William Dykenson, who were joint reeves, did not account for "any profit forthcoming from the passage of the water of Wynandremer". A hundred and twenty years later the "Wynandermyer" fishing and ferrying paid an annual lord's rent to the Queen, this being £6. A lord's rent continued to be paid until 1937. The ferry was let to the Lancashire and Westmorland County Councils from the 1920's and bought by them in 1948.

The early ferry boats were broad wooden boats, which were rowed across the lake, and the remains of one of them are on display at the Steamboat Museum. The first steam-powered ferry entered service in 1870, the engineer responsible for it being George Dixon of Balla-wray. It was a small boat, originally using a chain but later a wire rope to guide itself across the lake. In 1914 a new and larger ferry was built, its continuing in use until 1954 when the 'Drake' was built. 'Drake' was originally steam driven and had a tall funnel, but this was removed on its conversion to diesel. The present ferry is 'Mallard', a larger vessel introduced to service in 1990.

There have been accidents involving the ferry over the years. The most tragic was on 19 October 1635 when wedding guests were returning from Hawkshead around sunset. A gale was blowing and the ferry was overloaded.

The boat sank with the loss of 47 lives and eleven horses. Another accident, of a very minor nature was in 1944 when a rower somehow collided with the ferry and claimed it was the ferry's fault. He wrote to Westmorland County Council about this, but they found that the rower was entirely to blame for the collision.

After passing the piers, follow the road along as it passes round the bay and past buildings backing onto the lake. Shortly, by a marina, the road turns to the left. To the right, between the road and the entrance to the marina, is an iron gate to pass through. Follow the path along as it passes Cockshott Point, from where there is a good view of the Round House on Belle Isle, and turns left to reach another iron gate. From this gate, turn right along the path and follow it up to the road. Turn right for the ferry, which is taken across the lake.

The ferry sails every twenty minutes unless there is some reason preventing it, such as the waters of Windermere being too high. On the far side of the lake, go along the road and past the main buildings. On the right there is a gate leading onto a footpath by the edge of the lake. At the end of the path there is a gate leading onto a very minor road, where turn to the right. (This road can also be reached by going straight along the road from the ferry and turning right at the next junction.) Follow the road along close to the shore of Windermere.

The Claiffe shore of Windermere, prior to the local government boundary changes of 1974, was in the Furness District of Lancashire, known as 'Lonsdale North of the Sands', the sands being Morecambe Bay.

The ferry promontory on the Lancashire side of the lake was formerly called Swines Ness. Ferry House, that is now the headquarters of the Freshwater Biological Association, was formerly a hotel.

Above the lake is Claiffe Heights, which are said to have at least one example of every tree native to this country. The area also abounds with wildlife.

In June 1930 Sir Henry Seagrave attempted to break the then world water speed record on Windermere, an event capturing the interest of the nation. Sadly, it ended in tragedy with Seagrave and his mechanic being killed. Seagrave's body was first taken to Belle Grange after the accident. For many years there were two white posts a mile apart to be seen on the lake shore, these marking what was known as "Seagrave's Mile".

Not visible from the attractive little village of Wray is Wray Castle. The castle was never defensive but is a Victorian folly that was built in the 1840's by Dr. James Dawson from Liverpool. The building, which is in Victorian Gothic style, was used as a training college for Merchant Navy electronics and radio officers for many years from 1950. Now it is privately owned, but the grounds are owned by the National Trust and are open to the public with a footpath passing through them.

A cattle grid is crossed. As the road is followed, there are good views back towards the ferry, across to Belle Isle and up towards the Fairfield Horseshoe. Pass another cattle grid and the road then becomes an unsurfaced track which is not suitable for cars. The road is rather undulating, and normally quite close to the lake. A wildlife viewing platform is passed on the left.

A bridleway to Hawkshead is reached by the boundary wall of Belle Grange. This is part of the road between Windermere and Hawkshead from when a ferry is believed to have crossed to here. Pass along the roadway in front of the grounds of Belle Grange to where Sir Henry Seagrave was brought after his ill-fated attempt on the world water speed record.

A gateway is reached beyond which the road is tarred again. Here, there is a small car park to cross, Red Nab Car Park, towards the lakeshore and then turn left along a bridleway. After passing along the track for some distance, the houses of Balla Wray can be seen above and to the left. Further on, there is a footpath leading up the fields to Wray village. Pass that path, which is close to a field gate by which there is a stile on the right. Cross the stile and pass round the top of Wray Bay.

There is a wooden gate to pass through by a large field gate. From here, for a shorter walk, the bridleway can be followed straight along to the road for Ambleside, which is joined by the Lodge to Wray Castle. For a more interesting walk, there is another wooden gateway on the right a few dozen yards along the bridleway. Once through it, follow the grassy path ahead, passing behind a boathouse.

On reaching woodland, the path turns up the hillside and then to the right again towards the trees. There is a stile to the left of a gate and the path then carries along through the woodland. The lake is seen below and then the path drops down to go behind a large, black boathouse.

At the junction with another track turn left to reach Wray Castle. Go round to the left in front of the castle and at its end turn right. The path bears round the building to the main driveway out. There are signs indicating the way. Follow the driveway along and come to the Ambleside road by the lodge and turn right onto it.

On reaching the junction with the main Hawkshead road, turn right towards Ambleside. Keep along the road and pass the junction with the road leading up to the Drunken Duck. A few yards beyond the junction there is a permissive path on the right. At the end of that path the road is followed again for a short distance until another permissive path is reached, again on the right. It is only a short one. On leaving it, cross the road and go through a gap in the wall onto another permissive path and turn right for Ambleside.

This path comes out onto the road, which is then followed by the River Brathay to the bridge leading to Clappersgate. Once over the bridge, turn right for Ambleside. At a pathway by the road on the right there is a footbridge over the river, avoiding crossing the busy road bridge. Cross it and turn left for the main road and then turn right for the town centre, crossing over the road from Waterhead. On reaching a junction where traffic can go left or right but not straight ahead, turn right for the buses, this being Kelsick Road.

WALK 33, WINDERMERE, TROUTBECK, WATERHEAD.

Easy
6 to 6.5 miles
Allow 3.5 hours.

From Windermere station, cross the road to by the Windermere Hotel, which looks down from the right. Turn to the left and a few dozen yards ahead there is the roadway for Orrest Head going to the right. Go straight up the road, ignoring the way to the Troutbeck road (38). The tarmac road zigzags its way upwards until, at the last house, it changes to an unsurfaced track.

Follow this track for a short distance then, as the wall on the right goes away from it, follow the path along amongst the trees, going upwards. At the top, another path is joined where turn right and follow it to a kissing gate in the wall on the left. Go through the kissing gate and straight up the path ahead to the summit of Orrest Head, where there are good views along Windermere and across to the fells around High Street and Kentmere.

Cross behind the main seat on the summit of Orrest Head and turn left along the path behind towards Causeway Farm and Near Orrest, which can be seen ahead. The stony path goes over a stone slab stile into a field. There, follow the grassy path along, its bearing to the right, pass a small conifer plantation and then cross over a small stone footbridge. Another stone slab stile, which is by a field gate, is crossed onto the road close to Causeway Farm.

Turn right along the road for Near Orrest. On reaching the entrance to the farm there is a stile of concrete slabs on the left leading into the field. Cross it and go along by the wall on the right to a kissing gate into the next field. Cross the field bearing slightly right. At the end of the wall on the opposite side there is another kissing gate. Go through it and the extremely short stretch of plantation to the stile across the next wall. The path then goes straight ahead towards the right-hand tree of the row in front.

At the corner of the wall by the trees there is a stone stile leading over the wall into the next field. From there, go along by the wall on the right, ignoring a gateway, to a wooden ladder stile at the end of the field. From there follow the clear grassy path as it bears left over the field to where it comes to another ladder stile to cross. Bear left

Along Robin Lane, Troutbeck

towards the buildings of Far Orrest. At the farm, go through a wooden kissing gate, over the farm track, through another kissing gate and over to the left. Continue straight along the grassy field path with the farmhouse just over to the left.

As the house is passed, come to another wooden kissing gate to go through and then along a lane to the right (37). Another kissing gate leads into an open field to pass over and then into the open, rocky area of Allen Knott, with a wall to the left. Follow the grassy path along by the wall until a small stile in it is reached (36). Go through the stile and straight down the field, quite close to the wall on the right. On reaching a roadway, turn right along it.

Cross a cattle grid and continue along the road until a road coming down the valley is reached. Cross straight over that road and go through the yard in front. At the end of the yard there is a wooden stile to cross and then turn right along the path, passing on the way a seat in memory of Annie Leaver, who loved the views from there.

Follow the clear path along, cross a beck and then bear a little to the left going over the next field. The path then drops down to the main road up the Troutbeck valley. Turn right along the road and in around five minutes, at the brow of a hill, there is a kissing gate on the left, by a large field gate. Go through it and drop down the path as it winds down towards Trout Beck. At the bottom of the field there is a wooden gate leading to the two wooden footbridges taking the path over the Beck.

Go straight up the path, Ford Lane, from the beck and come out onto a road where turn right for Town End, Troutbeck. Go along the road to Troutbeck Post Office (31). A few yards before the Post Office there is a turning to the left for the bridleway, Robin Lane. Follow the lane along and come to two field gates. Go through the kissing gate by the left-hand gate and continue straight along the track. Go through two gates by each other and onto a roadway, where turn right.

Follow the road along towards High Skelgill. The track goes through the farmyard and then through the field gate, which is just to the left of the farmhouse. Another field gate is passed through and the track followed along, passing through another gateway and into woodland.

A sign to the left indicates a short diversion to Jenkins Crag, a rocky outcrop with a flat top, which forms a viewpoint for Lake Windermere.

Back on the main path, it shortly splits and then joins up again. Cross a stream and follow the path down to the left by it. The path leaves the stream and shortly another path is reached going to the left. Follow it down, cross another path, and continue down to a wooden stile into a field. Pass along the right-hand side of the field and over a stone stile in the wall from where turn right along the path. Follow the stony path along and come out onto the road by the Waterhead bus stops.

Waterhead of the 1850's was a quiet hamlet, only a few boatmen living there. All this changed with the coming of the steamers, its being a place of importance by the 1890's. As its name implies, Waterhead is at the end of the lake and there are many private boats moored around here as well as there being commercial vessels from the piers. In the winter the lake sometimes froze over and there was skating.

By the head of the lake is the attractive Borrans Park. In the adjacent field, and reached from the park, is the site of Galava, the Roman forts. The first fort was probably built in the first century and only occupied for around 30 years. The second fort covered two and a half acres and was twice the size, its being constructed in the second century and lasting around two hundred and fifty years. The last known date of the fort's existence is a coin dated 378 A.D. A number of tools found at the fort show that there was a variety of tradesmen on the site. The fort was on the Roman road from Watercrook to Ravenglass via Hardknott with another road going to Penrith via Ullswater.

Walkers by Elterwater.
Loughrigg Tarn, and Loughrigg.

At Loughrigg summit.
Across Grasmere to Helm Crag and Dunmail

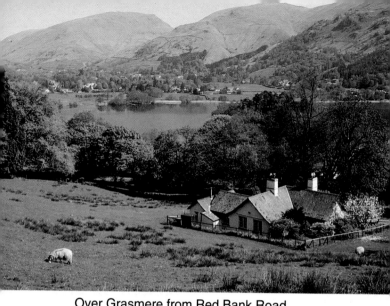

Over Grasmere from Red Bank Road.
Grasmere village from near Alcocks Tarn.

Easdale Tarn.
Down to Town Head, Grasmere from Helm Crag.

Alternatively, instead of turning left for Waterhead, after leaving the stream, continue straight ahead, pass a path going backwards to the left (it is the one crossed on the way down to Waterhead) and continue onwards. The track skirts the edge of the woods with a field over to the left. The roadway next turns sharply to the left and then follow the lane down to a road. Cross that road and then come out onto the main Ambleside road opposite the garden centre and by the bus stops, which are just to the right.

31. Walks 25, 33 and 34 meet at the Post Office.
36. Walk 30 passes this stile.
37. Walk 30 goes through the field gate to the left for Crosses Farm.
38. Walk 30 ends by coming along that path.

WALK 34, BROCKHOLES TO AMBLESIDE VIA TROUTBECK AND WANSFELL PIKE.

Moderate
5 miles
Allow about 3.5 hours for the walk excluding Stock Ghyll Force.

On leaving the bus stop at Brockholes go southwards in the direction of Windermere. Shortly, the way up to a farm is reached on the side of the road for southbound traffic and immediately afterwards there is an old farm track. Here, there is a signpost indicating 'Wain Lane'. Turn up this lane, which is a bridleway. It can be very muddy at the bottom end. Continue along the lane and come out onto a road at a corner in it (32). Go straight ahead and Town End at Troutbeck is shortly reached.

Continue straight along the road through Troutbeck (31) and, a few yards after passing St. Margaret's Well in the wall on the left, there is Lane Foot Farm. Here, turn left and go through the gate onto the track for Wansfell Pike. It is generally a good, stony track, rather rough in places. The track winds its way up the hillside with a stile to be crossed beside a gateway spanning it on the way. Shortly, after leaving the gate, the track ahead changes from being stony to being grassy. Here, on the left, there is a gateway for Wansfell.

The Wansfell path steadily ascends the hillside, passing through another gate and over a wooden footbridge. From up here there are good views down Windermere and of the Eastern Lakeland fells.

To Kirkstone Pass from Wansfell Pike

At the summit, there is a stile in a fence. Once over the stile and onto the rocks, there is a good view of Ambleside way down below and of the route of the path dropping down the hillside. The first part of the descent is steep and rather rough. After this, whilst it is still steep, the path is stepped, which makes for easier walking.

Next, there comes a section of loose stones. A gap in a wall is passed through. Another stepped stretch of path is crossed, a footbridge is crossed then comes an ordinary stretch of path. On the descent of the path, there are good views to Kirkstone Pass to the right.

A long stretch of stepped path is descended, this being part of erosion control, the old route having got into a very bad state. At the bottom of this path there is a lane going to the left (to another part of Ambleside) but for this walk pass through the kissing gate. Walk along the grass by the stream on the right and then on a proper stone path. Follow the path to two stiles together and cross these onto a minor road (39). Turn left down this road and Ambleside is straight ahead. Go down the road, crossing a cattle grid on the way. By continuing down the road, keeping to the right, the centre of Ambleside is reached. On the main road, turn left and cross it and then turn down Kelsick Road for the buses.

However, there is a pleasant diversion which can be taken shortly after crossing the cattle grid. Over to the right there is a turnstile in the wall. By going through it and to the right, you can go round by the top of Stock Ghyll Force cross the bridge and then follow the path down on the far side of the Force. The path comes out onto the road down to the centre of Ambleside, as above.

31. Walks 25, 33 and 34 meet at the Post Office.
32. Walk 25 passes the top of Wain Lane.
39. Walk 35 follows the road to the right.

WALK 35, AMBLESIDE, KIRKSTONE PASS, AMBLESIDE.

Easy/moderate
7.5 miles
Allow 4.5 hours.

Ambleside is most famous for its Bridge House, a small building straddling Stock Beck. The land on which it stands was part of the extensive property surrounding Ambleside Hall, which stood between the present Smithy Brow and North Road, and was owned by the local Braithwaite family for around 200 years from the 16th century. It is thought probable that Bridge House originally served as a summerhouse and a way across the stream to an orchard and pastures beyond, there then being no road in front. In later years, the house was used as a small dwelling and a fireplace installed. It would be then that a rear door, traces of which are still to be seen, would be blocked up. Later, Bridge House was used by a shoe repairer and an antiques and gift shop. 1956 saw its being opened by the National Trust, to whom it had been handed in 1926, as its first recruitment and information centre in the country.

Close to Bridge House, Stock Beck is spanned by Stock Low Bridge, in the middle of which is a marker stone dividing "Above Stock" from "Below Stock". This is a reminder of the times when Ambleside was split between the parish of Grasmere to the north and the parish of Windermere to the south. In 1675 St. Anne's Chapel was built as a chapel of ease, but it was not registered for the recording of marriages and deaths, these having to be registered in Grasmere and townsfolk taken there for burial. The original chapel was replaced in 1812 and, in turn, replaced by St. Mary's Church in 1854.

The architect of St. Mary's Church was Sir George Gilbert Scott. It was following the building of this church that Ambleside became a parish in its own right. Inside the church at the back there is a mural painted by Gordon Ransom in 1944, depicting the annual Rush-Bearing which is still held every year. Ransom was a lecturer at the Royal College of Art during its period of evacuation to Ambleside during the Second World War. The rush bearing is an old custom from when houses and churches had earthen floors and rushes were strewed for warmth. A procession followed by a church service is still held here annually.

At the top of Church Street stands the Old Stamp House where William Wordsworth was the Distributor of Stamps for Westmorland from 1813. His salary for this post was £500 a year, his duty being the selling of government excise stamps, not postage stamps.

Ambleside "Above Stock" was an area where the Norse-Irish farmers settled. This would be drier ground than the area around the old Roman fort at Waterhead and the local people must have moved up to there after the Romans left. The name of the town comes from Old Norse referring to a shieling by a river-bank.

In 1650 a charter granted a weekly market to sell wool and cloth, its being held near the present day Post Office. A market hall was soon built and it was replaced in 1796 by a larger building which was used until 1825 when the decline in the wool market led to its closure. However, a market is still held in the town on Wednesdays, but it is now behind the Kelsick Road bus stops.

The Market Cross now stands opposite the Tourist Information Centre and the shopping centre built in 1997 on the site of the former bus station, further up the main street from its original site in Market Place. Also in Market Place there was a Bedlam or Bethlehem, a 17th century Poor House.

Following the establishment of the market, more buildings were constructed around it, leading to the gradual moving of the centre of the town from "Above Stock" to "Below Stock". The coming of tourism in Victorian times, particularly following the arrival of the railway to Windermere and steamers on the lake, led to the construction of many of the buildings seen today.

Several water-powered mills were built along the banks of Stock Ghyll, a woollen mill of 1797 by Bridge House now being a restaurant. Further upstream stands another mill where goods can now be purchased and the wheel seen turning, its having been restored after many years of disuse. On the opposite side of the stream is Bridge Street, which was formerly known as Rattle Ghyll owing to the clanking of the waterwheels.

At the top of Bridge Street, on North Road, is Stock High Bridge. Prior to the coming of the turnpike road (the present road) to Rydal in 1833, North Road was the coaching route through Ambleside to the north. Originally, there was a ford up here.

In the early 1900's Ambleside had a 9-hole golf course, 'Loughrigg Links', situated on Loughrigg. Green fees were 2s. 6d. a day, 10s. 0d. a week or a pound for a month.

There are many items of interest relating to Ambleside history to be seen at the Armitt Library and Museum, which is close to the road for Kirkstone Pass.

Another attraction on the main street in the village is 'Homes of Football', easily recognised by the model footballer outside.

Kirk Stone

From the Kelsick Road bus stop in Ambleside, go straight up to the main street turn left and then go along Cheapside, which is to the right of the White Lion. There is a sign indicating the way to Stock Ghyll and Wansfell Pike. As the road is followed, Stock Beck is over the fence on the left. A track to the left, leading to Stock Ghyll Force is reached. (If desired, the road can be followed straight ahead without visiting the fall.) Follow the path along through the woodland, going upwards, and not crossing the Ghyll. Once there was a charge of 6d., and earlier 3d. to go to the Force, but now it is free.

Come to where part of the Force is to be seen and then to another path by a picnic table. Turn right onto this path and shortly come to a turnstile leading out onto the road. Here, turn left and shortly cross a cattle grid. Pass the stiles from Wansfell (39), keeping straight along the road. Cross a cattle grid by Low Grove house and continue following the road to Grove Farm, where the tarmac road comes to an end.

At the farm, go straight ahead through a gate, ignoring the other gate by it, and follow the farm track along just to the right of a wall. Ford a small stream and then pass through a gate and out into an open field. The track is followed ahead with the occasional stream to ford. All the time, Kirkstone Pass is in view ahead and to the left.

On one stretch of the path there used to be a proper wall on either side, but there are just its remains now. Go through a field gate and down towards Grove Gill, cross it and go up on the other side. There, at the top the path is grassy as the field is crossed to the trees in front. Go through a gate and pass the trees, which are growing all around the remains of High Grove. From High Grove there is a clear path to follow again, part of it having recently been reconstructed.

A stile at the end of the track leads out onto the road at the bottom of "The Struggle". Climb up the road and at the top, where the A592 from Troutbeck joins, there is the Kirkstone Pass Inn, 1500 feet above sea level and dated 1496.

Follow the road on past the Inn for around five minutes to where there is a group of large stones on the hillside to the left of the road. As these are approached, it will be seen that one of them looks very like a church building in shape, the Kirk Stone.

From the Kirk Stone, retrace your steps along the road past the Inn and down "The Struggle". From there, the road is undulating but overall downwards. Pass the entrance to Kirkstone Quarries. In about 2.5 miles from Kirkstone Pass Inn, at a bend in the road, there is s signpost indicating the way to Ellerigg to the right. Pass through a large field gate and then follow the track.

From by two seats there is a good view across Ambleside to the church. Continue along the track and then cross over a stile by a large gate. Follow the path along by the wall and then through a gate which is part of a stile in the wall and drop down the path in front. To be seen in front, on the other side of a wall, is a very attractive garden. On reaching that wall, turn left and pass through another gated stile and follow the path down in front, at the back of some houses.

Shortly, reach a roadway and turn down it to the left for Ambleside. Come to a junction and again go to the left (40). Continue dropping down and come out onto the Kirkstone road. Here, turn right and pass down Smithy Brow to come out onto the A591. Turn left along the road, passing over Stock Ghyll on the opposite side of the road from Bridge House. Continue along the main road through Ambleside until Kelsick road is reached on the right, the first turning after Church Street, and go down it for the bus. Alternatively on reaching the A591, turn right and there are bus stops on either side of the road at the northern end of the Health Centre's grounds.

39. Walk 34 comes over these stiles.
40. To the right is walk 36 for High Sweden Bridge.

WALK 36, AMBLESIDE, HIGH SWEDEN BRIDGE, AMBLESIDE.

Easy
4 miles
Allow 2.5 hours.

From the Kelsick road bus stop, go straight up the road to the main street and turn left. Cross the pedestrian crossing in front of the Tourist Information and then turn left to Bridge Street which is shortly reached. Go up there to Stock High Bridge, cross it, and follow North Road to Smithy Brow. Cross over the road and continue straight ahead and then turn left onto Sweden Bridge Lane. Pass Belle Vue Lane and the junction with Ellerigg Lane. At the end of the tarred road there is a wooden gate leading onto a stony track.

Follow the track along, passing an old quarry on the right. Over to the left is Scandale Beck. Pass through a wooden gate and, further on, another gate. From here the ground is more open and suddenly High Sweden Bridge is seen over to the left, spanning the beck.

High Sweden Bridge is a lovely old packhorse bridge which, although it looks fragile, is so constructed that it has easily withstood the traffic of the centuries passing over its top. All around here is noted for wild flowers.

Cross the bridge and turn left. A few yards on the track turns sharp right by a wall and then passes up the hillside to the left of the wall.

At the top of the stretch of path up the hillside there is a ladder stile to cross. From there, there are two paths, one to the left and one going further up hill. Continue along the one up the hillside and shortly it bears left. On turning left, another ladder stile is seen ahead. Just before reaching it, the path comes out onto a farm track. Turn left and, as there is no gate in the wall in front, pass through rather than use the stile. There are good views down Windermere from up here.

Follow the farm track along as it steadily winds its way downward. Ambleside comes into view. There are various gateways to pass through on the way, the gates having been removed, the stiles now being ignored. A hairpin bend is reached, at the end of which is Low Sweden Bridge, again crossing Scandale Beck. Cross the bridge and pass through a gate which must be shut afterwards.

High Sweden Bridge

On reaching a metal gate, go through it and past all the farm buildings. At the end of the farm there is a kissing gate by the gate spanning the roadway. From it, continue straight down the road, turning right and then right again at road junctions to come out onto the A591. Turn left and pass Bridge House. Cross Stock Bridge, noticing the stone in the middle of the parapet, indicating "Above Stock" and "Below Stock". Continue straight along the road, passing the shops, until Kelsick Road is reached for the buses.

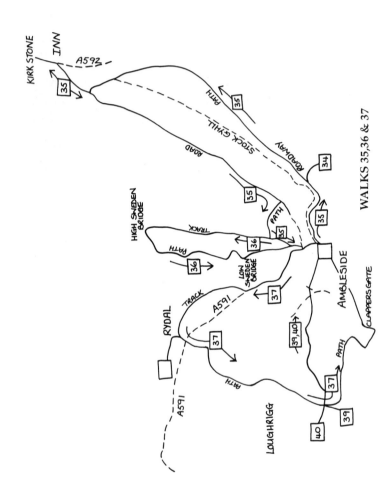

WALKS 35, 36 & 37

WALK 37, AMBLESIDE, RYDAL, LOUGHRIGG, CLAPPERSGATE, AMBLESIDE.

Moderate
6 miles
Allow 4 hours.

From the bus stops in Kelsick road, go straight up to the main street of Ambleside and turn left. Follow the street along until the northern end of Ambleside is reached, all the main buildings having been passed. A beck is crossed at Scandale Bridge. Actually, there are bus stops either way just to the north of this bridge. By the bridge, on its eastern side, the footpath is indicated. The path, part of the old coffin route, goes along by the left bank of the beck. A gate crossing the track is reached and by it there is a wooden stile to cross.

Shortly, follow the main track to the left as it passes through Rydal Park. It is not then far to a junction where there is a sign indicating the way to go is to the right. Whilst you do turn up to the right here, you immediately turn to the left again to pass amongst the buildings of Rydal Hall. Follow the signs, going left again, and pass the back of the hall and then the path comes out onto a road. Here, if wanting to go to Rydal Mount turn right, otherwise turn left for the A591 road below. There are bus stops on either side of the main road if not wishing to continue the walk through to Ambleside..

Rydal was in the Norman Barony of Kendal. As the walker will appreciate, around all this area are paths on the hillsides that were at one time parts of the routes linking farms and townships. In Celtic times the valley bottoms were a morass and not the cultivated land of today, resulting in farms being some way up the various hillsides. The slopes of the hills were forested and largely impenetrable to strangers, a very different scene from today. When ways were constructed, they tended to be from farm to farm as that way existing routes could be extended rather than building completely new ways. Quite a few Rydal farms were also inns in the 1600's.

Rydal church, dedicated to St. Mary, was built by Lady le Fleming of Rydal Hall, her laying the foundation stone in 1823, there being no church here until then. As the church is built on rocky ground, there are still no burials here. The dead from Rydal used to be taken to Grasmere along the 'Coffin Trail', the path to be followed in walk 41 from there to Grasmere.

William Wordsworth regularly worshipped in Rydal church, having been influential in its being built.

Next to the church is Rash Field, which is known as Dora's field and is in memory of William Wordsworth's daughter who died in 1847. He had intended building her a house on the land. Wordsworth lived in Rydal Mount, a short distance up the road, from 1813 until his death in1850. Dora's field is easily reached by passing straight through Rydal churchyard, and is particularly beautiful when the bluebells are in bloom. Rydal Mount is still owned by descendants of Wordsworth and is open to the public.

Close to the shore of Rydal Water about half way along the lake is 'The Nab', which was owned by Margaret Simpson who married De Quincey in 1817. He bought the whole estate in 1829. Later in the 1830's 'The Nab' was occupied by Hartley Coleridge, who rented it from William Wordsworth. The roadway in front of the building used to be part of the main road before the present road closer to the lakeshore was constructed.

For the walk, turn right along the main road and opposite the pub, Badger and Bar, there is a path leading down to the River Rothay, which is crossed by a wooden footbridge (41). From the bridge, follow the path up the field to a kissing gate at the top and then through woodland to a gate onto a road. Turn left for a few yards to pass a cottage and then to its right, at a signpost, turn up the grassy path up the hillside.

Ignore a path soon crossed and continue on to a waymarker sign where turn uphill to the right. At the top there is a gate to pass through and then the path is followed along amongst the bracken with a wall on the right. It becomes a good stony path to follow. There is a wooden stile to cross on reaching another boundary wall. Once over there, continue along the path, still by the wall on the right.

The wall comes to an end, but the path continues onwards ahead amongst the bracken, another way down through the bracken to the right being ignored. A rather boggy area is reached, this being crossed bearing left towards the track seen going round the hillside in front. On reaching that path, turn to the left.

A crossroads of paths is reached with a rather vague path going right, a clear path going half left and another clear path going full left. Take the middle path, going half left. It goes upwards and then skirts the hillside on the right before crossing over the dip on the ground to skirt the hillside on the left. Continue straight along the path, passing a cairn on the way.

Keep on going ahead, ignoring ways off to the left and the right. A fork is reached, the right-hand path being taken. Keep going ahead, ignoring ways off to the left and right until another fork is reached and then again take the right-hand path. Shortly, the path comes out onto a main track just above a ford at a stream. Turn right and cross the ford (42).

Once over the ford, turn to the left down another path, which soon crosses the stream again and continues downwards on the opposite side of it. It is a clear, stony path to follow with views back up Loughrigg and down to Windermere.

A junction of a few paths is reached, the one to take being to the right towards a kissing gate to be seen in front. Pass through the gate and then straight up by the wall on the right. Follow the main path, ignoring side turnings. A small tarn, Lily Tarn, is reached and passed round, either to the left or to the right.

At the end of the tarn there is a good, clear path round to the right. Follow it as it goes to the right, across a dip and to the right of the hillside in front, many walkers going up to a top for a view down Windermere. Keep going right round the hillside and reach another path coming down from above. Turn down that path, which zigzags downwards. At a seat by a wall the path turns left at a hairpin bend. It is a stony path to follow as it

Lily Tarn, Loughrigg

drops down and into woodland. Pass through a wooden gate and then continue down the track, coming out onto the Ambleside/ Coniston road at Clappersgate.

Turn to the left along the road for Ambleside. As it is approached, there is a path to the right of the road, this leading to a footbridge over the river. Cross it and turn left and then turn right when by the road bridge over the Brathay. Go straight up the road to a crossroads, the road ahead not being accessible to traffic. The road to the right is Kelsick road for the buses.

41. Walk 41 from Grasmere is met at the bridge.
42. Walks 37, 39 and 40 meet here.

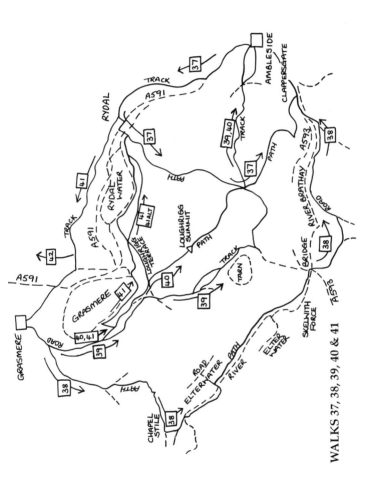

WALKS 37, 38, 39, 40 & 41

WALK 38, GRASMERE, CHAPEL STILE, ELTERWATER, SKELWITH FORCE, AMBLESIDE.

Moderate
7.5 miles
Allow 5 hours.

Grasmere is a scattered community with a main central village. Just to the south of the main village is Town End, the original turnpike road is the one running past Dove Cottage, a former inn called the 'Dove and Olive Branch', and over White Moss Common, but it was by-passed by what is now the A591 in 1823.

Dove Cottage is now a Wordsworth Museum visited by thousands every year. It was here that William Wordsworth and his sister Dorothy lived from 1799 to 1807 before moving to larger quarters in Grasmere for the five years prior to the move to Rydal Mount. After that, in 1809, the Wordsworths' friend De Quincey took over the cottage for the following twenty years.

At the time the Wordsworths lived in Grasmere, the roads were so little used by wheeled traffic that Dorothy once recorded that a chaise had passed that day. William, his wife Mary and Dorothy thought nothing of walking over Dunmail Raise to Keswick.

William Wordsworth is buried in a railed plot of St. Oswald's churchyard, another place of pilgrimage for many. The church is as Wordsworth knew it. St. Oswald was a 7th century king of Northumbria and it is believed that he preached here. The earliest parts of the building date from the 13th or 14th century. The first Rector to be recorded was Henry de Galdington in 1254.

St. Oswald's has a lych-gate. By the gate is the building that was the village school for over two hundred and twenty years from its opening around 1630. Early in the 19th century, one of the teachers at the school was William Wordsworth. Now, the building is Sarah Nelson's famous Grasmere Gingerbread shop, the delicious smell of its being baked often tickling the taste buds of tourists.

On the opposite side of the road from the church is the National Trust shop. Here, there used to live a Mr. Alcock, who was a keen fisherman. He had Alcock Tarn constructed so as to be able to stock it with trout.

Now, there are no mills in Grasmere parish, but in 1453 there were six producing cloth.

Whilst many Lakeland villages have their own sports days, probably the most famous is Grasmere Sports, where there are events peculiar to the area, such as Cumberland and Westmorland Wrestling and fell racing.

On leaving the bus at Grasmere, go towards the Red Lion and pass to its right along Langdale Road. This road comes out onto Red Bank Road opposite the Tourist Information Centre, where turn right. Follow the road for about a quarter of a mile to a signpost indicating a public footpath to the right. Turn right up the stony track, starting at a kissing gate. Pass through another kissing gate and follow the path up the hillside quite close to the wall on the left. The path is quite a rough one to follow here. See Grasmere and Rydal Water over on the left.

A corner of the wall is reached, with the path starting to drop down on the left. Ignore the path going to the right. Cross over a piece of path which is generally muddy. Continue along the path by the wall or as close to it as is reasonable. Watch out for a gate in the wall with a stile by it where another path comes up from The Wyke. A few yards beyond there a path goes off uphill to the right, this being the way to follow.

The path up the hillside is a grassy one amongst the bracken. It goes to the right of and above an old building. Ignore a path going over to the right. Another path is crossed before reaching the top of the hillside.

Once over the top, there is another track to ignore as it is crossed and then the path starts its descent amongst the bracken. Elterwater and its quarry can be seen to the left and the road down below. The path zigzags down the hillside, care needing to be taken as there are erosion problems. Chapel Stile is seen over to the right.

Chapel Stile

The path levels out at a grassy part and then turns right to go down a good path towards Chapel Stile, where it comes out onto the road at End Cottage. Turn right past the cottage and go into the village. On reaching the Parish Church, take the very minor road down to the left and drop down to the main road up Great Langdale, where turn to the left.

Chapel Stile church, Holy Trinity, dates from 1857, its becoming a parish in 1863, and is the church for the Langdale valley. However, the first recorded chapel on the site was founded in 1571, and was rebuilt in the 1750's. Baptisms, marriages and funerals had to be taken at St. Oswald's, Grasmere, for many years. There is a former corpse road via Hunting Stile, a short stretch of which is used at the beginning of walk 39.

The township has its own independent Co-operative store, which was founded by the mining company in 1884.

Pass the Langdale Co-operative Village Store and pass Wainwright's Inn and a few yards beyond, by the car park, there is a turning to the right. Go through a wooden gate and cross a bridge over the River Brathay.

Follow the path along to the left, passing beneath the spoil heap for the slate quarry. The path comes to a quarry road where turn to the left. Across the river from here used to be a gunpowder works.

The quarry road comes out by the bridge over the river, which is then crossed into the attractive little village of Elterwater, with a maple tree on the green in front of the Inn.

Elterwater comes from Old Norse plus Old English for "swans' lake".

The present holiday complex by Langdale Beck is on the site of a gunpowder mill covering twenty acres. The mill was established by David Huddleston and production started in 1824. It was a good site as there was tree cover to provide screening in the event of a blast. Silver birch was available for charcoal, with alder being brought in from Leighton Moss, near Carnforth, and the Rusland Valley.

Elterwater gunpowder was a coarse, black blasting powder that was particularly suitable for use in slate quarries. Close to the entrance to the mill were the stables. There were very strict rules for the carters, who had to leave a space of at least 50 yards between carts. The horses wore special slippers to prevent their shoes from possibly causing sparks to fly. Prior to the coming of the railway to Windermere, the raw materials were brought either up Coniston Water or up Windermere to a pier near Clappersgate.

Production continued for over 100 years until the works closed in 1928. All the buildings used in the manufacture of the powder then had to be burned to ensure that no powder remained in any crannies. After that, the machinery was removed for scrap.

The maple tree in the centre of Elterwater village, giving the name to Maple Tree Corner, was planted in 1935 to commemorate the Silver Jubilee of King George V.

For the walk, after crossing the bridge, turn right through the car park and go through a gate and then follow the path by a wall by the river. It is a good track to follow and passes through a gate into an open field by Elterwater itself. Here, there is a good view back of the lake and the Langdales. Continue along the path by the river, at the end coming to a field gate with a kissing gate to pass through by it.

Continue along the path in the woodland, the river on the right and the road above to the left. The path passes the way down to Skelwith Force, which is always worth a closer look. From there, continue straight ahead and pass through the yard of Kirkstone Slate, with a shop at the end. On reaching the road, turn right across Skelwith Bridge, the river here formerly being the boundary between the counties of Lancashire and Westmorland.

Ahead is a road junction, the way to take being straight ahead along the minor road and not the main Coniston road. It is quite a steep pull up to Skelwith Fold. The road being followed meets another road, Bog Lane, where turn to the left. By the road junction is the Old Farm and Old Farm Cottage.

Of Brathay church, which is dedicated to the Holy Trinity, Wordsworth said that he thought it had one of the most perfect settings for a church outside of the Alps. Unusually, because of the lie of the land, the building is on a north to south axis rather than east to west.

The road is followed, Brathay Church passed, and then shortly come to the road from Hawkshead. Follow it, crossing the bridge over the Brathay and turning right for Clappersgate. Continue along this road until a footbridge is crossed to the right. From there, turn left to the road bridge over the Brathay and there turn right to the centre of Ambleside, crossing the Waterhead road on the way. On reaching a road junction where traffic cannot go ahead, turn right up Kelsick Road for the bus stops.

WALK 39, GRASMERE, LOUGHRIGG TARN, AMBLESIDE.

Easy/moderate
5 miles
Allow 3 hours.

Starting from the main bus stops close to the Red Lion in Grasmere, go along College Street, which is the road leading off the Green, passing the bookshop and the Methodist Church. At the end of the road, turn left along the main road to the church and then cross over and follow the road past the Tourist Information Centre. Pass footpaths leading off to the right and continue along the road until reaching a junction by a cottage with a letter box in the wall. Follow the right-hand road, as indicated by a signpost for Loughrigg YHA and Great Langdale.

The roadway is tarred until the last of the houses and then it becomes a broad, stony track. Pass by a gate indicating that Nicholas Wood is open to the public. A few yards past the gate is a corner with various gates and a seat. Go through the kissing gate that is signposted for Loughrigg Terrace and follow the path along in the woodland. It is a good woodland path to follow. Go through a kissing gate and follow the path along with the road below to the left.

Shortly, the path and the road join. Continue along the road, passing the way down to Loughrigg Terrace (43), and come to a junction where the left-hand road is taken. After about five minutes walk, a decision has to be taken as to which of two routes to follow. A stile is reached on the left and one route is to cross it and turn right along the grassy path to the wall in front. At the wall, cross a stile in the fence spanning the track there and then follow the track on again.

Loughrigg Tarn

Cross a stile by a stream and a few yards beyond there is a gate to go through. Continue along by the wall. Shortly, come to a junction of paths with Loughrigg Tarn to be seen below. Take the right-hand path down by the fence, pass through a gate and come onto a track below. Turn left to pass some dwellings.

For the alternative route, continue along the road past the stile for a few hundred yards to where there is a farm lane going off to the left. Go down the lane and, by a field gate, there is a kissing gate to pass through. Follow the lane straight on to Loughrigg Tarn and the dwellings mentioned above.

From the tarn, follow the track straight along to its end at a gate. Pass through the gate and turn sharp left for Ambleside. The path passes through another gate and then goes upwards by a wall. It continues along by the wall after passing through another gate. A junction to the left is ignored. Eventually, the path continues across open country once the end of the wall has been reached. Close to where a stream is forded (42), ignore the paths to the right and to the left, and keep on ahead and through a gate. Continue following the path, which is passing the area that was once a golf course.

Pass through a kissing gate if a large field gate is not open. The rough stony track becomes smoother and later is tarred as it drops down Miller Brow and passes Brow Head Farm. A minor road is reached at a kissing gate. Turn right along the road, cross a cattle grid and then turn left to cross a bridge over the Rothay. Turn right, across another bridge and then go straight across Rothay Park.

On leaving the park, come out onto Vicarage Road and follow it to a main road. Cross this road at a pedestrian crossing and then go up The Slack and come out by the Queen's Hotel in the centre of Ambleside. Turn right for Kelsick Road, which is the second road down on the right, towards the end of the shops on the main street.

A diversion, which can be made on leaving the Loughrigg Tarn track before turning onto the Ambleside path, is to Skelwith Force. Go straight down from the gate and bear right. Next turn left down to a minor road with a letter box in the wall opposite. Turn right along the road to a nearby junction where turn left. Go straight down this road to the A593. There, turn right to the entrance to Kirkstone Slate just by Skelwith Bridge and pass through their yard. Follow the path along just above the river until Skelwith Force is reached. Retrace steps to the original path turning for Ambleside on the path which was originally being followed before going to the Force.

42. Walks 37, 39 and 40 meet here.
43. By going down the track to Loughrigg Terrace walk 40 is joined.

WALK 40, GRASMERE, LOUGHRIGG SUMMIT, AMBLESIDE.

Moderate
5 miles
Allow 3 to 3.5 hours.

On leaving the bus stops in the centre of Grasmere, turn along the main road towards Red Lion Square, which is to the west, and follow it round, past the Gingerbread shop, to the church. Opposite the church, cross over and follow Red Bank Road past the Tourist Information. Continue straight along the road for about a mile, passing the beginnings of various footpaths used in other walks on the way.

On reaching the beginning of a very steep stretch of road there is a track leading off to the left. Turn onto the track and then turn right to go in front of a cottage. Continue along the good woodland track and come to a wooden kissing gate at its end and then turn left along the track for Loughrigg Terrace (43). A few yards along it there is a metal kissing gate to go through and then cross over a stone slab bridge. Here, the Loughrigg Terrace path is straight ahead whilst to the right is the path to take, climbing steeply up the hillside.

On ascending the path, there are good views looking back down to Loughrigg Terrace and Grasmere. The well-worn path climbs up the hillside, passing cairns on the way. In part it is quite rough and stony, in other parts it is grassy. The summit appears ahead and the path circles round to it.

Grasmere from Loughrigg

For the descent, circle round the summit to where a quite broad grassy path can be seen below, going southwards in the direction of Windermere. (Great care needs to be taken in mist as it is easy to end in the wrong place owing to the large number of paths on this fell.) Drop down a steep and stony stretch of path and onto this grassy path. The path goes between two hillsides, passing over another steep section on the way. (The path to the right is to be ignored as it leads to Langdale.) A more grassy path is then followed straight ahead, bracken on either side.

Continue along this main grassy path, ignoring other paths to the left and the right, until it reaches another main path in front. Here, turn right and soon reach another main path, where continue ahead in the direction of Windermere. It is quite a broad, stony path, dropping gradually downwards, again paths to the left and right are ignored.

On suddenly reaching a lip there is a steep, rough section to drop down. (This can be avoided by going down a path to the left shortly before reaching the lip. As it is not possible to tell it is the path down before reaching the lip, it would be necessary for the walker to go back a little way.) There is a cairn at the bottom of the lip. From there, go straight along the path in front towards another path which can be seen crossing ahead. This path is the main path from Loughrigg Tarn to Ambleside.

Cross the ford (42) and turn left up the main path for Ambleside, its being the clearest stony path. Follow it along and in about a quarter of a mile pass through a wooden gate. Continue down the path and through a wooden kissing gate by a field gate. Follow the good track along, quite close to the wall on the left.

Continue straight ahead, pass Brow Head Farm and drop down to a kissing gate leading onto a road. Turn right, pass a cattle grid and then turn left and cross the bridge over the Rothay. Go through the metal gate straight in front and along the path towards the top end of Ambleside. Pass through a wooden kissing gate and out onto a road that is a cul de sac. Turn left for the main A591 road and then right along it for the centre of Ambleside. The nearest bus stops are about 100 yards to the left of where the walk comes out onto the main road.

42. Walks 37, 39 and 40 meet here.
43. An alternative start to this walk can be made by following walk 39 to here.

WALK 41 GRASMERE, RYDAL, GRASMERE.

Easy/moderate
5.5 miles
Allow 3.5 hours.

From the bus stops in the centre of Grasmere, follow the main street past Red Lion Square to St. Oswald's Church. Turn right down Red Bank Road, opposite the church, and pass the Tourist Information offices. Go straight up the road for about a mile, passing cottages on the left, one of which has a letter box in the wall. Shortly, a permissive path leaves the road for the shore of Grasmere. Turn down here and on reaching the lake turn right.

After passing through a gateway either go along the shore or along the path amongst the trees just above the shore. At its end, the higher path goes through a kissing gate and then drops down to by the lake. At the weir the path can be followed straight ahead by the River Rothay, past the footbridge and on to another footbridge and then turning right for Loughrigg Terrace. However, it is suggested that at the weir turn right up the path going up the hillside to the right and leading to the Terrace. At first it goes straight up and then runs more or less parallel with the river down below.

South along Loughrigg Terrace

At the end of Loughrigg Terrace, turn right to go along it for the views up Grasmere. Return the same way to the junction of paths and take the one dropping down to the left rather than the one ahead to the right. A kissing gate is passed on the way down, this being the way up from the low level route by the river. Ignore the gate and continue down the track until the shores of Rydal Water are reached, part way along the lake.

Continue along the shore of Rydal Water and towards its end come to a junction of paths. Take the left-hand path and go through a metal kissing gate into Rydal Woods.

Follow the path along, through another metal kissing gate and out into an open field. At the end of the field, go over to the left to the bridge spanning the River Rothay (41).

Having crossed the river and come out onto the road, turn right for a few dozen yards to a road junction. Go up the road on the left, past Rydal church and continue on to Rydal Mount. A few yards after passing Rydal Mount, turn left and go along the roadway running behind the house. Next, go through a field gate to the left onto the bridleway and follow the track along.

The track being followed is part of the old coffin road from Ambleside to Grasmere from the days when bodies had to be carried there for burial. On coming to a junction just through a gate, take the right-hand path. Continue following the path along past some houses. The path becomes a tarred roadway to follow.

Drop down the road (44) and it comes to the junction of the road for White Moss Common and Dove Cottage. Turn right for Dove Cottage. The main road is reached shortly after passing Dove Cottage. There are bus stops to the left, the northbound one being across the road to the left, but the southbound stop is opposite the far end of the Thistle Hotel.

For Grasmere centre, cross the main road at the junction and go straight ahead towards the church and, beyond it, the main Grasmere bus stops.

* * *

Good alternative beginnings to this walk are to start as for either walk 39 or walk 40 and then walk straight along Loughrigg Terrace and continue as described.

An alternative route from the end of Loughrigg Terrace is to take the path to the right, passing along the side of the fell. It is a good,

lear path to follow and reaches Rydal Cave, a former slate quarry
nd not natural. From there, descend the path and reach the shore of
ydal Water, where turn right to follow the walk through Rydal Woods
s described above.

1. Walk 37 from Ambleside via Rydal is met at the bridge.
4. A path to the right leads to Alcock Tarn, walk 42.

WALK 42 GRASMERE (DOVE COTTAGE), ALCOCK TARN
GRASMERE VILLAGE.

Moderate
3 miles
Allow 2.5 hours.

The bus stop from the south is at the northern end of the Thistle Hotel
whilst that from the north is on the other side of the road at the south
end of the hotel. In either case, go to the road junction to the north of
the hotel and turn right onto the minor road leading past the
Wordsworth Museum and Dove Cottage. Continue along the road
climbing upwards, to where there is a small pond to the left and a
junction in front. At the junction, turn left up the rather steep road
this being the way for Rydal.

Shortly, another junction is reached (44), to the right being the road
for Rydal and to the left is the signposted track for Alcock Tarn, which
goes behind the house above the pond. On coming to a junction where
there is a large field gate to the left and a path up the hill to the right
go along the lower track through the gate and follow it along. Pass
through another field gate, just beyond which there is a good view
over Grasmere.

Keep following the track onwards and upwards to the right
ignoring another track going down to the left. Note an old larch tree
which has fallen over and developed itself into a row of nine larches.
Near here there is a small pond to the right of the path, this formerly
being used by packhorses on their way over the route. The track swings
around as it goes onwards and upwards, giving a view down onto
the pond recently passed. Go through a metal gate with a National
Trust sign for Alcock Tarn on it. You are still quite some distance from
the tarn.

Cross a beck by an unusual little stone bridge. After this the path
winds upwards close to the rock of Grey Crag. The path then levels
out as it goes towards a wall and through a gap in it. Pass over the
grassy path and there is the earthen dam of Alcock Tarn just in front.
From up here there are views down Windermere and across to
Coniston Water.

Turn left by the dam to pass to the left of Alcock Tarn. After passing
the tarn, come to a wooden stile set into an old gateway in a wall.
Cross it and follow the wall along to the left. Pass another very small

By Alcock Tarn

tarn and then start the steep descent down the very well worn and clear stony path. The path can be muddy and care needs to be taken.

The path becomes a grass track as it approaches Forestside Plantation. It becomes stony again as it drops down by the boundary wall of the plantation on its way to Greenhead Gill. Go to the left by the Gill and then cross its waters by a bridge and through the gate at the left. From here there is a tarred roadway by some of the Grasmere residences to follow.

Drop down the roadway until another road is reached, where turn left. Continue down this road which comes onto the A591 by the Swan Hotel. There, cross the busy road and turn left. Opposite the Roman Catholic Church, Our Lady of the Wayside, turn right onto the first footpath. (There is a second path which crosses the fields and comes out by the school and near St. Oswald's Church and the two paths are linked in the middle by the Millennium Bridge over the river and built to commemorate the Millennium.) Follow the footpath to its end where it comes out onto the road by the river. Turn left along the road for Grasmere centre and Green and the bus stops.

44. Walk 42 uses the right-hand road when coming from Rydal.

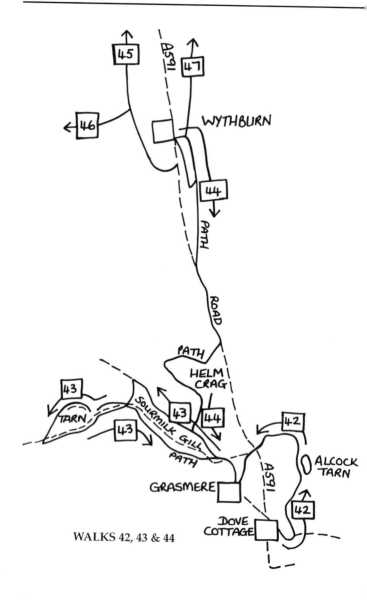

WALKS 42, 43 & 44

WALK 43, GRASMERE, FAR EASEDALE, EASEDALE TARN, EASEDALE, GRASMERE.

Easy/moderate.
5.75 miles.
Allow 3.75 to 4 hours.

This is an extremely popular walk and it is suggested that it be done outside the main holiday season.

From the main Grasmere southbound bus stop, cross the road and turn right to the road junction in front and then left up it, from the northbound stop, turn left on leaving the bus to Easedale Road and go up it, the road being only a few yards from either stop.

Follow Easedale Road, going along the permissive path on the left for part of the way, to its end. There, the road forks, left being to a farm and right onto a bridleway. As the bridleway is joined, the tarred stretch of road finishes. Pass through a field gate and 25 yards ahead is a junction with a path from the right (45). Go straight past the junction and continue along the good stony path ahead, sometimes fording streams.

Enter far Easedale, passing along by Far Easedale Gill. The path reaches a peaty stretch where a footbridge is seen to the left. Follow the path round to the bridge, cross it and continue up the good, clear path in front as it curves its way round the hillside. An indicator post is reached, showing that the path goes round to the right. Follow the gravelly path along as it turns to the

Up Easedale to Sourmilk Gill

right round the hillside, ignoring a grassy way ahead, beyond which walkers are probably to be seen, they are on the return route.

As the path is followed round it crosses some flat stones taking it over a boggy area. After this, the path becomes gravelly again. Reach Easedale Tarn, where Sour Milk Gill can be crossed by using the

191

stepping-stones at the foot of the tarn, shortening the walk by 45 minutes to one hour.

For the walk round Easedale Tarn, pass by the way down to the stepping-stones and instead follow the path to the right of the tarn. A number of streams are crossed on the way round. On approaching the end of the tarn a more grassy area is reached. Here, turn to the right away from the water rather than close by it. Some of the path is not very clear as it goes through bracken. Skirt above a boggy area and then come to the top of the tarn.

Pass over a muddy stretch and over a stream by some rocky ground to the right. Follow the path round to the right, still above the tarn, which it then leaves to go further up Easedale. It is not always clear to follow. On coming to where the main stream down Easedale does a bend in towards the path, drop down the grassy way to it, ford it, and go up to a gravelly path above. The stream may well be deeper than walking boots.

Over a hundred years ago there was a stone hut called 'The Tourist's Rest' at Easedale Tarn. This was run by William Wilson, who supplied tourists with simple food, such as bacon and eggs. Getting the food and fuel to cook it up to the tarn was a problem.

Turn left along the gravelly path and look straight down to Easedale Tarn. Follow the path along, passing the way up from the stepping-stones at the end of the tarn. In places there are easy stepping-stones taking the path being followed over streams. The path is a very clear one to follow as it makes its way downhill, passing by the falls of Sour Milk Gill, which are quite conspicuous from various points round Grasmere.

Come to a stone wall and then pass along by it to a wooden kissing gate by another gate. From there, continue along with Easedale Gill, which has been joined, on the left. Cross over a stream and then come to two good tracks passing through field gates, the one for Grasmere being the one on the left.

Follow the track along by the Gill and then through a metal field gate. Cross over a stone slab bridge and then over another stone bridge, but with a railing, and come out onto Easedale Road, where turn right to Grasmere and the beginning of the walk.

45. Walk 44 uses the right-hand path coming down from Helm Crag.

At the summit of Helm Crag.
Helvellyn from near Armboth.

Toward the head of Thirlmere.
Wythburn Church.

Castlerigg Stone Circle.
Looking down to Watendath Farm and Tarn.

Along St. John's in the Vale to Blencathra.
Skiddaw from High Rigg.

WALK 44, WYTHBURN, DUNMAIL. HELM CRAG, GRASMERE

Moderate, steep in places.
6.5 miles.
Allow 4.5 to 5 hours,

For details of Wythburn, see the beginning of walk 45.

The bus stops are to the south of Wythburn Church. The southbound stop (the northbound is opposite) is by a track leading to a car park. Go up this track to the car park, from where there is a gate leading to the church if it is wished to visit it. Go straight through the car park and through a wooden kissing gate which leads onto a right of way for Helvellyn. Turn right and go up the path.

It is a rather steep path upwards to a junction (46) where turn to the right along a track which is a permissive path. Go straight along the track to where it swings round to the right. A signpost on the left indicates the permissive path to Grasmere (47). Go through a wooden kissing gate and over a wooden footbridge to join the path. There is an attractive little waterfall on Birkside Gill just upstream from the bridge. As the Gill splits in two, there is another footbridge to cross a few yards further along. From there, follow the path along as it drops down to pass close to the wall on the right.

Continue along the path, crossing minor streams in places. Cross over a footbridge spanning a stream and then turn left along the field and come to a wooden kissing gate leading out to the A591 crossing Dunmail Raise and see the pile of stones between the carriageways.

The old county boundary between the counties of Cumberland and Westmorland was at the pile of stones. The cairn was displaced when the road was made in 1891but the stones were replaced in what was considered to be their original position. Now, the A591 passes either side of the cairn.

Tradition says that Dunmail, or 'Domhnall', who was one of the last kings of Strathclyde, was killed at the spot by Edmund, the Saxon king, in 945. Actually, he survived the battle and died thirty years later in Rome. There is also the tradition that Dunmail is buried under the stones and each year his supporters come and tap on the stones and ask if he is ready yet, to which he replies not yet and that they must wait a while.

The two former counties ceased to exist in 1974. ' Westmorland' came from 'the land of the people who live on the western moors', a name which must have been given by the people living to the east of the Pennines. 'Cumberland' and 'Cumbria' have the same base referring to the 'land of the Cymry'. Virtually the whole of the modern Cumbria was part of the Kingdom of Strathclyde, the inhabitants of which were from Strathclyde, Cumbria and Wales. Following the battle of Chester in 615, most of the area came under the control of Northumbria.

The ancient dialect way of counting sheep harks back to the Celtic days and can sometimes still be heard. Whilst there are differences between the valleys, there are very strong similarities in the numbers and the words for one, five and ten are very similar to their Old Welsh, Cornish and Breton equivalents. Probably the best known way of counting to ten are the Borrowdale area words of yan, tyan, tethera, methera, pimp, sethera, lethera, hovera, dovera and dick.

For the walk, continue along the field, quite close to the wall and A591 until it is necessary to turn left to cross a stream before returning to continue along by the fence close to the road. The path to follow is not a particularly good one along here. Come to a stile by a field gate close to the Dunmail Summit bus stops, which are at either side of the road. Here, cross the road and turn left along the wide grass verge towards Grasmere.

Follow the road for about a mile, passing the Dunmail Raise Water Treatment Works and also Toll Bar cottage. On reaching a minor road to the right, turn down it and pass Town Head Farm and Town Head Cottages. Cross Raise Beck by a packhorse type bridge and then turn right along a private driveway which is also a public footpath. On reaching the last of the houses, go through the wooden field gate and onto National Trust land, "Green Burn". At the wall just in front, turn right to follow the track along to a field gate.

Once through the gate, continue along the track for another fifty yards to a slope down to the left, this leading to a bridge spanning Green Burn. Once over the stream, go up the field hillside to a wooden kissing gate in the wall in front. There, cross a track and pass through another gate. Follow the steep, grassy path up the hillside amongst the bracken and come to a high wooden ladder stile near the corner of two walls.

Cross the stile, which has a shorter drop on the far side. Continue along the steep, grassy slope up the hillside, not far from the wall on the right, and then come to a more gravelly stretch of path. From there, it is not far to the path along the top of the ridge, on joining which turn to the left. Over to the right is Far Easedale and further over is Easedale with Sourmilk Gill tumbling down the hillside.

It is a zigzag path to follow as it makes it way to The Howitzer on the summit ridge of Helm Crag. The path passes just below the summit rocks and then drops a little to the right of the summit ridge. This stretch of path comes out at the end of the summit ridge and then drops steadily downwards.

On reaching a more level grassy area turn right, there is a small cairn at this point. (However, there is a good diversion to a viewpoint straight ahead that can first be made.) The path to follow down the side of the crag is a clear one to follow on the way down to Easedale. On reaching a wall, the path drops down a steep and stony stretch to the right where care needs to be taken, particularly after rain as water flows down the path as well.

Part of the path is railed as it makes its descent and passes an old quarry area before joining another path at the bottom. There, turn right for about thirty yards along by a wall to a track continuing downwards on the left. Follow this track down and come to another track where turn left for (45) Grasmere. Go through a large metal field gate and along the track past the first houses of the village.

On coming out onto Easedale Road, you can turn left for Grasmere. Alternatively, cross the road, go through the field gate and along the grassy track towards a bridge to be seen ahead. Cross the bridge over Easedale Beck and turn left along the track (48). Follow the track along and over a stone footbridge to come out onto Easedale Road again, where turn to the right, following the permissive path where possible. The road

Over Gibson Knott, Helm Crag

comes out in Grasmere village with the northbound bus stop a few yards to the left and the southbound stop across the road and a few yards to the right.

45. Walk 43 follows the track to the right.
46. Walk 47 is joined here,
47. Walk 47 is left here.
48. From here is also the ending of walk 43.

WALK 45, WYTHBURN TO THIRLSPOT

Moderate
Basic walk 6 miles, nature trail extra.
Allow 4 hours with a further half hour for the nature trail.

Now, Wythburn is noted for its church, which dates from 1640, with a chapel having stood there from 1554. Wythburn is a parish in its own right, but shares a vicar with the neighbouring parish of St. John's-in-the-Vale, and has done since 1926. The former vicarage at Wythburn has been demolished.

Wythburn had several more buildings in the past, including an inn, the Nag's Head, which stood opposite the church and was demolished in 1966. Further down a road, to Launchy Gill was the hamlet known as "The City", which is now beneath Thirlmere. Also beneath the waters of the lake is the "Steading Stone" where the manorial courts of Legburthwaite were held as was a local 'parliament'.

The only dwellings that now remain inhabited are those at Steel End.

Thirlmere was originally Brackmere or Bracken Water, this coming from the Viking 'Braikere'. Later, it became Leathes Water after the name of the principal landowner. It has also been shown as Wythburn Water. The lake was in two parts joined by a narrow neck in the middle, the lower one being close to the dam.

A road ran from Dale Head and crossed the lake by a ford by which there was also a Celtic bridge. The road led across to Arnboth House, turning right before reaching Fishergill. Dale Head was owned by the Leathes family, and the estate had been in their possession since 1577. The Lordship of the Manor of Legburthwaite was held by a Mr. Leathes, who was very much against the scheme for Manchester Corporation to extend the lake so as to provide water for that city. He would not allow access to his estate or give permission to go over his land to see the lake.

During the time of negotiations with Mr. Leathes, Sir John Harwood and Alderman Grave needed to see what the margin of the lakeshore was like. On one very wet day they went from Keswick and crept on their hands and knees past Dale Head Hall to reach the lakeshore without being observed. The pair returned to Keswick in very wet clothes and both were laid up with colds afterwards.

Following the death of Mr. Leathes, his son who was his successor was much more interested in the money than the family tradition and, in spite of family opposition, sold out to Manchester Corporation. As a result, the dam was built and the pipeline to Manchester constructed, the first stone of the embankment being laid on 22 August 1890. On 3 February 1894 the new road on the west side of the lake was opened by Alderman Anthony Marshall, Lord Mayor of Manchester. In spite of their problems with the original Mr. Leathes, the Manchester Corporation officials clearly respected him far more than they respected his son who sold them the land they required.

The water from the lake is still taken to Manchester, but now under the auspices of North West Water, who have opened up access to the lake and other woodland.

It was the acquisition of the land around Thirlmere by the Manchester Corporation that led to the closure of the Wythburn lead mine on the slopes of Helvellyn. The mine opened in 1839 and closed in 1880. Although the workings were quite extensive, very little ore was extracted.

The "King's Head" at Thirlspot is an old coaching inn. In 1861it was also the Post Office for the area, including Wythburn, John Atkinson being both the landlord and the 'receiver' for mails. Letters from Windermere arrived at 8.30 a.m. and were dispatched to there at 4.15 p.m.

The bus stops in each direction are at the end of the road leading past the head of the lake and eventually to Arnboth. Go along the road and shortly after passing Steel End there is a permissive path starting from the far side of the car park. All this area around Thirlmere is owned by North West Water and includes 4,800 hectares of farms, woodland and open fields. Turn left through a kissing gate and shortly the shore of Thirlmere is reached, with Helvellyn on the opposite side. The path winds along close to the lakeshore, old tree stumps and roots having to be avoided. A gate is passed through and a piece of an old wall crossed. After this, wooden walkways cross over some of the more marshy ground. Another wall is reached where you have to turn left and then diagonally right up to the road. Turn right along the road and cross a bridge spanning Dob Gill.

At Dob Gill there are the Harrop Forest Trails, three walks of varying lengths, and a bridleway to Watendlath (48). A few yards along the road, after crossing the bridge and opposite the car park, there is a kissing gate leading back down to Thirlmere. The path swings round to the left and then turns right down to the lakeshore. A footbridge is crossed. Two stone walls are reached with the remains of a roadway in between, this route now being cut by the lake. The next stretch of path can be muddy before reaching a stony path. A number of old boundary walls meeting together are passed and the path then goes out onto the road at a gate. Turn to the right and pass through a rock cutting, at the end of which there are some steps leading up to a viewpoint. By there, a gate leads to a slope down to the lakeshore path to Arnboth.

At a junction in the path, take the left hand arm, it shortly drops back to the lake shore, the right hand path being over a rough area. Continue along the path, which is undulating until it goes leftwards towards a gate onto the road. There is no need to go onto the road as the path crosses Launchy Gill by a footbridge to the right before getting there. However, it is well worth diverting to follow the nature trail at Launchy Gill, which is a Site of Special Scientific Interest, its being protected as an outstanding example of oak and birch woodland.

For the nature trail, go up the steep, rough path opposite the gateway until a junction is reached. There, take the right-hand path and drop down steps to a wooden footbridge over the Gill. Continue down the path to the road. Opposite the car park there is a gate with a path leading down to a fence and a gate onto the main path by Thirlmere. Allow about half an hour for the Launchy Gill walk.

If not visiting Launchy Gill, after crossing the footbridge, the path goes back down towards the lakeshore, passing the way from the far end of the Launchy Gill walk. It is an undulating path as it goes along toward Arnboth, where there are toilets by the car park and a signpost for Watendlath (49). Cross a wooden footbridge, pass through a gate and turn leftwards up the hillside before swinging right again down to Thirlmere. There are good views back to Helvellyn along here.

Next comes the easiest part of the walk as the path is in the best condition. A way out onto the road is ignored. The dam is to be clearly seen ahead. The path goes up to the road and then follows it for a short distance before going through another gate back to the lakeshore. A signpost for Arnboth is reached and steps lead up to a gate. That is the end of the permissive path and the way off. Go through the gate onto the road and turn right. Pass a junction, keeping right, cross the outflow from Thirlmere and the main part of the dam. On the way across, at a rock cutting there is an inscription up above explaining that the road was opened on 12 October 1894. A little further on is a large memorial plaque explaining that the first stone for the embankment was laid on 22 August 1890 by Alderman Sir John James Harwood.

Former road enters Thirlmere

Having crossed the dam (50), continue along the road to its end. The northbound bus stop is just to the left of the junction whilst the southbound stop is just to the right.

Alternatively, the walker needing refreshment can turn right down the road for about a mile to Thirslpot to the King's Head, passing the road to the hamlet of Legburthwaite on the way. Bus stops are at either side of the road by the pub.

48. Walk 46 follows the bridleway.
49. Walk 48, coming the other way from the dam, leaves here for Watendlath and Keswick.
50. The permissive path up steps to the right a few yards from the end of the dam is used in walk 48.

<u>WALK 46, WYTHBURN, WATENDLATH, KESWICK.</u>

Moderate
10 miles
Allow seven hours, there is much to see.

From the bus stops at Wythburn, which are close to the junction of the road to Arnboth, take that road to pass by the present West Head Farm. Go past Steel End car park and shortly reach some farm buildings on the left. Here, go through the farmyard to the gate on the right and then another gate immediately after it. Follow the track on ahead. At a junction, take the right-hand track and pass some old farm buildings that are largely demolished, this formerly being West Head.

Go through another gate and straight along by the wall. Pass through another gateway and then drop down the grassy path towards another gate that leads out onto the road. Turn left and follow the road to the next bridleway sign on the left, which is just before the bridge over Dob Gill (48). The first part of this walk forms part of one of the Harrop Trails. Go through the gate and then through another one after which the path is steep and stony as it ascends the hillside with a fence on the right.

There is a point where the path goes to the left for a few yards, but it soon returns to the right. Continue along by the fence until it is crossed into the woodland by a ladder stile. The path is then followed through the woodland, partly over a wooden walkway. A ford is reached, its being crossed by stepping-stones. To the left of the ford is Harrop Tarn. Having crossed the ford (or cheated by crossing the footbridge about twenty yards downstream), go straight ahead along the forestry track.

The track then skirts round Harrop Tarn and is followed to a junction where the left-hand path is taken. This path by Mosshause Gill shortly comes out onto the main forest track which is then followed again for a short distance. (From here, forestry work can affect the route to be taken, but which is correct at the time of writing.) A path to the right of the forestry track and going straight above it is followed to where it again joins the main track.

Follow the main track ahead and upwards to where it branches, the main track going to the right. Follow that track for a few hundred yards to its end at some rough ground. There, turn to the right and go

Harrop Tarn

through the woodland. A proper footpath is soon joined and an arrow on a tree in front indicates the way to the left. This path, which includes a short wooden walkway, is followed upwards, passing another footpath going off to the right on the way. The path reaches a double gate in a fence at the top. (The essential thing is to reach the double gate in the fence and not to have crossed Mosshause Gill.) Close by are the remains of an old building, presumably a shepherd's accommodation.

(Note, for those walkers not wanting to go through to Watendlath for any reason, by taking the path to the right shortly before reaching the fence, it is arrowed, one of the Harrop Trails can be followed. It goes down to the road by Thirlmere where turn right for Wythburn or left for Arnboth. There are some good views to be had on the way.)

Once through the gates the path ascends the hillside in front. It is a mixture of grassy, gravelly and stony as it climbs up the hillside towards the apparent top of the hill, passing two small cairns on the way. It then bears a little to the right, passing another cairn, with another one to be seen at the top. On reaching that cairn, it can be seen that the top of the hillside is further ahead. Some parts of the path are rather boggy and a way has to be found across. The path goes a little to the left, still being cairned. In one place there are some stepping-stones over a soft stretch of ground.

A fence is reached, running along the top of the ridge. The ground round here is rather boggy and a route has to be found across to a gate in the fence. From up here, there are views back to Helvellyn and in front to the hills around Borrowdale.

From the fence, the descent starts to Blea Tarn, which is soon reached. The grassy path bears to the right, going along above the tarn, and having several wet patches to cross. At the end of the tarn there is a signboard indicating that the way then to follow is up the hillside and not across the Beck. The way up the hillside tends to be wet. On looking upward, a cairn to the left of the apparent summit can be seen, and this is to be aimed for.

On reaching the cairn, another one is seen ahead and then follow the path along the hillside, not far from the top. Look straight along the Watendlath hanging valley and to Derwentwater beyond, with Skiddaw in the distance. The next part of the path is stony and this is followed by a muddy stretch to go round before reaching another cairn.

The path continues on in a similar fashion from cairn to cairn, going basically downwards, some parts being stony, some grassy and some muddy. An old wall is crossed. The path is followed round the hillside, in some places being very vague. As it is followed, the trees near Watendlath Tarn come into view and the Tarn itself. There are still cairns to be passed.

Suddenly the path becomes a good, clear one. Watendlath and its tarn are seen below and a wall passing along the ground a short way to the left. Continue along the undulating path, which bears towards the wall with the Tarn well below. Two streams are crossed on the way. When the path is directly above Watendlath it is joined by another path coming down the hillside (51) from High Tove.

On reaching the junction, the path turns to the left and crosses a stream. On the way down the steep path there is a marvellous view of Watendlath below. At the bottom of the path, go through a gate at the left of the stream then reached and pass along by a wall, ignoring a ladder stile to the left. The path then comes out onto the roadway at Watendlath.

Watendlath Valley is an excellent example of a hanging valley. During the last ice age the main glaciers came down from the hills, forming Borrowdale and scooping out what was to become Derwentwater. This ice was much more powerful than the smaller glacier coming down from Arnboth Fell, scooping out Blea Tarn and the Watendlath valley, its being held back at its end until the main glacier receded. The small glacier left behind Watendlath Gill and formed the cascades of Lodore Force where it dropped over the ledge of rock formed by the vanishing main ice. A smaller valley coming to a drop down to a main valley like this is known as a 'hanging valley'.

The name 'Watendlath' is Norse and probably has some reference to the 'end of the lake', but its full meaning is not clear. The valley was granted to the Cistercian Monks of Fountains Abbey in 1195, their retaining it for over three hundred years. Following the dissolution of the monasteries by Henry VIII, Watendlath was sold to Richard Graham. His family sold off the land in blocks.

The hamlet stood on an important packhorse route from Keswick, over High Tove to Arnboth and onto Grasmere and the south. Also, there was the route the monks used from Borrowdale coming over the fell from Rosthwaite. The packhorse route would be in use for hundreds of years until the coming of the more modern roads. Spanning Watendlath Beck at the mouth of the tarn is the delightful packhorse bridge. The sides were added following an accident in which a horse slipped over the edge.

The pinfold, from the days when stray sheep were kept until the next shepherds' meet, has been restored. This circular area is just above the hamlet and best seen on dropping down the path.

The drystone walls around the valley have been built over the centuries, taking in land for fields and pasture from the rough fellsides. In the 1500's there were sixteen tenants and their families living in the hamlet of Watendlath, all making a living from the land. Crops were grown near the buildings and animals grazed on the higher lands. Now, there is just one working farm here, no crops being grown apart from grass for hay and silage. A National Trust recruiting Land Rover is generally parked close by, the whole area now being owned by the Trust.

Watendlath also became famous as the home of Judith Paris in the Herries novels by Hugh Walpole. She was only a fictitious character and never actually living in the hamlet.

Refreshments can be obtained at Caffle House close to the bridge.

For Keswick, turn to the right down the road. The permissive path on the opposite side of Watendlath Beck is used in other walks (52) (53). The road is narrow, running between two Lakeland drystone walls. However, these would be constructed many years apart, the left-hand one being probably mid nineteenth century, its having dressed stones and a different top to it. The right-hand wall is of more rounded stones, some at the bottom being quite large, this wall probably dating back another hundred years.

A stone barn by the road is reached. Just after leaving it, note how the Beck crosses over towards the Borrowdale Valley and, in spite of the trees, it can be seen that at the end the valley drops steeply down at the lip where the glacier had been blocked by the glacier coming down Borrowdale. As the road is followed, it can be seen that it is following higher ground than the hanging valley below and to the left.

Surprise View is reached, looking down to Lodore below, up Borrowdale and down Derwentwater to Keswick. Shortly, Ashness Bridge, an old packhorse bridge is crossed. The road drops down and soon comes out onto the Borrowdale road beside Derwentwater (54). Turn right and follow it for Keswick. For much of the way, there is a path to follow a little to the left of the road (55). On reaching a junction, go straight ahead along Borrowdale Road, not following the main traffic. The Moot Hall is reached. Continue along the pedestrianised area, pass the Post Office and continue along the left-hand side of the street to a mini roundabout. Here, turn left and cross the road for the bus stands.

48. Walk 45 crosses the bridge over Dob Gill on the way to Thirlspot.
51. Walk 48 is joined here.
52. The permissive path is used by walk 48 going to Keswick and also walk 55 on its way to Watendlath.
53. By crossing the packhorse bridge and turning left, walk 55 for Rosthwaite is joined.
54. Walk 51 round Derwentwater follows the road to the left.
55. On reaching a good track to the left, walk 52 via Friar's Crag can be followed into Keswick.

WALK 47, THIRLMERE DAM ROAD END TO WYTHBURN CHURCH.

Moderate
6.5 miles
Allow 4.5 hours.

From the bus stops, the road to follow is on the West side of the main road, only a few yards from either of them. Go straight down the road, strictly not quite to the dam, but most walkers will want first to have a look up Thirlmere from there. A few yards before reaching the dam there are steps up to the left leading onto the permissive path. Go through a kissing gate at the top and follow the path along through the woodland at the edge of the lake.

The path passes through mixed woodland and has views back to the dam. It is an undulating path, sometimes some way above Thirlmere and sometimes close to the lakeshore. On reaching some other paths, turn to the left along the main path   A signpost is reached at a cross-roads of paths. Before turning right on the St. Coppice car park path, it is suggested that a diversion is made to the left up Great Howe.

The path is followed up the hillside. A sign is passed, stating that this is the route to Great Howe summit and return by the same route. A junction is reached. There, turn left for the tree-clad summit of Great Howe with its cairn. There is a seat by the cairn with a view across to Castle Crag above Thirlmere. After leaving the summit, return to the junction and follow the other path to another seat. There, a good view is to be had down Thirlmere. On turning to return to the junction there is an excellent view of Skiddaw. Return to the signpost for the St. Coppice car park along the path used for the ascent.

Go straight along the St. Coppice path, which is a good one to follow, at first being at the edge of woodland with a field wall to the left. The path drops down onto another path and then turns left to go through a kissing gate. From there, turn left and follow the path along to another kissing gate which is passed through. In this area are the old field walls from the days before the dam was built and the area afforested. At a junction shortly after the gate there is a waymarker showing the path to take is the one to the right.

Pass along this path, over a more open area near Dalehead and then into woodland again. Pass through another wooden kissing gate and then through an old wall. The path then turns to the left to a major track. On joining the track, an arrow indicates that the way to walk is to the right. Helvellyn is to be seen looming in front to the left. The track continues onwards, goes fairly close to the lakeshore and then reaches a stream tumbling down from the hillside (Helvellyn Gill).

The path goes up by the Gill, through a kissing gate and then up to another kissing gate at a car park by the A591. At this point, there is another permissive path going round to a viewpoint and on round the hillside to the left, which can be followed as a short detour.

For the walk, cross straight over the road and through a kissing gate and follow the path to a car park for

Looking up Birkside Gill

climbers of Helvellyn. To the right of the toilets there is a stile leading onto a track which is the permissive path for Dunmail. Go straight along the track, passing through a field gate near its beginning. Continue straight past the markers for the Swirls Nature Trail and go over a stile by a field gate.

On reaching another field gate there is a sign indicating that the forest track is to be left by turning left up the hillside and onto an old forestry path. This is followed, its shortly becoming a typical woodland path as it is followed along, now quite a bit higher that the forestry road below.

The woodland path is undulating as it passes amongst the trees and there are roots to avoid and muddy and stony patches to cross, so passage is a lot slower here. A wooden footbridge spanning a ghyll is crossed, after which there is a view to the top end of Thirlmere. A more open stretch of ground is reached with two footbridges to cross. The following stretch of path is easy to follow. Some streams flow down the hillside and across the path.

Two large streams are crossed, the second being a waterslide. Shortly afterwards a cross roads of paths is reached, to the left being for Helvellyn and the right for Wythburn Church (46).

Continue straight along the track and over a stile by a field gate. On reaching a point where the track swings round to the right by a signpost (47) follow it downwards. The track comes out onto the A591 by the end of the road for Arnboth at Wythburn.

From Steel End there is a wooden kissing gate to pass through, close to the road, this leading onto a permissive path avoiding the road. Follow the undulating path along, fairly close to the road. When Thirlmere is low, the outlines of old walls can easily be seen from up on this path. On reaching an old forestry track, follow it and then cross a wooden footbridge onto a grassy path and then a gravelly path amongst the trees. This comes out onto a track where turn left for the main road and the bus stops for either direction.

For Wythburn Church, turn right along the roadway on leaving the permissive path and come to the car park behind the church. Here, there is a gate leading into the churchyard.

46. Walk 44 coming up from Wythburn Church is joined here.
47. Walk 44 leaves here to continue to Dunmail and Grasmere.

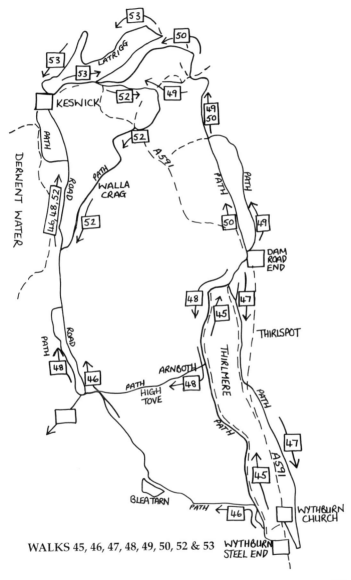

WALKS 45, 46, 47, 48, 49, 50, 52 & 53

WALK 48, THIRLMERE DAM TO KESWICK VIA WATENDLATH.

Moderate
9 miles
Allow six hours, there is a lot to see on the way.

The bus stop from the north is to the south of the road end, whilst that from the south is to the north of the road end. The road branches off westwards from the main Keswick road. Go along it, pass over the dam and come to a triangular road junction. At the end of the left-hand corner of the junction there is a kissing gate with steps leading down to the permissive path to Arnboth. Turn to the right to follow the path along by the shores of Thirlmere.

Mainly, the path follows the shore of the lake, but after about half a mile there is a quite steep rise up to the road, which it is necessary to follow for a short distance until a kissing gate takes the path down to the lakeshore again. The path goes round the back of a knoll, through a kissing gate and across a bridge to the car park at Arnboth, where there are toilets (49). Go out onto the road and turn right to a kissing gate on the left, a few yards away. Go through the gate, which is by a sign indicating Watendlath, and turn left over a small bridge crossing a stream. Next comes some farm penning. There are no stiles, but the pieces of penning spanning the path in two places close together can be moved to get past (and then put back again).

Once past the penning, follow the grassy path up the steep hillside in front. To the left, over the fence, there is a plantation of conifers, first larch and later spruce, whilst to the right is the craggy hillside of Cockrigg Crags. The path becomes stony as it continues onwards and upwards, and can have water running down it in places.

As the path makes its way upwards, there are the Crags above to the right and Fishergill over the fence on the left. Where the fence starts to bear right, the path turns sharp right for a short stretch at the end of which there is a small cairn. Here, turn left and go upwards again towards an isolated tree. Pass the tree and continue on up the hillside. The path is not always clear as it goes over the rough ground towards the plantation fence again. There is another cairn on the way. By continuing onwards, a wall comes into view in front. At the corner of the wall and the fence there is a gap through which to pass.

Once through the wall, the path bears left towards Fishergill and then turns more to the right again. It is a grassy path as it goes up the hillside with the Gill being left behind as the path turns to the right, where it goes by a flat-topped rock convenient to sit on for a breather. The path crosses near to the source of a stream, which is a tributary of Fishergill. Continue along the path as it goes up the hillside, bearing a little to the right.

From here, the route is very grassy as it passes amongst heather and bracken. The ground becomes soft and the path sometimes vanishes. It continues upwards virtually straight ahead to where the highest point of the land in front, High Tove, is seen. On the way there is another cairn with a better stretch of path as it is passed. A cairn can be seen on the top of High Tove. Cross the bed of a small stream and pass another small cairn. From here, the path can be seen making its way up to the summit, some of it being rather wet and some stony.

The summit plateau of High Tove is peaty. It is crossed to a fence with a gate in it. Once through the gate, two small cairns are to be seen indicating the way of the path down to Watendlath. Follow the path downhill. Some of it is soft and peaty and a way across has to be found, but some of it is firm and stony. The path goes more or less straight down the hillside, more little cairns being passed on the way. The trees above Watendlath come into sight.

Watendlath packhorse bridge

211

A wall across the land in front is reached. By the wall is the bridleway (51) coming from Wythburn. Turn right by the wall and continue downwards, crossing a stream. This first part of the bridleway is rather rough. Shortly, there is a marvellous view of Watendlath and Watendlath Tarn below.

The path drops quite steeply down towards Watendlath Farm. At the bottom, cross the stream by a bridge, pass a stile over a wall, and come out at the end of the roadway leading down to Keswick. Instead of following the road (52), cross the picturesque packhorse bridge over Watendlath Beck (53) and turn right through the gate onto a permissive path. Follow this good, clear path for about a mile and a half. It then comes to a junction with the right-hand arm going over a footbridge over the beck. This is the path to take (the other comes up from Lodore and is used in walk 55). A triangular stone in the ground acts instead of a signpost.

Once over the footbridge, go through the gate a few yards ahead, leading into the woodland. The woodland path is followed for about a third of a mile to where it emerges onto the road. Turn left down the road, pass a good viewpoint on the way, cross the famous Ashness Bridge, and drop down to the road beside Derwentwater. Here, turn right for Keswick (54). For much of the way there is a path which can be used instead of walking along the road (55).

On reaching a roundabout go straight ahead along the minor road, part of Borrowdale Road, which leads into the town centre at Keswick. On reaching the main street, pass the Moot Hall and continue onwards, passing the Post Office, until a main road to the left is reached. Turn down it and then cross over to the bus station, which is close by.

49. The route from the bus stop to here is used in reverse by walk 45.
51. Walk 46 uses the bridleway.
52. Walk 46 uses the road.
53. By turning left, walk 55 for Rosthwaite is joined.
54. Walk 51 round Derwentwater follows the road to the left.
55. On reaching a good track to the left, walk 52 via Friar's Crag can be followed to Keswick.

WALK 49, THIRLMERE DAM ROAD END, ST. JOHN'S IN THE VALE, CASTLERIGG STONE CIRCLE, KESWICK.

Easy
6 miles
Allow 3.5 hours.

From the bus stops at Thirlmere Dam Road End, the northbound stop being to the north of the junction and the southbound to the south of the junction, turn northwards towards Keswick for about fifty yards to where there is a wooden ladder stile on the eastern side of the road. Cross it and follow the clear path along. Take the left-hand, waymarked, path at a junction, not the lower, grassy path to the right. Shortly, another junction is reached and here take the lower right-hand path. (The left-hand path is used in walk 50.)

The path then goes through woodland above St. John's Beck, which takes water from Thirlmere to the River Greta. Shortly before reaching a farm go through a kissing gate by a field gate. On reaching the farm, the path goes to the left above the buildings, but you may be tempted down for refreshments.

On reaching a junction follow the left-hand path. It is a very clear one through woodland and easy to follow. On reaching a slate sign indicating Old Bridge End behind and St. John's Church ahead, a five

Sosgill Bridge, St. John's in the Vale

minutes diversion can be taken down the field to the right, passing some old buildings, to Sosgill Bridge, a packhorse bridge.

Back on the main path, follow it along, crossing stiles and passing through gates on the way. On getting well up the Vale, the path turns leftwards and climbs up by the wall. It comes out onto a minor road where turn left for St. John's-in-the-Vale Church a short distance ahead.

Whilst the Church now seems to be located in a remote spot, it must be borne in mind that the road in front of it was once part of an important road from the Naddle Valley (through which the A591 passes to Keswick) across to Wanthwaite and Matterdale. Although the present building only dates from 1845, there has been a church on this site from 1554 and probably much earlier. It was one of five chapels of Crosthwaite, but became a separate parish in 1865 and then joined with Wythburn in 1926.

By the church there is a building that is now Carlisle Youth Centre, but was formerly a school. Chapel House used to stand at the other side of the church, but this is long gone. At Legburthwaite there is still a mission chapel to St. John's Church, its having originally been founded in 1881.

On the right-hand side of the road, roughly opposite the church, there is a stone step stile over the wall, leading to the open country beyond (56). Cross over to the right, fording a stream, and then follow the grassy path round leftwards towards where there is a dip to be seen in the distant wall. On reaching the wall there is a stone step stile to cross.

Once over the wall there is a waymarker showing that the path to follow bears to the right towards Tewet Tarn with the right-hand end of Skiddaw being seen beyond. On reaching a gate in a fence, continue along the grassy path in the direction of Blencathra. The path passes to the right of Tewet Tarn and at the next wall, to the right of a fenced off gateway, there is a stone step stile to cross.

The path then follows the line it had been taking before the fenced gateway to another waymarker and there turns to the right towards the wall in front. Go along by the wall, drop down and bear round to the left. Pass through a gateway in the wall in front and then drop down to the right-hand corner of the field and out onto a minor road.

Once on the road, turn left. On reaching a road junction, again go left and at a further junction left again (57). A few hundred yards along the road Naddle Bridge crosses the very small Naddle Beck. Once over the bridge, on the left, there is a stone step stile dropping into the field where turn right towards a ladder stile over a wall. There, turn left to the nearby gateway and once through it go diagonally right up the field to the far corner. At the top go through a gate and across a narrow field to a gate out onto a road.

Turn left along the road for about a quarter of a mile, passing another footpath on the way (58). A footpath sign at a notice board by a gate indicates that the field with the stone circle has been reached.

Castlerigg Stone Circle is not a true circle, but is distorted by flattening on its eastern side. There are thirty-eight stones forming the main circle with a further ten making a rectangular enclosure on the south eastern side, its being unique. To see the circle when it is being struck by the sunlight but Blencathra is in the shade behind is very atmospheric. At the north side there are two stones forming a definite entrance to the ring.

It is thought that Castlerigg is one of the earliest stone circles and would be constructed around 3000 B.C., in Neolithic times. The stones are from the Borrowdale Volcanic Group, the type of rock to the south of here. The reason for the construction of the circle is not known, but Professor Alexander Thorn considers that such circles were for astronomical purposes. Another theory is that it was a place of trade, particularly for stone axes, which were made locally, three of which were found within the circle. Nothing has been found to support the popular belief that the circle was a place of Pagan worship and human sacrifice.

On leaving the field, continue straight along the road again towards Keswick. This minor road eventually joins the busy main road. At the next junction go to the right along the town centre road. In 250 or so yards a bridge crosses the track of the former railway line. Drop down onto the track and turn to the right and then follow the track bed along to the former Keswick station and walk the length of the platform.

Turn left at the end of the platform to drop down to a road and go straight down it, passing Keswick Museum, to a junction. Cross the pedestrian crossing and turn right down the road. At the bottom, by the Post Office, cross the end of the pedestrianised area and turn right along the road to the next junction. There, turn left and cross the road for the bus stands.

56. The next section of path is also used by walk 50.
57. Walk 50 is left here.
58. The path is used in walk 52.

Reflections in Derwentwater, Nichol End.
Ashness Bridge and Skiddaw.

Derwentwater from Walla Crag.
In Brundholme Wood.

Cloudcapped Skiddaw from Uzzicar.
Bridge over Newlands Beck at Little Braithwaite.

Pony by packhorse bridge at Watendlath.
Yew Tree Farm, Rosthwaite.

WALK 50, HIGH RIGG, ST JOHN'S IN THE VALE, OLD RAILWAY, KESWICK

Moderate
7.5 to 8 miles
Allow 4.5 hours.

This walk starts at the Thirlmere Dam Road end bus stops. From the stops, turn northwards, the Keswick direction, for about 50 yards to where there is a wooden ladder stile on the eastern side of the road. Cross it and follow the path, ignoring a way down on the right, to where there is a junction of paths. Turn up the left-hand path, which climbs quite steeply up the hillside, the right-hand one being used in walk 49.

On its way up, the path goes to the left of the rocky hillside in front before turning right to a top and some pines. From there, the path continues to climb upwards with part of St. John's in the Vale to be seen below to the right. It then continues along, just to the left of the top of the ridge before coming right out onto the top, with a view straight along the Vale to Blencathra, and over to the left to Skiddaw.

Shortly after leaving that viewpoint the path drops down quite steeply to an old drystone wall before climbing up again to the top of the hillside. The path continues along the ridge in an undulating fashion and does wind about between the Keswick side and the St. John's side. A stile in a fence is crossed, near which there is a very good view back towards Helvellyn. Here, the grassy path is on the Keswick side of the ridge.

A dip in the ground is reached and the path then turns to the right and passes an area of rough stone. After this, the path drops to the left and then crosses a wall by a ladder stile before going straight up the hillside, quite close to a wall. A rather boggy stretch is crossed and the path then continues close to the wall again. A very good view of Skiddaw is reached. Shortly after this, the path goes up the hillside and to the right, from where there is a very good view of St. John's in the Vale. The path goes round a rocky outcrop which is the summit of the ridge and then drops down the hillside.

The grassy path splits and then joins up again as it drops steeply down the hillside on the way to St. John's Church. Pass through a

217

kissing gate in a wall just above the former school and then follow the grassy path round the back of the building and onto the roadway.

Turn right along the road for a few yards and, before reaching the church (56), there is a squeeze stile crossing the wall at the top of some stone steps on the left. Bear to the right, crossing over a stream and join a grassy path passing straight through bracken on either side. The path is going towards a dip in a wall some distance ahead. On reaching the wall there is a stone slab stile to cross.

Once over the stile, go along the grassy path, which is initially in the direction of the right-hand end of Skiddaw. Shortly, Blencathra comes into view as well and Tewet Tarn is seen in front. Go through a wooden field gate and continue along the grassy path which passes just above Tewet Tarn. To the right of the fenced gateway in the next wall reached there is a stone slab stile to cross. From there, the path crosses the field, continuing the line as though it had gone straight through the gateway.

Cross a small gully and turn to the right, the path going up to the wall and then round by it to the right. At the end of the wall, turn through a gateway into the next field and drop down the path, bearing right towards the gate at the bottom right hand corner. There, go out onto the road and turn left.

High Rigg from Low Rigg

Follow the road to a junction where go left. At the following junction (57) continue straight on ahead, going towards the main road to be seen in front. Turn left at a bend and here there is a metal crash barrier. On the other side of the barrier there is a wooden stile leading down to a permissive path down to the main road. On reaching the busy road, turn right for a few yards to the end of the crash barrier on its far side, close to which a stile is to be seen. There, cross straight over, taking great care as it is a fast and busy stretch of road with motorists not expecting pedestrians.

Cross the stile into the field and then drop down the permissive path to the bottom of the field. There, the path crosses a stile to the bridge which takes the permissive path along the old railway line to Keswick.

At the time of writing, the possibility of reopening the railway line from Penrith to Keswick is under serious consideration, together with the possibility of raising the necessary finance. Primarily, the line would be for tourist traffic, but that is not why the Cockermouth, Keswick and Penrith line was originally built. The growth of the iron industry in the West Cumberland brought about the need for a railway line to bring coke across the Pennines from the South Durham coalfield. Originally, the North Eastern Railway operated the freight traffic and the London and North Western Railway operated the passenger operations.

The line was opened to freight from 4 November 1864 and to passengers from 2 January the following year. The making of coke from West Cumberland coal improved, resulting in that traffic having disappeared by the middle of the 1920's, but the line, by then part of the London, Midland and Scottish Railway, continued with passenger and local goods traffic. The car undermined the profitability of the railway so that in April 1966 it was closed west of Keswick. The rest of the line struggled on until it too closed on 6 March 1972.

Keswick station had extensive facilities for passengers, there being three platforms (only one now being left), a turntable and carriage sidings. The building housed the head offices of the railway company, which was originally independent even though other companies ran the trains. The adjacent Keswick Hotel was originally promoted by the railway.

Go through a gate onto the former line and turn left across the bridge. Continue straight along the path, seeing the River Greta through the trees and from bridges along the way. At Low Briery there is a platform from the days when timber was brought to the bobbin mill there. Now there is a holiday complex. Shortly after leaving the complex the path leaves the railway track to go up through the wood until it reaches the main road and then it drops down to the track again. It passes under the award winning bridge taking the A66 over the former railway and the River Greta.

Continue straight along the railway track and pass under a road bridge (59) and continue along to the station buildings. At the end of the former platform turn left, past Keswick Leisure Pool, and left again onto the road. Go straight down the road to a junction. About a hundred yards to the left there is a bus stop for the south. Alternatively, cross the pedestrian crossing and turn right down the road. At the bottom of it, cross the end of the pedestrianised area and turn right along the main road and at the next junction turn left for the bus stands.

56. The next stretch of path is also used by walk 49.
57. Walk 49 is left here.
59. Walk 52 uses the road bridge going to the Stone Circle.

WALK 51, KESWICK, ROUND DERWENTWATER, PORTINSCALE, KESWICK

Easy

12 miles

Allow 5.5 to 6 hours.

Keswick is derived from the Old English for 'cheese farm', showing the town's agricultural origins. In the 1800's there were fairs in October and May for the sale of cattle, rams and cheese. In addition, at Whitsuntide and Martinmas there were hiring fairs for the hiring of farmhands and servants. Those servants for hire had a straw stuck in a hat or from the corner of the mouth to indicate that they were available for hire and not staying with their original employer. In addition, there was the weekly Saturday market which had been held from 1276 when Edward I granted its charter, and which is still held today.

Also held each Saturday were the Petty Sessions, the equivalent of the modern Magistrates' Court, these taking place in the Town Hall. In addition, there was a fortnightly meeting of the Board of Guardians, a monthly County Court and a Court Baron on 22 May.

The Town Hall, or Moot Hall, now housing the Tourist Information Office, was built in 1813 on the site of an old courthouse. In 1861, from a directory of that year, Mr. Reginald Dykes Marshall, who was the lord of the manor, owned the Town Hall.

As now, Keswick had a wide variety of shops in 1861, but some of the goods stocked or made locally were very different from today, there being cloggers, shoemakers, a wool repository, a saddler and harness maker, a watchmaker, a straw bonnet maker, a nail manufacturer and others besides the types of establishments still to be found around the town.

Back in the sixth century Saint Kentigern, the patron saint of Glasgow, planted his preaching cross in a clearing by where the 'river of the oak trees' left one lake to flow into a second, the river being the Derwent (but its name could also mean 'clear water') and flowing from Derwentwater into Bassenthwaite Lake. The present church of the Parish of Crosthwaite is on the same site. Its foundations date from 1181 whilst the main building is 16th century with restoration work having been done in 1844.

Until 1856 the whole of Keswick was in the parish of Crosthwaite, but from then it was split with the part of the town to the south and to the east of the Town Hall becoming separate and in the parish of St. John the Evangelist.

One of the attractions of Keswick is the Pencil Museum. Originally graphite (also known as black lead, wadd or plumbago) from the mine at Seathwaite in Borrowdale was used in the making of pencils, its being the best graphite to be found. However, the mine has long been closed and imported materials are now used. The pencil industry started in Keswick during the reign of Queen Elizabeth I and still continues. However, pencils are now made by machine and not by hand as was done originally.

Another unusual attraction in the town is the 'Cars of the Stars' Museum, where various cars that have been used in films or on television are to be seen.

16 August 1999 saw the main contractor formally hand over the keys to the Theatre by the Lake and just three days later the first performance took place in the last theatre to be opened in the twentieth century. It had long been hoped to build a permanent theatre in Keswick. From 1975 there had been the Century Theatre's mobile 'Blue Box' on the Lakeside car park, but it was not a permanent building. Without a £3.1 million lottery grant in May 1996, the theatre would probably not yet have been built. The 'Blue Box' was dismantled and taken away in November 1996 in readiness for the permanent theatre to be built on the site.

In November 1997 planning consent was obtained and in June the following year the building work was started. At that time the new theatre had no name and was called the theatre by the lake. After public consultation, in December 1998, 'Theatre by the Lake' became its official name as there was nothing more appropriate, its being so close to the shores of Derwentwater and the boats being only a few hundred yards away. The original sketch for the building was done by a man named Christopher from Theatre Futures whilst sailing round the lake on a passenger launch.

The theatre has two houses, the Main House and the Studio, which is a much smaller and very intimate theatre. During the main season, the repertory company performs plays in both theatres, the one in the Studio having a cast of only one or two actors. The first two plays in the Main House were the opening production which was Brandon Thomas's 'Charley's Aunt'. This was followed by a play written by James Plumtre in the 1790's but not professionally performed before, 'The Lakers'. It is set in the area around Keswick and took a wry look at early tourism. The two plays then alternated so that visitors could see both of them and 'Two' in the Studio. In 2000 there were three Main House plays and two Studio plays alternating. There are many other events held in the theatre, including a play for the Christmas season, and there are not many days in the year when it is closed.

From the bus stands at Keswick, cross the road and turn left to go round The Headlands (do not go down the road to the right) and then along The Heads. At the end of The Heads, turn right along a very short stretch of road to parkland. Follow the main pathway and then road along as it passes by Hope Park and the Theatre by the Lake on its way to the piers at the edge of Derwentwater.

Go straight along the roadway above the piers and at its end follow the track along to Friars Crag where there are a number of paths. Here, there is a memorial to John Ruskin. From the end of Friar's Crag, turn back a few yards and take a path to the right, leading down to a wooden gate and into the field bordering Derwentwater. Follow the path along and into some woodland. Pass through a gate into a field where there is an unsurfaced roadway. Turn right along it and continue straight along, through a gate by a cattle grid, and passing a National Trust sign indicating it is a path to Calfclose Bay.

At a junction in the track, take the left-hand path and continue on round the edge of Derwentwater. Pass through a gate and follow the path just above the lakeshore. Reach a point where the path is by the Borrowdale road, and then it turns a little to the right again, coming back to by the lake. Cross a small wooden footbridge and turn up to the road again and follow it to the right.

Whilst it is shortly possible to follow a path again below the road, it is not worth doing so. Continue along the road, which passes the Ashness Landing (52). Shortly afterwards come to a fence with a stile to cross and follow the path along by the lakeshore again. Cross over a small wooden footbridge and continue along the grassy path by the shore of the lake until it comes out onto the road.

Cross the road by a car park and there is a permissive path opposite, avoiding the traffic on the road. Turn right along the path and follow it along, passing where another path joins it from the right. Go through a wooden gate and then along a stony stretch of path and then through another wooden gate. At a junction shortly reached there is a waymarker indicating the left-hand path is taken. Continue straight on along the main path, ignoring another coming from the road and one going to the left. At the next junction, turn right to drop down and cross a footbridge spanning Watendlath Beck.

(A diversion to Lodore Falls can be taken at the junction of the paths by going left up to the falls and then returning the same way.)

Launch at Hawes End

Once over the bridge, turn left round the back of the Stakis Lodore Hotel (where there is an honesty box for those visiting the Falls) and out onto the road. Turn left, pass the public conveniences and about the same distance further on there is a stile in the wall to the right. Cross it and follow the path over the footbridge spanning the River Derwent. From there, go straight over the wooden walkway in front, crossing a marshy area.

On reaching a rocky knoll by the head of the lake (60), cross over it and onto another stretch of wooden walkway quite close to the lake, passing through a gate on the way. Firm ground is reached and continue along the path by the lakeshore. Follow the path along, over some more wooden walkways and come to a point just after one of them where there is a path going over to the right. Go down it to the shore of the lake and turn left. Follow the path along as it wanders amongst the trees and close to the water. At Myrtle Bay there is a fence with a stile to cross and then turn left up to the main path, which is part of the Cumbria Way, where turn right along it.

The path turns inland through some woodland before reaching the next bay, Abbot's Bay. From there, follow the stony track along, sometimes closer to the lake shore than at others. Pass the Manesty Cloutie Tree, which has raised money for the peoples of Tibet. Every ribbon tied to the tree represents a wish or a prayer. This tree is at Brandlehow Bay.

Go through a kissing gate by a field gate and then to the right for Brandlehow. At the lake, cross a stile and follow the path to the left as it goes right round on the shore. The land around Brandlehow was the first in the Lake District to be purchased by the National Trust, this being to stop the building of a railway from Keswick to the mines.

Continue along the path, walking through the woods close to the lake. At the next bay, go straight over the field and by the fence. At the end, turn right to go through a wooden gate by a field gate. Continue along the trackway with open country on the left, looking up to Cat Bells. Continue round to the right by the lakeshore, ignoring a footpath for Lingholm and Keswick going off to the left. Reach the path down to Hawes End landing stage, pass it and continue along the path up to a road where turn right.

A few yards along the road pass the one from the Newlands Valley on the left (61) and the entrance to Derwent Bay Sawmill on the right and a few yards further there is a kissing gate to the right. Follow the path from the gate, pass through a small gate at the end of a footbridge and then go straight over an open field. A kissing gate by a field gate leads into woodland and shortly come to a wooden gate leading onto a driveway, which is crossed and the path goes along by a wall. A path going to the left is passed (62). Cross straight over a driveway and continue along the path. Shortly, Nichol End, with its Marina, is reached. There, turn left up to the road for Keswick.

Turn right along the road for a third of a mile to Portinscale. On reaching that village, the main road for Keswick turns sharply left, but the walk turns to the right, there is a footpath sign. The buildings along the road are a reminder of the times of various rural crafts, Farrier House, Smithy Cottage, Force Cottage. Pass the Derwentwater Hotel, outside which are the stone steps of a mounting block. At the end of the roadway there is a suspension bridge for pedestrians spanning the River Derwent.

Portinscale is said to mean 'the harlot's hut'! The only industry there now is tourism related, but this was not always so. A stone axe finishing factory was located here, their having been roughly shaped out on the fells, but brought here for shaping and polishing.

After crossing the bridge there is a pathway off through the fence to the right. This path comes out onto the roadway again, but immediately turn right to follow another path for Keswick. Go through wooden gates onto the path and then straight along it At the end of the path, pass through another wooden gate and then turn left up to the main road. There, turn right, cross the bridge over the River Greta and, on reaching the main road junction in about 175 yards, turn right for the bus stands.

51. Walks 46, 49 and 52 are met here.
60. Walk 55 crosses the walkway to Lodore here.
61. Walk 54 joins here.
62. Walk 54 uses this other path, which is part of the Cumbria Way.

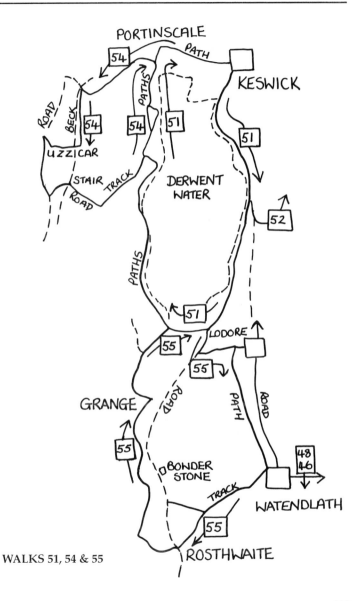

PORTINSCALE

PATH

KESWICK

54

54

54

51

51

ROAD

BECK

UZZICAR

STAIR

TRACK

ROAD

52

DERWENT WATER

PATHS

51

LODORE

55

55

GRANGE

ROAD

PATH

ROAD

55

48
46

BONDER STONE

WATENDLATH

TRACK

55

ROSTHWAITE

WALKS 51, 54 & 55

WALK 52 KESWICK, CASTLERIGG STONE CIRCLE, WALLA CRAG, ASHNESS BRIDGE, KESWICK.

Moderate
8.5 miles
Allow 4.5 hours.

From the bus stands at Keswick, follow the bus route back, going up to the main road and turning right. Go to the start of the pedestrianised area where turn left up Bank Street. Follow this road up to a pedestrian crossing, which cross, and go straight up Station Road, passing over the River Greta and by Keswick Museum. Station Road turns right, passes in front of Keswick Hotel and then passes under a bridge taking the former railway track into the station. Once under the bridge, turn right up some steps to join the track bed just beyond the end of the station and turn left away from it at the top.

Go along the railway track to an over bridge, pass under it and turn left up the steps to the road (59). Turn left and cross the bridge. Cross the road before reaching the junction with the Windermere road just ahead at Chestnut Hill. Cross over the top of Windermere Road and continue along the main road for about fifty yards to where a minor road leads off to the right and take it. A sign indicates that this is the road for Castlerigg Stone Circle. Come to a road junction to the right and pass over it to the gates leading into the field in which there is the Stone Circle. The stone circle can also be reached by going down the road to a gate there.

After exploring the stone circle, come out at the gates at the top and turn right along the road for about 150 yards to where there is a wooden gate leading onto the path for The Nest (58). This path can be very muddy. Go by the fence on the right and then continue ahead along the grassy field path as the fence bears off to the right. The path crosses a stream and then comes to a wooden ladder stile into the next field. Go straight over that field and over another wooden ladder stile continuing straight ahead. Cross another wooden ladder stile and then go by the fence on the left of the field. The path becomes a farm track shortly before reaching The Nest. Go through a field gate, past the buildings of The Nest, and then along a tarred roadway.

Pass through a wooden gate by a cattle grid and continue along the roadway to the A591 ahead. Go to the right along the road for about 80 yards to the junction with the road down from by the Stone Circle, and which can be followed instead of the footpath to this point. There are 555 bus stops here.

At the junction, cross straight over the A591 onto the good, gravelly path for Walla Crag going up the field in front. At the top of the field a wooden stile is crossed into the next field and the path followed fairly close to the fence on the right. Come to a wooden ladder stile to the left of a field gate and continue by the fence, which becomes a wall, on the right to the next ladder stile at the corner of the field, also to the left of a field gate.

In the following field the path is rather sunken as it passes along by the wall on the right, and keeps along by the same wall after crossing another stile. Part of Derwentwater comes into view. The path comes out onto a roadway where turn left to its end at Rakefoot, ignoring the path opposite for Great Wood.

The roadway comes to a junction where take the right-hand track to pass by Rakefoot. At the roadway's end, cross a wooden footbridge over the stream and then go onto the Walla Crag path. The path to follow is to the right of the farm track, which has forded the stream. Shortly there are good views right round from Derwentwater to Blencathra. A wooden stile by a field gate is crossed and the stony path is followed, ignoring the farm track. Follow the path up the hillside, passing close to a wall and then leaving it again. Cross a small stream and then go straight up the path in front, ignoring the one to the right.

The hillside path passes through a wooden kissing gate and then continues along it from there. Very shortly the route is passing along the top of Walla Crag, again with excellent views all round. Continue along the top of the crag, its being a little undulating, and come to its actual summit. From there the path drops downwards and crosses a wooden stile. Once over it, turn right to a junction of paths. Ignore the grassy one going down to the right and follow the leftwards path over the open country. The path passes a small cairn.

The path is a mixture of grassy and gravelly as it continues on its way, basically above Derwentwater, and passing over some small streams. It reaches a point where it looks up the Watendlath Valley to the left of Borrowdale. From there, the path steadily descends, at one point going a little to the left, on its way to Ashness Bridge. Go through a small wooden gate in a wall, seeing the bridge down below to the

Friar's Crag, Derwentwater

right. The path goes ahead towards Barrow Beck and then turns right to drop down towards the road. Cross a wooden stile to the right of a gate and drop down to Ashness Bridge.

From Ashness Bridge (53) turn right down the road to the main Borrowdale road by Derwentwater (54). Turn right along that road for about a mile, on the way coming to the path by the wall on the left, avoiding walking along the road itself. On reaching a good track leading off to the left, turn down it. Pass through a gate by a cattle grid. On reaching a point where the track bends to the left there is a wooden gate by a field gate over to the right. Go through this gate (60) and follow the track along.

Go through another wooden gate and over a bridge by a stream and follow the path along close to the lakeshore. As Friar's Crag is approached go along the path above the lake, through a gate, and turn left up some steps. Pass along the path, above Derwentwater and pass Ruskin's Monument on the right. Go right round the viewpoint and then continue along the path above the lake. This reaches a point where either the roadway or the shingle can be followed to the landing stages.

From the landing stages continue along the road, pass the Theatre by the Lake and go on the left-hand side of the road and then over the pathway by the park, leaving the road. This path comes out onto a road where turn left for about 50 yards to a junction where cross over the junction. Follow the road in front of the hotels along The Heads and keep on round a corner to the right, where the bus stands are seen just ahead across the road.

53. Walks 46 and 48 from Watendlath are met at Ashness Bridge.
54. Walk 51 round Derwentwater follows the Borrowdale road to the left.
58. Walk 49 from St. John's in the Vale is met here.

59. Walk 50 is met at this bridge.
60. Walk 51 use the track from Keswick to here and then continues along to the left to pass round Derwentwater.

WALK 53 KESWICK, BRUNDHOLME WOOD, LATRIGG, FITZ PARKS, KESWICK.

Easy
6.5 miles
Allow 4 hours.

From the bus stands, go straight back up to the main road and up Bank Street and cross the road at the pedestrian crossing. Continue straight along Penrith Road, which is the route the bus follows, close to the River Greta. Follow the road along and come to an iron gate on the left, just before reaching Blencathra Street, which is across the road. Go through the iron gate and follow the path along by the river. Return to the footpath by the road at another iron gate and pass an old railway bridge.

An area of parkland, Town Head Trust, on the left is entered by another iron gate. Pass over there and follow the path above the river. (Alternatively, you can go straight across the field.) The path comes out onto a roadway where turn left to Force Mill. Pass a few buildings until a bridge spanning the River Greta is seen to the left. Cross the bridge and turn right to go through a wooden gate and onto the permissive path along Forge Brow.

The path passes beneath the award winning bridge carrying the A66 over the Greta. It is a good path to follow. On reaching a junction, take the left-hand path, the one to the right leading to the walk along the former railway. Continue straight on along the path through Brundholme Wood, ignoring another path to the right to the former railway. Follow the path ahead until it reaches an open field in front. Here, it turns left on a hairpin bend and in a few yards a minor road is reached.

Turn right along the road. From along the road there is a good view towards Helvellyn in one direction and Cat Bells in another. The road is followed for about a quarter of a mile to a signpost indicating Skiddaw and Underscar on the left. (From here it is a very pleasant diversion to go on down the road and then left along the footpath, which crosses Whit Beck, and perhaps up to Blencathra Centre, returning the same way.)

At the signpost, cross the stile to the left of a field gate and immediately there is a path to the left with a much broader main track to the right, one well used by horses. Follow the main right-hand track along for a little over half a mile and go through a field gate. Here there is a choice, either bear left up a grassy field path until it joins a main path or continue along the bottom path until just before another field gate is reached and then turn left up the hillside to join the main path. (Walkers seem to split fairly evenly which way is followed.)

The path goes gently up the hillside and then to the left of some wire fencing. Follow it along with a steep drop down on the left. Pass

through a gate in the fence in front and continue along the path at the top of a quite steep drop to the left. It goes gently along, passing over the highest point of Latrigg on the way. From up here there are good views of Derwentwater, into the Newlands Valley, Skiddaw and Blencathra.

The path turns sharply to the right on reaching a seat looking out over

Summit of Latrigg

Bassenthwaite Lake. It is a grassy path going down the back of Latrigg for about three quarters of a mile and zigzags down the hillside at one point. The path comes out onto a stony track in front of a plantation, where turn to the left and follow the boundary fence on the right. Pass through a kissing gate by a field gate and then past a recent plantation. Continue dropping down the path, over a point where there has been water erosion, and eventually reach a kissing gate to the left of a field gate.

Pass through the kissing gate and along the broad track in front, crossing the A66 by a large bridge. Shortly after, come out onto a residential road and turn to the right. In about two hundred yards, after passing the sight of a former railway bridge, there is a metal gate on the left. Go through it and straight ahead by the former railway track until the path swings to the right at the end of Fitz Parks. Come to one path turning left and another going right, which is the one to follow down to the River Greta.

On reaching the river, turn left to follow its bank along to some steps leading out onto a road bridge. Cross the bridge and go down Station Road to the junction, cross at the pedestrian crossing and turn right straight down the road for the town centre. Cross the end of the pedestrianised area and turn right along the main road to the next left turn, where cross over and turn down the road for the bus stands.

WALK 54, KESWICK, PORTINSCALE, NEWLANDS VALLEY, PORTINSCALE, KESWICK

Easy
7.5 miles
Allow 3.5 to 4 hours.

From the bus stands in Keswick, go back up to the main road and turn left to cross Greta Bridge and immediately afterwards turn left onto the footpath for Portinscale. The first few yards of the path are tarred and then turn right to pass through a wooden gate onto the path by the hedge on the right hand side of the field then entered. Follow this path to its end, passing through a kissing gate on the way. The path comes out onto a roadway where turn left to the suspension bridge spanning the River Derwent.

Pass over the bridge and into Portinscale. Follow the main road along through the village for about two hundred yards from its centre, ignoring a road to the left going towards Borrowdale. To the left of the road is a signpost indicating the footpath for Ullock, which is followed. It is a good track, terminating at a gate out onto a roadway. Turn left along the road for about fifteen yards to where there is a footpath on the right, passing between two hedges.

A small wooden footbridge spans a stream and then the clear, gravelly path is followed in front. Close to the dwellings at the end there is a wooden gate to pass through and then turn left along the last stretch of path to the road. Turn right along the road for about half a mile, passing through Ullock, and then at a junction turn right along the road for Braithwaite.

The road crosses a very minor stream and then comes to a very attractive stone bridge over Newlands Beck. Do not cross the bridge, but immediately before it turn left to pass through a wooden kissing gate leading onto the bank of the beck. Follow the path by the beck for about three quarters of a mile to where there is an attractive little stone footbridge to cross. From there follow the farm track up to Uzzicar where it turns right to go up to a minor road.

Names such as Uzzicar and Ullock have Norse Origins, referring the 'the place where wolves play' and 'a dwelling house with a cultivated field'.

The lovely, quiet Newlands Valley was once the scene of much mining activity. During the reign of Queen Elizabeth I the Company of Mines Royal was incorporated to work some of the mines in the valley, it probably being the first such company in the north of England. The miners, because of their greater experience, came from Germany, but were at first distrusted locally. For safety, they at first lived on Derwent Island and sailed over to Nichol End. At that time, copper was the main metal extracted in the valley. It was smelted at Brigham, by the River Greta, and the ingots received the official mark at the Queens Receiving House in the Moot Hall. Cromwell's forces destroyed the smelters during the Civil War and, as a result, the mines closed.

During the nineteenth century mining was revived, this time being mainly for lead. Barrow Mine was an extensive lead mine, most of the workings being on the west side of the road, later workings being on the east side. Operations ceased in 1889.

A major mine for both periods of workings was the Goldscope Mine, the name having nothing to do with gold but being a local corruption of 'Gottesgab' (God's Gift). Now, just spoil heaps, roadways and the sites of entrances are all that remain of this former industry in the Newlands Valley.

At Stair, a small village in the valley, a mill was built for the manufacture of woollen blankets and other goods, its power coming from Newlands Beck. The mill has now been converted to dwellings.

Towards Blencathra from Skelgill

On reaching the road, turn left and pass above Uzzicar Farm. On reaching a footpath on the right, which is not followed, look over the fields and see the circular hollow of the disused Barrow Mine. Continue along the road, pass Stoneycroft, and at the next road junction turn sharp left to go down to the village of Stair.

Newlands Beck is crossed again at Stair. About fifty yards from the bridge is another road junction where the very minor gated road ahead is taken, not the road to the left. The road followed is for Skelgill. On the way up this road there is a good view up the Newlands Valley. Pass through a gate across the road and go up towards the farm at Skelgill in front. Turn left to pass in front of the farmhouse and then turn left again to come to another gate across the road.

Follow the road for about half a mile, passing a car park and the footpath up Cat Bells and come to a road junction. There, take the left-hand road and shortly pass through a wooden gate to the right of a cattle grid and follow the path down again towards the road. It then comes to a corner where it turns left, but the track to follow is straight in front. A signpost indicates Hawes End. Follow the path straight ahead through some woodland and come to another minor road which is crossed (62). To the left at the other side is a wooden kissing gate to pass through and follow the path for Lingholm. There is a plantation on either side of this stretch of path. The path is followed for roughly 200 yards and then a bridge over a stream is crossed and the gravelly path followed in front. At its end there is a wooden kissing gate by a field gate into more woodland.

Some houses in the woodland are reached. Pass through a small wooden gate, over the roadway and then continue along the gravelly path by the wall for a hundred or so yards to where another path leading into the woodland is seen on the left (63). Follow it through the woodland, its being part of the Cumbria Way.

The path comes out onto the road for Portinscale where turn right, passing the way up from Nichol End. On reaching the middle of Portinscale, turn right to follow the road to the footbridge and having crossed it turn right along the path across the fields which had been used at the start of this walk. At the end, turn left to the road where turn right, cross the bridge and take the next turning right for the bus stands.

62. Walk 51 is joined here.
63. Walk 51 is left here.

WALK 55, KESWICK FOR LODORE, WATENDLATH, ROSTHWAITE, GRANGE-IN-BORROWDALE, LODORE FOR KESWICK.

Moderate
7.5 miles
Allow 4.5 to 5 hours from Lodore Hotel for the full walk via Rosthwaite.

From the bus stands at Keswick, either walk to Lodore by road or following the beginning of walk 51, or go on the Seatoller bus. If desired, the falls, which are reached from by the Stakis Lodore Hotel, can be visited before doing the walk. From Lodore, continue along the road towards High Lodore and, on reaching the farm on the left, High Lodore Farm, at the beginning of High Lodore, turn left along the public footpath, which is indicated. (If not going to the falls, the reader can stay on the bus to Borrowdale Hotel and then turn back a short distance along the road from Keswick to the farm.)

The path goes in front of the farm and then turns to the left round the buildings. Follow the stony path upwards until a bend to the right is reached. Over to the right a seat is to be seen with a path going in front of it. This is the path to follow, not the one going ahead at the bend. It is a stony path to follow as it goes quite steeply up the hillside, first going to the right and then turning back to the left. From up here there is a good view of Derwentwater.

The path reaches more level ground at the top and passes through a wall. It continues on its undulating way and comes to Watendlath Beck, flowing below towards the falls. Continue along the path and into woodland. A wooden stile in a fence is crossed and the path followed to where it joins another path, and there turn right.

Follow this good path along and go through a kissing gate. Shortly, a junction (63) is reached, where there is a triangular marker in the ground, and there turn right along by Watendlath Beck. Follow the permissive path up the beck. Generally, the path is close to the stream, but at one point it does turn right and up some steps at the top of which there is a wooden gate to go through before turning back again to the left.

The path is back by Watendlath Beck again as the hamlet is reached. For the walk, it is not necessary to cross the packhorse bridge spanning the beck (53), but most people have a rest around here and partake of some refreshments.

From by the bridge, continue straight along the track, through a wooden kissing gate by a field gate and just beyond take the higher right-hand track at the junction. It is a good path to follow as it climbs up the hillside and then crosses over the more level ground at the top.

Go through a kissing gate by a field gate. The top end of Borrowdale is to be seen spread out in front. As the path drops down, it becomes rougher The view expands, taking in Stonethwaite, Rosthwaite, Seatoller, and across to Honister Pass and the surrounding fells. A kissing gate leading down to the road for Keswick and the Bowder Stone is passed, an alternative ending for this walk.

A field gate on the right is reached and passed through, the path which was being followed to here going onto Stonethwaite. Follow the track downwards, through another field gate and then along a wooden walkway above the track to avoid fording two streams. On reaching a signpost by a bridge spanning Stonethwaite Beck, turn right to cross it. The track leads to the main road where turn left into Rosthwaite.

Rosthwaite is a township in the Borrowdale valley, and is near where there would anciently have been another lake following the retreat of the glaciers, but which has now become dry ground. Even as recently as 1861 Borrowdale was regarded as 'at once awful, grand and interesting' and had 'promontories and sudden projections of naked rocks, intersected by fearful and fathomless chasms'.

In past times Borrowdale was part of the ancient manor of Castlerigg, which was owned by the Derwentwater estate. The Court Baron was held annually at the inn at Rosthwaite. Following the dissolution of the monasteries it became Crown property.

Roads in the area were to connect with the monasteries and ran east and south rather than north to Keswick. The route from Watendlath was an old coffin trail and a resting stone is still marked on the Ordnance Survey map. The monks used this route on their way to Wythburn via Harrop Tarn.

The name Rosthwaite comes from 'a clearing with a heap of stones'. Nearby is a very famous boulder, the 2,000 ton Bowder Stone, deposited by a glacier some 12,000 years ago. Until the 1800's the road up Borrowdale passed by its base.

Down Rosthwaite track to Watendlath

At the road junction opposite Rosthwaite Post Office, turn right along the minor road, passing the village hall, to the very attractive Yew Tree Farm, where refreshments can be obtained. Continue along the track beyond the farm, its being for Grange, and pass over an attractive little Lakeland stone bridge and then turn right along the path. Pass through a field gate, cross the field and come to two field gates side by side. There, cross the stile by the right-hand gate and follow the path along by the River Derwent.

The riverside path is part of the Cumbria Way and is a good path to follow. It turns a little inland from the river and passes a path going up the hillside to the left. Continue straight along the main path, which enters the woodland in front at a kissing gate by a field gate.

On reaching a junction, take the much better left-hand path. Pass some very minor paths and pass the entrance to an old slate quarry. There are two slate cairns by the path along here. Continue through a gap in the wall reached in front and then pass along the right-hand edge of an old slate spoil heap. Continue along the main path, ignoring minor ones to the left and right.

Just up from the quarry area, at a proper junction of paths, take the one to the right.

Go through a gap in a drystone wall and turn right to follow a reconstructed path. Drop down to the river again and continue along the path by it.

Go over a stile by a field gate and continue along the path, passing two small weirs. Follow the track round by a wall with a car park above and come out onto a minor road where turn right. This is by Hollows Farm. Keep straight along the road to Grange in Borrowdale.

Grange in Borrowdale gets its name from when the Cistercian Monks of Furness Abbey placed a few of their number at the entrance to Borrowdale to receive and guard their crops. Here was their granary or 'Grange'.

Whilst there was not much mining in Borrowdale, Grange was one place where it took place. Nearby there was a slate quarry. Close to Derwentwater was a lead mine, but it was not very successful.

The National Trust's first acquisition in the Lake District was Brandlehow Woods so as to prevent a railway being built from Keswick to the mines in the area. The beginnings of the Trust were in Lakeland, Canon Rawnsley of Grasmere having been one of the founders and much land later was donated to the Trust by Mrs. Heelis, otherwise known as Beatrix Potter.

For the walk, on leaving the very minor road, turn left up the main road through Grange, passing the church. (Most walkers will no doubt want first to look at Grange and the well-known bridge before continuing with the walk.) Pass along the road for about half a mile to where, shortly before reaching the houses of Manesty, there is a small wooden gate by a field gate on the right and a signpost indicating Lodore.

Cross over the field track, over a stream and through a kissing gate. Go through a field gate and turn along the grassy path to the right. Shortly, the path starts across a wooden walkway over some marshy ground. It passes some birches on firm ground and then turns to the right at the head of Derwentwater. Come onto another wooden walkway and pass through a gate and onto a rocky knoll (60). Cross it and onto another wooden walkway which terminates by a footbridge over the River Derwent.

Cross the footbridge and follow the path straight over the field and out onto the road at a stile in the wall at the top. There, turn left for the bus stop for Keswick opposite the Stakis Lodore Hotel.

An alternative ending to this walk can be taken from the kissing gate mentioned before reaching Rosthwaite, this enabling the Bowder Stone to be visited.

Go through the kissing gate and follow the good, clear path down to the road where turn right. Follow the road along for about a third of a mile, passing a footpath sign on the way, to where there is a good track on the right for the Bowder Stone. Follow this track along, to its end, passing the Bowder Stone on the way. On re-joining the road, turn right towards Keswick. On reaching the bridge to the left at Grange, cross it and continue straight up the road and proceed as instructed above from by the church.

53. By crossing the bridge, the road can be used to Keswick as in walk 46 or the woodland and road as in walk 48.
60. Walk 51 follows the path to the left here.
63. Walk 48 can be followed from here to Keswick.

SELECTED FURTHER READING.

The following list of further reading is not a bibliography as many documents, newspaper cuttings and other works were consulted in the preparation of this book. Those books which are no longer in print can often be found in second-hand bookshops. They are all books that help give the flavour and history of the area.

Ashworth, Susan & Dalziel, Nigel. *Lancaster and District in Old Photographs*, Alan Sutton.

Bingham, Roger, K. *The Chronicles of Milnthorpe*, Cicerone Press.

Bingham ,Roger, K. *Kendal, A Social History*, Cicerone Press.

Cottam, John, Alan. *Elephants on the Line*, Helm Press.

Duff, Margaret. *Life in Old Kendal*, Dalesman.

Ffinch, Michael. *Kendal and the Kent Valley*, Hale.

Griffin, A. H. *Inside the Real Lakeland*, Guardian Press.

Hindle, Paul. *Roads and Tracks of the Lake District*, Cicerone Press.

Hutton, Guthrie. *A Tour Through Old Lakeland,* Richard Stenlake Publishing.

Lofthouse, Jessica. *The Curious Traveller through Lakeland*, Hale.

Marsh, John, *The Westmorland Lakes in Old Photographs,* Alan Sutton.

Orrell, Robert. *Saddle Tramp in the Lake District.*

Rollinson, William. *The Lake District Life and Traditions*, Weidenfeld & Nicholson.

Sisson, Malcolm. *A Century of Heversham and Leasgill*, Helm Press.

Swain, Robert. *A Walker's Guide to the Lancaster Canal*, Cicerone Press.

Timetable of buses Keswich to Lancaster.

Carlisle - Keswick - Kendal - Lancaster (LAKESLINK)   555/556

Monday to Friday

Service No	555	556	555	555	555	555	555	555	556	555	555	555	555	555	555	555	555
Code				D													
Carlisle, Bus Station									0910				1305				1625
Wigton									0935				1330				1650
Castle Inn									1000				1355				1715
Keswick, Bus Station							0930	1020	1030	1130	1230	1330	1415	1440	1545	1645	1735
Grasmere, Swan			0722		0810		0948		1048	1148	1248	1348		1458	1603	1703	
Ambleside, Kelsick Road	0700		0740		0828	0915	1015		1115	1215	1315	1415		1525	1630	1730	
Windermere, Railway Stn.	0715		0755		0843	0935	1035		1135	1235	1335	1435		1546	1645	1750	
Kendal, Bus Station arr.	0739		0819		0907	0959	1059		1159	1259	1359	1459		1610	1709	1814	
Kendal, Bus Station dep.		0651	0820	0715	0909	1009	1109		1209	1309	1409	1509		1610	1714		
Milnthorpe Square		0711	0843	0735	0929	1029	1129		1229	1329	1429	1536		1630	1734		
Carnforth, New Street			0904	0800	0950	1050	1150		1250	1350	1450	1557		1651	1755		
Lancaster, Bus Station			0922	0818	1008	1108	1208		1308	1408	1508	1614		1709	1813		

Service No	555	555	556	555
Code		G		
Carlisle, Bus Station				
Wigton				
Castle Inn				
Keswick, Bus Station	1740	1840		
Grasmere, Swan	1805	1905	2031	2300
Ambleside, Kelsick Road	1825	1925	2049	2318
Windermere, Railway Stn.	1845	1945	2104	2333
Kendal, Bus Station arr.	1909	2009	2128	2357
Kendal, Bus Station dep.	1914		2135	
Milnthorpe Square	1934		2155	
Carnforth, New Street	1955		2216	
Lancaster, Bus Station	2013		2232	

Saturday

Service No	556	555	555	555	555	555	556	555	555	555	555	555	555	555	555	555	555
Code																	
Carlisle, Bus Station							0910				1305				1625		
Wigton							0935				1330				1650		
Castle Inn							1000				1355				1715		
Keswick, Bus Station					0930	1020	1030	1130	1230	1330	1415	1430	1545	1630	1735	1840	
Grasmere, Swan			0810		0948		1048	1148	1248	1348		1448	1603	1648	1805	1910	
Ambleside, Kelsick Road		0742	0828	0915	1015		1115	1215	1315	1415		1515	1630	1715	1825	1930	
Windermere, Railway Stn.		0758	0843	0935	1035		1135	1235	1335	1435		1535	1645	1730	1845	1945	
Kendal, Bus Station arr.		0820	0907	0959	1059		1159	1259	1359	1459		1559	1709	1759	1909	2009	
Kendal, Bus Station dep.	0715	0820	0909	1009	1109		1209	1309	1409	1509		1609	1714		1914		
Milnthorpe Square	0735	0840	0929	1029	1129		1229	1329	1429	1529		1629	1734		1934		
Carnforth, New Street	0800	0901	0950	1050	1150		1250	1350	1450	1550		1650	1755		1955		
Lancaster, Bus Station	0818	0919	1008	1108	1208		1308	1408	1508	1608		1708	1813		2013		

Service No	556	555
Code	G	
Carlisle, Bus Station		
Wigton		
Castle Inn		
Keswick, Bus Station		
Grasmere, Swan	2031	2300
Ambleside, Kelsick Road	2049	2318
Windermere, Railway Stn.	2104	2333
Kendal, Bus Station arr.	2128	2357
Kendal, Bus Station dep.	2135	
Milnthorpe Square	2155	
Carnforth, New Street	2216	
Lancaster, Bus Station	2232	

Service No.	556	555	555	555	555	555	556	555	555	555
Code										
arlisle, Bus Station		0850			1120			1550		
gton		0915			1145			1615		
astle Inn		0940			1210			1640		
eswick, Bus Station		1000	1005	1140	1230	1340	1540	1700	1735	
rasmere, Swan			1023	1158		1358	1558		1758	
mbleside, Kelsick Road			1050	1225		1425	1625		1825	1830
indermere, Railway Stn.			1105	1240		1440	1640		1859	1909
endal, Bus Station arr.			1129	1304		1504	1704		1859	1909
endal, Bus Station dep.	0930									
lnthorpe Square	0945						1719			
arnforth, New Street	1002						1736			
ancaster, Bus Station	1020						1754			

odes:
- Operates via Levens Village for Dallam School
- Continues to Lancaster Rail Station, arriving 2236

ancaster - Kendal - Keswick - Carlisle (LAKESLINK) 555/556

Monday to Friday

Service No.	555	555	555	555	555	555	555	555	555	556	555	555	555	555	555	555
Code										Hol	Sch					
ancaster, Bus Station			0725		0830	0925	1020	1120		1220	1320	1320	1420		1520	
arnforth, Haws Mill			0745		0850	0945	1040	1140		1240	1340	1340	1440		1540	
ilnthorpe Square		0726	0823		0915	1010	1105	1205		1309	1405	1405	1505		1605	
endal, Bus Station arr.		0746	0841		0930	1030	1125	1225		1329	1425	1425	1525		1625	
endal, Bus Station dep.	0705	0750	0845		0930	1030	1130	1230		1330	1430	1430	1530		1630	1705
Windermere, Railway Station	0733	0818	0913		0958	1058	1158	1258		1358	1458	1458	1558		1658	1733
mbleside, Kelsick Road	0750	0833	0928		1018	1118	1218	1318		1418	1518	1552	1618		1718	1748
rasmere, Swan	0808	0851	0946		1036	1136	1236	1336		1436	1536	1608	1636		1736	
eswick, Bus Station		0911	1006	1025	1056	1156	1256	1356	1425	1456	1556	1630	1656	1740	1756	
astle Inn				1045					1445					1800		
igton				1110					1510					1825		
arlisle, Bus Station				1135					1535					1850		

Service No.	556	556	555	555	556
Code					
ancaster, Bus Station	1620	1725	1820	2020	2315
arnforth, Haws Mill	1640	1745	1840	2040	2330
ilnthorpe Square	1709	1814	1905	2105	2348
endal, Bus Station arr.			1925	2125	0004
endal, Bus Station dep.	1745	1835	1930	2155	
Windermere, Railway Station	1813	1903	1958	2223	
mbleside, Kelsick Road	1833	1923	2013	2243	
rasmere, Swan	1851		2031	2259	
eswick, Bus Station					
astle Inn					
igton					
arlisle, Bus Station					

Continued ....

Lancaster - Kendal - Keswick - Carlisle (LAKESLINK) 555/

Saturday

Service No.	555	555	556	555	555	555	555	556	555	555	555	555	555	555	556
Code															
Lancaster, Bus Station				0830	0925	1020	1120		1220	1320	1420		1520		1620
Carnforth, Haws Mill				0850	0945	1040	1140		1240	1340	1440		1540		1640
Milnthorpe Square				0915	1010	1105	1205		1309	1405	1505		1605		1709
Kendal, Bus Station arr.				0930	1030	1125	1225		1329	1425	1525		1625		
Kendal, Bus Station dep.	0705	0740		0930	1030	1130	1230		1330	1430	1530		1630	1705	1745
Windermere, Railway Station	0733	0808		0958	1058	1158	1258		1358	1458	1558		1658	1733	1813
Ambleside, Kelsick Road	0750	0823		1018	1118	1218	1318		1418	1518	1618		1718	1748	1833
Grasmere, Swan	0808	0841		1036	1136	1236	1336		1436	1536	1636		1736		1851
Keswick, Bus Station			0901	1025	1056	1156	1256	1356	1425	1456	1556	1656	1740	1756	
Castle Inn				1045					1445				1800		
Wigton				1110					1510				1825		
Carlisle, Bus Station				1135					1535				1850		

Service No.	555	555	556
Code			H
Lancaster, Bus Station	1820	2020	2315
Carnforth, Haws Mill	1840	2040	2330
Milnthorpe Square	1905	2105	2348
Kendal, Bus Station arr.	1925	2125	0004
Kendal, Bus Station dep.	1930	2155	
Windermere, Railway Station	1958	2223	
Ambleside, Kelsick Road	2013	2243	
Grasmere, Swan	2031	2259	
Keswick, Bus Station			
Castle Inn			
Wigton			
Carlisle, Bus Station			

Sunday & Bank Holiday Mondays

Service No.	555	555	555	555	555	555	555	555	555	555
Code										
Lancaster, Bus Station				1020						1754
Carnforth, Haws Mill				1038						1812
Milnthorpe Square				1055						1829
Kendal, Bus Station arr.										1844
Kendal, Bus Station dep.	0805		0915	1115		1315	1515		1745	
Windermere, Railway Station	0833		0943	1143		1343	1543		1813	
Ambleside, Kelsick Road	0850		1000	1200		1400	1600		1830	
Grasmere, Swan	0906		1016	1216		1416	1616			
Keswick, Bus Station	0928	1000	1038	1238	1400	1438	1638	1700		
Castle Inn		1020			1420			1720		
Wigton		1045			1445			1745		
Carlisle, Bus Station		1110			1510			1810		

Codes:
H - Commences Lancaster Rail Station at 2311
Hol - Operates on School holidays only
Sch - Operates on School days only.

N.B. Timetable correct at time of print. Timetables are subject to change without notice. For further timetable information, contact Traveline on:-0870 608 2 608

Stagecoach in Cumbria

Service 555
LAKESlink

- Carlisle
- Keswick
- Grasmere
- Ambleside
- Windermere
- Kendal
- Lancaster

Stagecoach are pleased to be associated with this publication and hope that you are able to enjoy as many of the walks as possible.

Service 555 is one of many services operated by Stagecoach throughout Lancashire and Cumbria and which are used by over 50 million travellers each year.

Our Explorer tickets offer the freedom of a vast network stretching from Manchester to the Scottish borders.

The Best Way to get around the "Lakes"

. . . take the 'bus'

Comments to:
Stagecoach North West
Broadacre House
16-20 Lowther Street
Carlisle
CA3 8DA

For timetable Information
contact Traveline on

0870 608 2 608